THE SEARCH FOR HARMONY

ESSAYS ON SCIENCE AND MORMONISM

Edited by

Gene A. Sessions and *Craig J. Oberg*

Signature Books   Salt Lake City   1993

COVER ILLUSTRATION: *ROYAL CUBIT*, BY DOUG HIMES, 1989, OIL ON PAPER
COVER DESIGN: JULIE EASTON

97   96   95   94   93   6   5   4   3   2   1

Library of Congress Cataloging-in-Publication Data

The Search for harmony : essays on science and Mormonism / edited by
    Gene A. Sessions, Craig J. Oberg.
        p.   cm.
    Includes bibliographical references.
    ISBN 1-56085-020-5
    1. Religion and Science—1946- 2. Church of Jesus Christ of
Latter-day Saints—Doctrines.   3. Mormon Church—Doctrines.
I. Sessions, Gene Allred.   II. Oberg, Craig J.
BL241.S4257   1993
261.5'5—dc20
                                                        92-16811

CONTENTS

The Mormon Retreat from Science

BY THE LAST DECADE OF THE TWENTIETH CENTURY FEW MEMBERS OF THE Church of Jesus Christ of Latter-day Saints would doubt the truth of the following statement: The ideas of organic evolution, particularly as they apply to the development of humankind, are false. In addition, "so-called intellectuals who rely upon the scientific method as an always valuable and legitimate way of searching for knowledge fail to realize that faith must take precedence over empiricism, no matter how voluminous or convincing supporting data may be." Attempts to reconcile faith in God and the "evolution of man" are seen as a rejection of moral law.[1]

Moreover, such statements characterize the common percep-tion among Mormons of the intellectual underpinnings of evolution-ary biology and in the larger context the scientific method itself. In league with fundamentalist Christians, Mormons tend to accept the whole cloth of "creation science"—the notion that geologists, biolo-gists, and others have participated in a gross misinterpretation of the geologic and fossil record and in so doing subvert the truth of a divine creation. Dwelling on semantical extrapolations of such terms as "law" and "theory,"[2] these attacks on science comprise a central component of modern anti-intellectualism.

Yet in spite of the above, the Mormon church has demon-strated repeatedly a deep affection for and strong bond with science. Part of that fondness developed from a sense that the doctrines of Mormonism dovetail with the findings of science, even the notions of evolutionary biology, as Mikel Vause argues in "Eternal Progress:

The Higher Destiny" and as David Bailey suggests further in "Scientific Foundations of Mormon Theology." Perhaps as a result, Mormon theology has refused to box itself into a strict anti-scientific stance in order to defend its basic premises. In addition, numerous Mormon leaders, many of them accomplished scientists, have expressed confidence in the unfettered pursuit of the scientific method. Spencer W. Kimball, a Mormon prophet, extolled often the virtues of "modern scientific findings," which "harmonize with revelation through the ages."[3] His successor, Ezra Taft Benson, once stated that Mormons "have no fear that any discovery of new truths will ever be in conflict with . . . any fundamental basic principle which we advocate in the Gospel." Affirming his comfort with "any new truths, whether discovered in the laboratory, through the research of the scientist, or whether revealed from heaven through prophets of God,"[4] Benson's remarks reflect accurately the historical position of the leadership of the Mormon church relative to science.

Unfortunately, this intellectual enlightenment has evaporated from the common discourse of the church as creationist notions have crept into its sermons and classrooms. Among Mormon scholars confronting this situation, three professors of biology at church-owned Brigham Young University published in 1979 a commentary titled "The New Biology and Mormon Theology." They noted that such early leaders as Orson Pratt were "willing and able to combine empirical and theological insights," but that such high-ranking Mormon officials "have all but disappeared from the Mormon scene."[5] The truth of their observation suggests an interesting set of questions: What has led Mormons to a marriage with Christian fundamentalism relative to organic evolution? How does this affect the attitudes of the common membership of the church, not only toward science and the scientific method but with respect to traditional Mormon virtues of education, the pursuit of knowledge, and the embrace of all truth? What is the overall effect of an all-or-nothing attitude of rejection when doctrinal issues appear to collide with scientific observations?

Even passive observers cannot fail to notice a recent bombardment from the ramparts. In written and oratorical form this warfare has operated on two levels. Visible and vocal general leaders have in recent decades assaulted evolution in particular and science in general. The founding father of this movement was Joseph Fielding

Smith, prolific writer and church historian during his years as apostle and prophet.

Smith published perhaps the most complete compendium of his attitudes about science in 1954 under the title, *Man, His Origin and Destiny*.[6] After stating that there exists no "conflict between truth revealed from heaven and truth revealed through the research of man," he launched into a nearly 300-page diatribe against organic evolution and the scientific method. Characterizing "the doctrine of organic evolution [as] only an hypothesis—a guess . . . and a bad guess at that,"[7] he argued that it is surely "Satan's chief weapon in this dispensation to destroy the divine mission of Jesus Christ."[8] A most telling remark came on page 138 where he asked, "Why is it that thousands of intelligent looking human beings are willing to accept these stupid teachings? Frankly it is because Satan has deceived them and they love darkness rather than life."

Smith's son-in-law Bruce R. McConkie followed closely this line of thinking for what he called "weak and puerile intellectuality."[9] As church apostle and semi-official theologian, McConkie called organic evolution one of the "seven deadly heresies" of the modern age.[10] Relentlessly damning the science that supported "the theoretical guesses and postulates of some organic evolutionists," he bemoaned those who "reject the revealed truth that there was no death either for man or animal or plants or any form of life until 6,000 years ago when Adam fell."[11] His harmonizing with Bishop Usher's biblical chronology stamped McConkie's stand as extreme among creationists.

At the base of the problem for Mormons are notions about the order of the universe. Church founder Joseph Smith stated it as "a decree of the Lord that every tree, plant, and herb bearing seed should bring forth of its kind, and cannot come forth after any other law or principle."[12] Four decades later, church president John Taylor restated the same position in light of Darwin's voyage aboard the *Beagle*: "These principles do not change, as represented by evolutionists of the Darwinian school, but the primitive organisms of all living beings exist in the same form as when they first received their impress from their Maker."[13] Also operating against acceptance of evolution for many Mormons is the doctrine of the fall of Adam and the atonement of Christ. But even with these accoutrements, only recently has the general tenor of church pronouncements joined in the marginalization of science and scientists.

Although David O. McKay, prophet during the 1950s and 1960s, expressed negative feelings about evolution in his books,[14] his now-classic letter to William L. Stokes made plain the church's refusal to join fundamentalist sects in disavowing organic evolution altogether.[15] The resulting historical schizophrenia manifests itself in an ongoing fashion as outspoken Mormons discredit Darwinism and its derivatives yet praise open-minded, scholarly pursuit of truth.

A second tier of Mormons has written a plethora of science-bashing works. Such authors as Melvin and Garfield Cook,[16] Dean R. Zimmerman,[17] Ernst Eberhard, Jr.,[18] and Reid Bankhead[19] deny that the church "has taken no stand; the scriptures themselves are the 'stand' taken by the Church."[20] They reject not only organic evolution but also the scientific age of earth prehistory. Bankhead refers to such ideas as "most pernicious" and "a trick of the devil."[21] Characterizing Darwin and Lyell as anti-Christs,[22] the Cooks and others argue the familiar creationist line about "the slow but persistent penetration of false theories and doctrines into science"[23] and suggest that those who accept evolution are deceived by Satan and are co-conspirators.

According to the typical lay church author, reliance on science for knowledge is fine unless it involves "special theoretical models of science which have been devised to eliminate the need for a God and thus promote deception."[24] Their usual conclusion is that it is impossible to "embrace Lyellian prehistory without utterly repudiating the teachings of the scriptures"[25] and the divinity of Christ. Along with their creationist-fundamentalist fellow travelers across the Christian world, they readily accept the benefits of scientific discovery that promise to improve their lives. But when the same methods yield findings that conflict with their views of the universe, such techniques are the machinations of evil people.

Mormon leaders, scholars, and theologians have not always shared with other biblical literalists this degree of hostility to Lyell, Russell, Darwin, and their successors. Their uneasiness about what seemed to be unequivocal scientific revelations from taxonomic, fossil, and geologic records rarely lead them into outright rejection of science. Early Mormon leaders felt that science would vindicate Mormonism. Joseph Smith himself repeatedly stressed that Mormonism would always accept truth from whatever source. His nephew and early twentieth-century successor Joseph F. Smith reiterated this long-standing attitude when he said, "We are willing to receive all truth, from whatever source it may come; for truth will stand, truth will endure. . . . True science is that system of reasoning which brings to the fore the simple, plain truth."[26]

It is also apparent that many of the most influential nineteenth- and early twentieth-century Mormon leaders, many of whom were prolific writers, were independent-minded—Orson and Parley Pratt, Orson Hyde, Lorenzo Snow, John Taylor. Church president Brigham Young found little difficulty harmonizing Mormonism and evolution: "God brought forth material out of which he formed this little terra firma upon which we roam. How long had this material been in existence? Forever and forever, in some shape, in some condition. We need not refer to all of those who were with God, and who assisted him in this work. The elements form and develop, and continue to do so until they mature, and then they commence to decay and become disorganized. The mountains around us were formed in this way. By and by, when they shall have reached their maturity, the work of disintegration and decay will commence. It has been so from all eternity, and will continue to be so until they are made celestial."[27]

Young also had little problem with accepting a Lyellian earth millions or perhaps billions of years old, and even less respect for the literalness of the Genesis account: "How long it [the earth] has been organized is not for me to say, and I do not care anything about it. As for the Bible account of creation we may say that the Lord gave it to Moses, or rather Moses obtained the history and traditions of the fathers, and from them picked out what he considered necessary, and that account has been handed down from age to age, and we have got it, no matter whether it is correct or not, and whether the Lord found the earth empty or void, whether he made it out of nothing or out of rude elements; or whether he made it in six days or in as many millions of years, is and will remain a matter of speculation in the minds of men unless he gives revelation on the subject."[28] Add to this his general encouragement of the study of science: "Every accomplishment, every polished grace, every useful attainment in mathematics, music, and in all science and art belongs to the Saints, and they should avail themselves as expeditiously as possible of the wealth of knowledge the sciences offer to every diligent and persevering scholar."[29]

Mormon sympathy with science derives mostly from the writings of three early twentieth-century members of the hierarchy. The first of these emigrated from England as a teenager. Shortly after his arrival in Utah, James E. Talmage enrolled at Brigham Young Academy where he came under the tutelage of Karl Maeser, who comfortably elevated science to the same level of reverence as religion. After extensive graduate training in chemistry and geology at Lehigh and Johns Hopkins universities, Talmage returned to Utah to occupy the Deseret Chair of Geology at the University of Utah, serving as president of the university, and become a member of the Quorum of Twelve Apostles. The LDS church published his doctrinal expositions on Jesus the Christ and the basic tenets of the Mormon faith. A fellow of the Royal Microscopical Society of London and of the Royal Society of Edinburgh, Talmage had no tolerance for anti-scientific prejudice and argued consistently for a rational and open-minded pursuit of knowledge about the nature of the cosmos: "Discrepancies that trouble us now will diminish as our knowledge of pertinent facts is extended. The Creator has made a record in the rocks for man to decipher; but He has also spoken directly regarding main stages of progress by which the earth has been brought to be what it is. The accounts cannot be fundamentally opposed; one cannot contradict the other; though man's interpretation of either may be seriously at fault."[30]

Talmage expressed an unwavering confidence in the scientific method and chided sectarians for their lack of understanding of Darwinism. His voice spoke eloquently for the possibility of "races of the human sort" before Adam.[31] His major caveat to the Saints related not to science but to scripture: "The opening chapters of Genesis, and scriptures related thereto, were never intended as a textbook of geology, archaeology, earth-science, or man-science. Holy scripture will endure, while the conceptions of men change with new discoveries. We do not show reverence for the scriptures when we misapply them through faulty interpretation."[32]

Mirroring Talmage's story, a second scholar immigrated from Norway to Utah and then eagerly received advanced training in chemistry at Harvard where he was president of the chemistry club. John A. Widstoe subsequently studied at the University of Goettingen in Germany from which he graduated magna cum laude with M.A. and Ph.D. degrees. After working with several prominent European chemists, he returned to Utah as director of the Agricultural Experiment Station and on to service as president of the Utah State Agricultural College and then of the University of Utah. After his appointment as an apostle, Widstoe expended a great deal of effort on questions surrounding the interface of religion and reason.[33] Following those of Talmage, Widstoe's general conclusions encircled the notion that "there can be no conflict between true religion and correct science."[34] "In summary: The Church supports and welcomes the growth of science. It asks only that the facts of science be as accurately determined as human powers permit, and that confusion between facts of science and inferences of science be earnestly avoided. The religion of Latter-day Saints is not hostile to any truth, nor to scientific search for the truth."[35]

While he expressed nagging doubts about the complete veracity of evolution,[36] he steadfastly supported a happy marriage between Mormonism and science, believing in an easy reconciliation between them, "since all proper human activities aim to secure truth. Every person of honest mind loves truth above all else. . . . Truth is truth, whether labeled science or religion."[37] Consistent with the teachings of Joseph Smith and Brigham Young, Widstoe argued eloquently for an open-mind. "A man who loves truth, and seeks it," he wrote, "frequently finds that the new truth is in opposition to his former, cherished beliefs. Then if this love of truth be genuine, he must replace the traditions of his life with the new-won knowledge."[38] After traversing Richard Sherlock's "Turbulent Spectrum," we know that Widtsoe's belief in such a courageous pursuit of truth led him to form to his own satisfaction a simple reconciliation between ideas of creation and organic evolution: "The law of evolution . . . does not require that all things, all life, shall have a common origin. It merely declares that everything in the universe is moving onward."[39] By the end of his career Widtsoe had also accepted the existence of "human like beings before the coming of Adam."[40]

The third member of this intellectual triumvirate also immigrated to Utah as a youngster. While not trained as a scientist like

Talmage and Widstoe, B. H. Roberts was a consummate scholar who spent his career as a church leader investigating the realities of his faith, both past and present, particularly as it crossed paths with the world of secular knowledge. Early on, Roberts seemed unwilling to accept Darwinism, discounting the theory of evolution as "contrary to all experiences so far as man's knowledge extends. The great law of nature is that every plant, herb, fish, fowl, beast and man produces its kind."[41] He was willing to allow the "claim that the fossilized remains in the different strata of the earth's crust reveal that in the earlier periods of the earth's existence only the simpler forms of vegetation and animal life are to be found, both forms of life becoming more complex and of a higher type as the earth becomes older, until it is crowned with the presence of man."[42] He also confirmed the incontrovertability of geologic evidence for an ancient earth and explained the fossil evidence of "lower forms" by arguing for extra-terrestrial transfers of species to the earth that could inhabit it successfully during its various stages of development. As changes in the earth came, so did mass extinctions.[43] Roberts obviously found himself trapped and attempted to force two positions into what would seem today to be a bizarre amalgamation.

In 1929, suffering from "an incurable ailment," Roberts presented to the church hierarchy for approval a 700-page manuscript entitled *The Truth, The Way, The Life*. This monumental work attempted in one grand sweep a complete doctrinal reconciliation of theology and science, a total analysis of a theistic cosmos. By this time Roberts had come to the conclusion that organic evolution had to take its place as a certain truth among the countless others his faith and reason had affirmed. The full extent of his logic on the matter took him right to the brink of accepting evolutionary theory as the basic explanation to all life, but he paused there to cling to the idea of special creation for Adam and his descendants, while accepting without reservation the existence of humans prior to a cleansing of the planet to make way for the Adamic dispensation. Several of the apostles, led by Joseph Fielding Smith, responded to the manuscript with an attack on the whole idea of evolution and a general debunking of the scientific method. Talmage, an apostle with seniority, jumped into the fray on the side of Roberts. While the manuscript never saw publication, Talmage managed to convince the First Presidency to take a neutral stand on the issue, which it did in April 1931: "The statement made by Elder Smith that the existence of pre-adamites is not a doctrine of the Church is true. It is just as true that the statement 'there were not pre-adamites upon the earth' is not a doctrine of the church. Neither side of the controversy has been accepted as a doctrine at all."[44] Talmage and Roberts died just weeks apart in 1933 while Smith lived another four decades, long enough to serve briefly as president of the church.

Roberts, like Talmage and Widstoe, testified to the worthiness of scientific investigation as a desirable pursuit. Such support for science among outspoken leaders of the church helped to encourage the development of a tradition at mid-century for Mormons to respect the scientific endeavor. It also created an atmosphere in which Mormon thinkers of the stripe of BYU religion professor Hugh Nibley,[45] Apostle Joseph Merrill,[46] and Frederick Pack[47] rose to state their devotion to reason and their rejection of any exclusivity between religion and science.

Merrill's attitude toward science, for example, stands in contrast to many current pronouncements that it is opposed to religious progress: "Assuredly there can be no conflict between two truths. But certainly there have been severe conflicts between interpretations of facts of science and some teachings of religionists. . . . I think no truth-seeker, no Mormon, need be seriously disturbed by these conflicts. They are usually due to misinterpretations and intolerance. Scientists and religionists of the present generation have found that there were faults on both sides among their predecessors. Yes, I believe the facts of science, rightly looked at and understood, are helpful to the development of a sound religious faith."[48]

As Steven Heath and Edward Kimball illustrate, the example of renowned scientist and believing Mormon Henry Eyring provided further inspiration to Latter-day Saints, who Pack asserted have "no part in the controversy concerning the origin of the earth."[49] The thinking Mormon, Pack continued, "knows that God is omnipotent, that he works by natural principles, and, therefore, that the truths of science are equally as sacred as those of the Written Word, for both proceed from the same source."[50] For Eyring, contradictions between science and religion resulted from "provisional and fragmentary" understanding that would disappear only as one "approaches the

Divine." Until then, he wrote, "we can only continue our quest for the balanced view that comes from weighing all evidence carefully in the search for enduring values."[51]

On one point, all of these Mormon thinkers, from Widstoe and Roberts to Nibley and Pack, agree completely. Mainstream Christianity misinterpreted biblical ideas of the origin of the earth and life thereon. Roberts suggested that insufficient understanding of creation among theologians was responsible for the theory of evolution in the first place. "Finding so much that was contrary to well-known facts," he wrote, "induced men of intelligence to look for some other explanation of the genesis of things."[52]

One of the major complaints of mainstream Christianity is that Latter-day Saints have other scriptures in addition to the Bible. Nibley studied these other scriptures as possible keys to untying the Gordian Knot of science and religion. Using the books of Abraham and Moses, he concluded that there were "people that lived thousands of years before Adam."[53] He also tried to distinguish between Mormons and other Bible-oriented people on such matters. "Latter-day Saints . . . have always been taught that things were happening long, long before Adam appeared on the scene."[54] He affirmed his belief in anthropoid forerunners of modern humans and pointed to Mormon scriptures as support. "The creation process as described in the Pearl of Great Price," he said, "is open ended and ongoing, entailing careful planning based on vast experience, long consultations, models, tests, and even trial runs for a complicated system requiring a vast scale of participation by the creatures concerned."[55]

Many essays have been written to bring some sense to the paradoxical problem of Mormonism's shifting attitude toward science. David Rees outlines that historical drift, and Duane Jeffery documents clearly the conflict among church leaders on organic evolution.[56] A few Mormon scientists, such as Frank Salisbury,[57] Eldon Gardner,[58] and William Harris[59] have written books designed to ease the tension, while Mormon theologian Keith Norman contemplated "Adam's Navel" to surmise that the whole controversy stems from misunderstanding the role of myth.[60]

Others lament the growing sense that science simply cannot coexist peacefully with religion in the minds of Latter-day Saints. Most notable among the latter are personal essays by Cedric Davern[61] and Richard P. Smith.[62] Davern accurately describes the dichotomy between evolution and creation as conflicting world views for Mormons. "The big question for me in this controversy," wrote Davern, "is whether freedom of inquiry, with the agonizing ambiguity that accompanies it, will be sacrificed to the interest of those who demand certainty in the hope of salvation."[63]

Some comfort for these troubled souls appeared in an article in the September 1987 issue of the official church magazine *The Ensign*. Morris Petersen, professor of geology at BYU, produced a brief essay in the "I Have a Question" section in which he took essentially the same position relative to the fossil record that Nibley took but without the specificity.[64] He also echoed Widstoe in requesting patience as science and religion both take their separate paths to the same ultimate truths. A similarly conciliatory article appeared in the January 1970 *Improvement Era*, predecessor to *The Ensign*. Titled "In the Beginning," it consisted of a collection of statements by Mormon scholars affirming their testimonies in light of scientific findings in their fields.[65]

Several reasons for this Mormon retreat from science parallel the current literalist/fundamentalist antagonism toward science: (1) paranoia over the implications of organic evolution, paleogeology, and astrophysics; (2) misunderstanding the nature of scientific inquiry and scientific terminology; (3) a general retrenchment against secularization and the apparent erosion of traditional values; (4) comfort in scriptural authority as a panacea for the turmoils of living in a complex world; and (5) the inability of science to satisfy emotional needs. (Non-scientists expect science to provide "exact" answers, and when those tentative answers are emotionally unappealing or contradict personal beliefs, they become targets for rejection as suddenly "unproven" or "mere theory," which is really what all scientific conclusions are in the first place.)

Persuasive commentaries exist that present detailed discussions of the forces behind the anti-scientific, and hence anti-intellectual, propensities of many of today's religious thinkers.[66] The present concern, however, is to come to a few conclusions about the Mormon struggle and its peculiarities. Among the first of these is a parallelism. During the 1970s, a renaissance promised to usher in a Golden Age of Mormon studies. The truth of the Restoration would come forth through the labors of church historian Leonard J. Arrington, his staff, and countless others who would flock to the church historical department to write a new and open history of Mormonism. But gradually, as the first works came forth, certain leaders decided that such an open-minded pursuit and the scholarly interpretation of it could damage faith. Too many questions might create too much discomfort. After all, they argued, the church is in the business of saving souls and should sponsor only activities that lead directly to that end. On that occasion the point man in the attack was Elder Boyd K. Packer, whose condemnation of non-faith-promoting history and resulting debate among Mormon intelligentsia made national news.[67] Vocal elements of current Mormon leadership apparently view scientific endeavors in the same light. In other words, anything that does not promote faith is counterproductive.

In the Mormon situation, there exists a strong personality factor. Differences between the perspectives of apostles like Widstoe and McConkie need no analysis. Plainly, their contrasting views and styles and resulting effects on the general population of the church have manifest themselves in the dramatic change we have seen. The degree of respect for science that comes across in common discourse both from the high pulpit of the tabernacle and in the lowliest Sunday school class in the church is eroding.

Part of these differences relate to historical changes in the church itself and the institution's view of its place in the world. In the nineteenth century, isolationist church leaders thumbed their noses, so to speak, at the sectarian world. With statehood and the end of polygamy, the new century brought the need for respectability and a desire on the part of church leaders to move Mormonism into the mainstream of placid American Christianity. As it steadily backed away from overt doctrinal and social radicalism, it absorbed other aspects of the conservative church at the very time when Darwinism and Freudianism were taking a toll on traditional notions of religious truth. American church membership and attendance went into a slide, and although Mormonism with its own growth dynamic did not share that fate, it naturally moved with the current into the fundamentalist reaction to the forces of dysfunction. By the post-war period, Mormon expansion into a national and then international arena demanded a conservative demeanor. It would not do to emphasize a formerly radical set of ideas and practices. Literalist inter-pretations of the Bible fit naturally into such a scheme.

Another reason for the Mormon retreat from science is particularly curious. LDS dogma, the same beliefs that inspired the liberal ideas of Nibley, have in other hands added more justification for the fundamentalist retrenchment. Literal interpretations of the books of Moses and Abraham, filled as they are with more detail about the Creation, provide even heavier cannon fodder for the fundamentalist than does the Bible.

Some suggest that anti-intellectualism in the Mormon church is cyclical, that the archives and minds of the church will reopen. Unfortunately, a multi-generational mindset now seems in place that retracts fetally to intellectual challenge. Contrary to bygone eras of Mormonism when support for science was intrinsic, Saints need no longer seek God's truth in the best books and through science and scholarship. Such pursuits become too confusing and challenge simple tenants of faith. If a literal interpretation of the scriptures suggests it, then so be it. In such a view, there can be no room for debate, a distinct departure from Henry Eyring's philosophy allowing "room in the Church for people who think that the periods of creation were twenty-four hours, one thousand years, or million of years. I think it is fine to discuss these questions and for each individual to try to convert others to what he thinks is right."[68]

The building notion that there is no room in the church for harmonizing and reconciling scientific and religious truths has slowly caused a retreat among many Mormons from a former reverence for science. Perhaps James E. Talmage left the most enduring advice inscribed on his tombstone: "Within the Gospel of Jesus Christ there is room for every truth thus far learned by man, or yet to be made known."[69]

Appreciation is extended to the following authors, publica-tions, and publishers for permission to reproduce, sometimes under a different title, many of the essays appearing in this collection: to *Dialogue: A Journal of Mormon Thought* for essays by David H. Bailey, James L. Farmer, William S. Bradshaw, F. Brent Johnson, Dennis Rowley, Richard Sherlock, Jeffrey E. Keller, Edward L. Kimball, Steven H. Heath, Duane E. Jeffery, William Lee Stokes, Keith E. Norman, and Richard Pearson Smith; to the *Ensign* for the essay by

Morris S. Petersen; to the *Journal of Mormon History* for the essay by Richard Sherlock; to Utah State University Press for the essay by Eldon J. Gardner; and to Signature Books for the essay by Gary James Bergera. The essays by L. Mikel Vause, Gene A. Sessions, and Craig J. Oberg are published here for the first time.

NOTES

1. Boyd K. Packer, unpublished discourse, 30 Oct. 1988, Brigham Young University, Provo, Utah. See also his October 1984 conference address, "A Pattern of Our Parentage," *Ensign* 18 (Nov. 1984): 66-69.

2. See Gale Rhodes and Robert Schaible, "Fact, Law, And Theory: Ways of Thinking in Science and Literature," *JCST*, Feb. 1989, 228-32, 288. For a good indictment of scientists' failure to communicate more effectively with the public and hence to avoid some of these problems, see Manfred Kroger, "The Why and How of Communicating Science," *Food Technology*, Jan. 1987, 93-99.

3. Spencer W. Kimball, *Modern Scientific Findings Harmonize with Revelation through the Ages* (Salt Lake City: Deseret Book, 1962). Kimball typically praised science, while urging followers to remember to accumulate spiritual knowledge along with the secular: "No conflict exists between the gospel and any truth . . . All true principles are a part of the gospel of Jesus Christ. There is no principle that we need to fear" (Edward L. Kimball, ed., *The Teachings of Spencer W. Kimball* [Salt Lake City: Bookcraft, 1982], 391).

4. Ezra Taft Benson, *Conference Report*, Apr. 1958, 60.

5. J. L. Farmer, W. S. Bradshaw, and F. B. Johnson, "The New Biology and Mormon Theology," *Dialogue: A Journal of Mormon Thought* 12 (Winter 1979): 71. See also sermon by Orson Pratt, *Journal of Discourses*, 26 vols. (Liverpool: Latter-day Saints' Book Depot, 1854-86), 21:197-206; also, E. Robert Paul, "Early Mormon Intellectuals: Parley P. and Orson Pratt, a Response," *Dialogue: A Journal of Mormon Thought* 15 (Autumn 1982): 42-48.

6. Joseph Fielding Smith, *Man . . . His Origin and Destiny* (Salt Lake City: Deseret Book, 1954), 1.

7. Ibid., 160.

8. Ibid., 184.

9. Bruce R. McConkie, *Mormon Doctrine* (Salt Lake City: Bookcraft, 1966), 256.

10. Bruce R. McConkie, "The Seven Deadly Heresies," *BYU Speeches of the Year* (Provo, UT: BYU Press, 1980), 74-80.

11. McConkie, *Mormon Doctrine*, 681.

12. Joseph Fielding Smith, comp., *The Teachings of the Prophet Joseph Smith* (Salt Lake City: Deseret Book Company, 1959), 198.

13. John Taylor, *Mediation and Atonement* (Salt Lake City: Deseret News Co., 1882), 164.

14. "Now, evolution leads men away from God. Men who have had faith in God, when they have become converted to that theory, forsake him" (David O. McKay, *Gospel Ideals* [Salt Lake City: Improvement Era, 1953], 283).

15. William Lee Stokes, "An Official Position," *Dialogue: A Journal of Mormon Thought* 12 (Winter 1979): 90-92.

16. See Melvin A. and M. Garfield Cook, *Science and Mormonism* (Salt Lake City: Deseret Book, 1973); and Melvin A. Cook, *Creation and Eternalism* (Salt Lake City: Deseret News Press, 1970).

17. Dean R. Zimmerman, *Evolution: A Golden Calf* (Salt Lake City: Hawkes Publishing, 1976).

18. Ernst Eberhard, *The Origin: A Mormon's View on Evolution* (Salt Lake City: Ernst Eberhard, Jr., 1981).

19. Reid E. Bankhead, *The Fall of Adam, the Atonement of Christ, and Organic Evolution* (Levan, UT: RAM Books, 1978).

20. Cook and Cook, *Science and Mormonism*, 162.

21. Bankhead, *Fall of Adam*, 14. Contrast this attitude with the position of George Q. Cannon, a late nineteenth-century Mormon leader: "Joseph Smith taught that a day with God was not the twenty-four hours of our day; but that the six days of the creation were six periods of the Lord's time. This he taught half a century ago; it is now generally recognized as a great truth connected with the creation of the world. Geologists have declared it, and religious people are adopting it; and so the world is progressing" (in Cook and Cook, *Science and Mormonism*, 126).

22. Cook and Cook, *Science and Mormonism*, 390-91.

23. Ibid., 386.

24. Ibid., 385.

25. Ibid., 391.

26. Joseph F. Smith, *Gospel Doctrine* (Salt Lake City: Deseret Book, 1939), 1, 6.

27. Sermon by Brigham Young, *Journal of Discourses*, 18:231.

28. Ibid., 14:115-6.

29. Ibid., 10:224.

30. John R. Talmage, *The Talmage Story: Life of James E. Talmage, Educator, Scientist, Apostle* (Salt Lake City: Bookcraft, Inc., 1972), 232.

31. Jeffrey E. Keller, "Discussion Continued: The Sequel to the Roberts/Smith/Talmage Affair," *Dialogue: A Journal of Mormon Thought* 15 (Spring 1982): 79-98.

32. Talmage, *Talmage Story*, 232.

33. Widstoe was particularly interested in Joseph Smith's insights into scientific discoveries of later years as well as the Prophet's curiosity about the nature of things. See John A. Widstoe, *Joseph Smith as Scientist* (Salt Lake

City: YMMIA General Board, 1909).

34. John A. Widstoe, *Evidence and Reconciliations: Aids to Faith in a Modern Day* (Salt Lake City: Bookcraft, 1943), 125. "The Church, the custodian of the gospel on earth," he continued, "looks with full favor upon attempts of men to search out the facts and laws of nature. It believes that men of science, seekers after truth, are often assisted by the Spirit of the Lord in such researches. It holds further that every scientific discovery may be incorporated into the gospel" (ibid.).

35. Ibid., 129.

36. Ibid., 149-56.

37. John A. Widstoe, *In Search of Truth* (Salt Lake City: Deseret Book, 1963), 16.

38. Ibid., 21. "The open mind is the sign of growth and progress," he said. "To stand before the unknown and undiscovered universe, in full desire for truth, and ready to accept it, insistent only that it must be the truth and nothing else, that has been and ever will be the attitude of those who have done most for the human race. The open mind is ready to accept truth; but more ready to reject error. It tests and tries; it philosophizes and prays; then it goes on its way rejoicing, ready for more truth at the next turn of the road" (ibid., 104).

39. Ibid., 71. "The Church, which comprehends all truth, accepts all the reliably determined facts used in building the hypothesis of organic evolution. It does not question the observed order of advancement or progression in nature, whether called the law of evolution or by any other name. In every field, the Church encourages the search for knowledge and welcomes each new fact as it appears" (ibid., 77).

40. Quoted in Keller, "Discussion Continued."

41. B. H. Roberts, *The Gospel and Man's Relationship to Deity* (Salt Lake City: Deseret News, 1961), 282.

42. Ibid.

43. Ibid., 280-81.

44. Quoted in Richard Sherlock, "We Can See No Advantage to a Continuation of the Discussion: The Roberts/Smith/Talmage Affair," *Dialogue: A Journal of Mormon Thought* 13 (Fall 1980): 63-78.

45. Among Nibley's publications, perhaps the most cogent to the present discussion is "Before Adam" (preliminary report, FARMS, Provo, UT, 1980). Nibley's advice on human evolution is not to "begrudge existence to creatures that looked like men long, long ago, nor deny them a place in God's affection or even a right to exaltation—for our scriptures allow them such. Nor am I overly concerned as to just when they might have lived, for their world is not our world. They have all gone away long before our people ever appeared" (Hugh Nibley, *Old Testament and Related Studies* [Salt Lake City: Deseret Book, 1986], 82).

46. See Joseph F. Merrill, *The Truth Seeker and Mormonism* (Salt Lake City: Radio Station KSL, 1945).

47. "Religion, when properly understood," said Pack, "comprehends the entire system of universal truth; it encompasses everything worthy of acceptance. Hence, the religious man who professes the proper conception of his own faith should be able to go into the field of learning and accept everything that is true. Any religion which does not possess this high standard can hardly hope to retain a membership of thinking people" (in Paul R. Green, *Science and Your Faith in God* [Salt Lake City: Bookcraft, 1958], 168).

48. Ibid., 102.

49. Ibid., 191.

50. Ibid.

51. Henry Eyring, *The Faith of a Scientist* (Salt Lake City: Bookcraft, 1967), 99. "All of these wonderful findings in nature should increase our reverence for the omniscient wisdom of the Creator in fashioning this exquisitely complex universe as a school for His children. Since the Gospel embraces all truth, there can never be any genuine contradictions between true science and true religion" (ibid., 41).

52. Roberts, *Gospel*, 254-55.

53. Nibley, *Old Testament*, 49.

54. Ibid.

55. Ibid., 69.

56. Duane E. Jeffrey, "Seers, Savants and Evolution: The Uncomfortable Interface," *Dialogue: A Journal of Mormon Thought* 8 (Autumn/Winter, 1973): 41-75. See also, Stephen and Kathy Snow, Dow Woodward, Norman Eatough, and Duane E. Jeffrey, "Seers, Savants and Evolution: A Continuing Dialogue," *Dialogue: A Journal of Mormon Thought* 9 (Autumn 1974): 21-38.

57. Frank B. Salisbury, *The Creation* (Salt Lake City: Deseret Book, 1976).

58. Eldon J. Gardner, *Organic Evolution and the Bible* (Logan: Utah State University Press, 1960).

59. William E. Harris, *From Man to God: An LDS Scientist Views Creation, Progression and Exaltation* (Bountiful, UT: Horizon Publishers, 1989).

60. Keith E. Norman, "Adam's Navel," *Dialogue: A Journal of Mormon Thought* 21 (Summer 1988): 81-97.

61. Cedric I. Davern, "Evolution and Creation: Two World Views," *Dialogue: A Journal of Mormon Thought* 17 (Spring 1984): 44-50. The late Professor Davern, a renowned scientist, spent most of his career as a non-Mormon scholar teaching at the University of Utah.

62. Richard P. Smith, "Science: A Part or Apart from Mormonism?" *Dialogue: A Journal of Mormon Thought* 19 (Spring 1986): 106-22.

63. Davern, "Evolution and Creation," 50.

64. Morris S. Peterson, "I Have a Question," *Ensign* 17 (Sept. 1987): 78-79.

65. Jay M. Todd, "In the Beginning," *The Improvement Era*, Jan. 1970, 33-48.

66. See Douglas J. Futuyma, *Science on Trial: The Case for Evolution* (New York: Pantheon Books, 1982).

67. Kenneth L. Woodward, "Apostles vs. Historians," *Newsweek*, 15 Feb. 1982, 77.

68. Henry Eyring, *Reflections of a Scientist* (Salt Lake City: Bookcraft, 1983), 57.

69. Talmage, *Talmage Story*, 240.

1.
Scientific Foundations of Mormon Theology

David H. Bailey

A 1974 ARTICLE IN *SCIENCE* IDENTIFIED MORMON CULTURE AS AN unusually productive source of American scientists and scholars, an achievement linked to such distinctive tenets of Mormon theology as rationalism, natural law, and its elevated concept of humankind.[1] Unfortunately, the church now appears to be backing off from these distinctive theological tenets and taking a more conservative stance towards science, perhaps due in part to the influence of fundamentalist Christian creationist groups. Many Latter-day Saints have become suspicious of science and consider a number of currently accepted scientific theories irreconcilably at odds with the teachings of the faith.

Compounding this difficulty is the fact that the scientific aspects of Mormon theology have not been thoroughly studied, especially in the last few decades during which a virtual explosion of scientific knowledge has occurred. Nearly thirty years ago Mormon philosopher Sterling McMurrin lamented that no one had yet seriously attempted to place Mormon theology on a scientifically rigorous and philosophically acceptable foundation.[2] Perhaps it is time to systematically examine the scientific foundations of Mormon theology.

Many recent developments of modern science have significant implications for LDS theology. Albert Einstein's theory of relativity is certainly one such development. Like all significant scientific discoveries, Einstein's theory was based on groundwork laid by

1

others. Crucial to this theory was the development during the late nineteenth century of a highly accurate method for measuring the speed of light. Numerous measurements revealed the startling conclusion that the speed of light coming from distant stars did not appear to vary in the slightest as the earth moved in its orbit around the sun, whereas a difference of about 67,000 miles per hour due to the motion of the earth would be expected. Physicists had previously noted the puzzling fact that the speed of light was directly calculable from Maxwell's electromagnetic equations without considering relative motion.

For years physicists unsuccessfully tried to accommodate these facts within traditional Newtonian physics. Einstein took a different approach. Rather than trying to explain away the constancy of the speed of light, he proposed this fact as an axiom of a new system of physics. In ordinary situations his theory did not contradict the well-established laws of Newtonian mechanics. However, his theory predicted that in exotic situations certain bizarre phenomena would occur. His assertions include the following:

There is no such thing as an absolute reference frame. All motion is only relative.

Rapidly moving objects increase in mass, contract in length, and experience a slower passage of time.

Two events that appear to be simultaneous to one observer may not appear simultaneous to another observer.

The speed of light is the ultimate speed limit of physical objects in the universe.

Mass can be created and destroyed (converted to energy).

Space and time are distorted near massive bodies.

It took years for these counterintuitive notions to gain acceptance, but since 1905 the theory of relativity has been confirmed in a large number of precise and exacting experiments. For example, the increase in mass and dilation of time are routinely observed in nuclear particle accelerators. Relativity is now considered to be among the most universal and firmly grounded of all scientific theories.

Although not as well know as relativity, quantum theory is at least as fundamental and has far more applications in the "real" world. Quantum theory essentially tells us that our notion of the universe as a collection of tiny particles zipping around in well-defined, deterministic paths is fundamentally inaccurate. For instance, an electron can only be regarded as a wave function with a corresponding probability distribution. This means that we can accurately calculate the probability that an electron will be found at a particular location, but that is about all.

One striking consequence of quantum theory is the Heisenberg uncertainty principle. This principle states that the position of a particle and its momentum (the product of its mass and velocity) cannot simultaneously be determined with absolute precision. Although this principle applies for all objects large and small, its effects are most noticeable at the atomic level. This inability to measure both position and momentum simultaneously has nothing to do with the limits of technology but is a fundamental limit transcending any possible means of measurement.

A related consequence of quantum theory is that there is a small but non-zero probability that a particle entirely confined in a force field will suddenly appear on the outside of this barrier and escape. This is like saying that a marble confined inside a wooden box can suddenly appear on the outside without even penetrating the wood. Indeed the radioactive decay of a nucleus demonstrates this principle: an alpha particle suddenly appears outside the nuclear force field (which normally confines it) and escapes.

Another quantum effect, one which has profound philosophical consequences, is known as the Einstein-Podolsky-Rosen (EPR) effect. The most commonly studied instance of this effect is the polarization of two photons (light particles) simultaneously emitted from a nucleus in opposite directions. Experiments indicate that when the polarization angle of one photon is determined at a detector, this orientation is somehow instantly communicated to the other photon. The traditional quantum theory interpretation of this paradoxical result is that the polarization of the photons, like the position of an electron, simply does not exist in any sense until it is measured. This implies that there is no such thing as an objective reality—the act of observation is an essential part of the phenomenon being observed.

A third area relevant to this discussion is cosmology, in particular the theory that the entire observable universe (space, time,

and matter) was created roughly 15 billion years ago in a single
cataclysmic event known as the "big bang." The big bang theory grew
out of a discovery made about sixty years ago by astronomer Edwin
Hubble. He observed that the farther away a galaxy was, as measured
by its absolute brightness, the faster it appears to be receding from
the earth, as measured by the "red shift" of its light spectra. This
implies that the universe is expanding and was thus at some previous
time much denser than it is today. In 1964 a theoretical physicist
showed that if the big bang had really occurred, then a remnant of
the initial fireball should still be observable as low-level microwave
radiation characteristic of that emitted by a body a few degrees above
absolute zero (-460 degrees Fahrenheit). At about the same time and
completely independently, two scientists at Bell laboratories were
attempting to reduce the level of noise in an experimental microwave
antenna. After eliminating every conceivable source of noise in their
equipment, they concluded that this noise was microwave radiation
of extraterrestrial origin. Astrophysicists immediately recognized
that it fit the pattern predicted by the big bang theory.

Since then other persuasive pieces of evidence have been
uncovered. As a result this theory is now generally accepted as the
correct description of the origin of the universe. I must emphasize
that the big bang theory is not as fundamental and well established
as relativity and quantum theory. However, the weight of evidence
supporting the theory has increased to the point that it must be
taken seriously by anyone attempting to form a scientifically tenable
theology.

Some remarkable aspects of the current big bang theory have
theological overtones. Physicists have concluded in recent years that
the fundamental constants of physics—the gravitational constant and
the masses of protons and electrons—all seem to be exceedingly
finely tuned for the universe to exist as we know it today. For example,
if gravitation was just very slightly stronger, the universe would have
long ago stopped expanding and would instead have fallen back and
obliterated itself in the opposite of a big bang. On the other hand, if
gravitation were significantly weaker, then after the big bang matter
would have dispersed too rapidly for stars and planets to have
formed. Some scientists have even claimed that the balance between
some of these fundamental constants is so sensitive that a change of

one part in 10^{40} would have rendered the universe uninhabitable as we know it.[3]

Cosmologists usually explain that such extreme coincidences are to be expected in any universe containing beings intelligent enough to pose the question. Many scientists consider the fact that our universe is conducive to the formation of stars, planets, biological evolution, and ultimately humans to be a highly significant piece of data leading to the conclusion that the universe we reside in must have certain characteristics. However, this notion, which is known as the "anthropic principle of cosmology," cannot be verified experimentally in a strict sense.

A fourth area of modern science with connections to theology is in the fields of geology and paleontology. The currently accepted outline of the history of the earth is as follows: the earth coalesced out of a cloud of stellar material about 4.5 billion years ago. Within approximately one billion years after the earth was formed, primitive single-celled organisms appeared, leaving traces in some of the oldest rock formations. Later oxygen appeared in the atmosphere, originating primarily from the photosynthesis of primitive plants. Beginning about 700 million years ago, there was a dramatic increase in the variety and complexity of life. Some members of the animal kingdom developed skeletons, and many new species of plants and animals eventually appeared, including dinosaurs and primitive mammals. Over the years many species appeared and disappeared, all the time increasing in complexity and approaching the species currently on earth. About four or five million years ago, new primate species arose that bore striking resemblance to modern humans, featuring a moderate-sized brain and bipedal locomotion. By about 40,000 years ago, the descendants of these hominids had changed into beings virtually indistinguishable in form from modern man and woman.

Studies of rates of deposition long ago established an age for the earth in the hundreds of millions of years. In the last fifty years, any remaining reasonable doubt has been removed by the development of very reliable dating methods. Many of these are based on radioactive decay. The rate of radioactive decay of a particular nucleus can be measured with high precision and is essentially invariant with time, temperature, pressure, and chemical combination. Thus dates obtained by radioactive dating techniques must be taken seriously. Other highly reliable techniques have been discovered as well. One of the most interesting of these new methods is known as "fission track" dating. It is based on the fission (splitting) of a uranium nucleus, again a basic quantum phenomenon. When a fission occurs in a certain crystalline rock, it leaves a distinctive track that is directly visible under a microscope. By counting the number of these tracks in a sample of known uranium content, a reliable date for the specimen can be determined. Geologic dates measured in this manner are entirely consistent with dates obtained by other techniques. Thus any scientifically tenable theology must acknowledge the above outline of the earth's history.

Surveys still show nearly half of adult Americans do not accept the basic notions of the theory of evolution. This skepticism is even greater in the LDS church. A survey of Latter-day Saints in the Salt Lake City area showed that 72 percent thought the theory either surely or probably false.4

Much has happened since Charles Darwin first outlined his theories in *The Origin of Species* in 1859. Some early conjectures have been proven incorrect, such as Lamarck's suggestion that acquired behavioral traits might be transmitted by heredity to the next generation. Recently scientists have questioned Darwin's general assumption that evolution is a uniform, steady process. However, the basic notions that species have changed and are continuing to change and that the entire biological kingdom is related are now rather firmly established.

The fossil record continues to provide strong evidence for evolution. True, there are troublesome gaps in the record, but an increasing number of these gaps are being filled. For example, some highly credible transition species between birds and reptiles have recently been discovered, and the transition between reptiles and mammals is now well understood.5 In addition, when these gaps are viewed in terms of molecular biology, many of them no longer appear discontinuous. The abrupt transitions between some species indicate to many paleontologists that evolution advanced in fits and starts with long periods of relative stasis in between. But none of this changes the basic conclusion that life has evolved on earth over many millions of years.

The discovery in the 1950s of the structure of the nucleic acids DNA and RNA marked a turning point in evolutionary biology. Since DNA sequences direct the synthesis of amino acids to form proteins, the mechanism of genetics could now be studied at the molecular level. Among the most significant recent developments is the tabulation of amino acid sequences for certain proteins across a wide variety of species. These tabulations provide a reliable, quantitative measure of the evolutionary distance among organisms. Now biologists no longer have to rely on subjective anatomical criteria to justify the evolutionary organization of the biological kingdom. For instance, the close relationship that had been theorized between humans and higher primates has been fully confirmed: the alpha chain of human hemoglobin, which is 141 amino acids long, is identical in chimpanzees, differs in only one amino acid location in gorillas, and yet differs in twenty-five locations in rabbits and in over 100 locations in fish.[6] Since these sequences apparently reflect the degree of genetic relatedness, they also provide a reliable measure of the length of time elapsed since two groups of species diverged.

Several aspects of the theory of evolution, however, can still be considered tentative and conjectural. One of these is the determination of the precise history and genealogy of an individual species. Another unsettled area is the actual causes and mechanisms of genetic change, such as determining the precise roles of environment and mutations. One important aspect of the theory of evolution that is still in the realm of hypothesis and speculation is explaining the development of the original, primitive, one-celled organisms. Scientists concede that they have not established a complete, satisfactory scenario for the origin of life.[7]

This overview of certain modern scientific developments, sketchy though it necessarily is, provides a suggestive context for examining some of the basic doctrines of Mormon theology.

The Nature of God. For many church members the doctrine that God the Father and Jesus Christ are separate personages is the most significant way their theology differs from traditional Christianity. However, other aspects of the Mormon concept of God are even more unusual. For example, the God of traditional Christianity is considered to be the totality of original existence, a being who created all natural laws and is beyond time and space. The LDS concept of God instead posits that God is a real, tangible being who co-exists with natural laws in the universe.8 Probably the most extreme Latter-day Saint "heresy" in the minds of other Christian sects is the law of eternal progression ("as man is, God once was, and as God is, man may become"). This doctrine, first enunciated by Joseph Smith[9] and later elaborated by other church presidents, is now a fundamental tenet of the faith.

   B. H. Roberts, who gave the first clear exposition of this finitistic concept of God in 1903, stated in effect that God's power and intelligence are not infinite in a literal, absolute sense. God cannot contravene natural law—like us he is apparently subject to natural laws himself. Thus there is no such thing as a miracle; God works through natural laws that he understands but that we do not yet. This doctrine provides a satisfying explanation to a host of philosophical dilemmas, such as why God, with presumably infinite power, is apparently unable to prevent human sin and suffering. Church members do not agree about whether God continues to progress in intelligence. Recently some authorities have insisted that he does not,[10] but many members continue to agree with the teachings and official statements of the early leaders this his growth is a natural corollary to the law of eternal progression.[11]

   From a scientific viewpoint, the notion of a finite, naturalistic, material God is an appealing idea, far more easily accommodated within scientific thought than an abstract immaterial being who contravenes natural law. It strongly suggests that studying scientific laws can help us understand God's handiwork more clearly. And while scientific knowledge alone cannot prove the existence of such a God, neither can it prove that such a being cannot exist.

   One example of how a finitistic God makes more sense from a scientific viewpoint is given by analyzing the concept of God's omniscience. For if we presume that all information requires at least some material for storage, then God's mind would have to be of infinite physical extent and mass to contain infinite information. An absolutely omniscient being also appears to contradict quantum theory, as I will later discuss.

   The Eternal Nature of God and Humankind. There is a story circulating in scientific circles that one day a professor was describing the currently accepted theories of the origin and destiny of the sun. When he mentioned that the sun will likely exhaust its nuclear fuel and die within five billion years or so, one of the students asked the professor to repeat the statement. Relieved, the student said, "Whew! I thought you said five *million*."

The notion that everything in our universe originated in a big bang approximately 15 billion years ago creates some problems for Mormon theology.[12] A God who exists in space and time should reside within the observable universe. In that case God is not eternal in a literal and absolute sense but instead came into being after the big bang. A straightforward solution to this dilemma is to abandon a strict interpretation of the word *eternal*, as is suggested in Doctrine and Covenants 19:6-12. After all, 15 billion years may not be forever, but it is so far beyond our comprehension as to be eternal for all practical purposes. In that event God is not the being who crafted the universe at the big bang. If there is such a being, it is a deity beyond him. Mormon theology, of course, allows the possibility of a hierarchy of deities (D&C 121:28).

Not all LDS scientists are satisfied with the concept of a material God residing within the observable universe. Russell T. Pack, for example, has argued that God does not reside in the universe created in the big bang and is not limited by the natural laws of our universe.[13] This theory allows God to craft the universe in the big bang and also to create numerous other universes about which we have no knowledge. Further it allows us to interpret God's omnipotence and omniscience in a completely different light than B. H. Roberts suggested.

While such a belief cannot be scientifically falsified, it does presuppose the existence of currently unknown scientific principles to avoid a mere deist concept of God, because current theories of fundamental physics and cosmology forbid any communication with or intervention by inhabitants of universes beyond the one created in the big bang. Clearly there are no easy answers to such questions, but perhaps further developments in physics and cosmology will shed some light.[14]

The traditional LDS concept of eternal elements (D&C 93:33) runs into a similar difficulty if it is literally interpreted to mean that matter has always existed and cannot be created or destroyed.

The conversion of mass to energy and the transmutation of matter, even of nuclear particles, are well established physical phenomena. Furthermore all matter originated in the big bang. A more tenable interpretation of this scripture is that it was intended to rebut the notion of the *ex nihilo* creation of the earth. This doctrine too might be reexamined in light of new scientific knowledge.

Determinism Versus Free Will. Quantum theory affirms the distinctively Mormon doctrine of free will and indeterminism. Though most of the effects of probabilistic quantum principles are restricted to the atomic and subatomic level, they can definitely have macroscopic effects. For example, a Geiger counter clicks when it detects the random decay of a single radioactive nucleus. Perhaps similar random quantum effects occur among neurons in the human brain, possibly inducing us to alter decisions. Thus human behavior as well as all other macroscopic phenomena may be fundamentally indeterminate. If this is true, then God's foreknowledge of human-kind's actions is not infinite in a literal and absolute sense, and God could be occasionally surprised by the outcome of some human events.

Quantum theory certainly does not imply that prediction of the future is impossible, either by God or humanity. For example, a knowledge of Newtonian mechanics (perhaps with some minute relativistic corrections) together with accurate astronomical observations allows engineers to predict with high precision the moment when an interplanetary spacecraft will reach its destination. Similarly parents do not exercise supernatural prescience when they predict that their teenage son will have an auto accident if he continues to drive in a dare-devil manner. Quantum theory does, however, limit the accuracy with which such predictions can be made. Thus God may be able to communicate to prophets glimpses of the future, but there must be a limit to the detail of such prophecy.

There is one difficulty in concluding that quantum physics is a basis for human free will. Even if certain quantum phenomena can change the course of human actions, how can a person be held responsible for truly random events? For example, if a neuron fires because of a quantum physics effect and induces a person to commit a crime, is that person really responsible for the crime? Perhaps the answer lies in the explanation that since quantum effects are generally of rather small scale, the person must have been already very close to a decision to commit this crime. We could then argue that the person was irresponsible in allowing him- or herself to approach the point of committing a crime so closely as to be affected by a quantum event. In any case some care must be taken before we conclude that quantum theory is the solution to the determinism/free-will controversy.

The Creation. One positive aspect of Mormon theology from a scientific viewpoint is its unequivocal rejection of the doctrine of the creation of the earth *ex nihilo*. Primitive Christians also rejected such a notion.[15] The creation *ex nihilo* doctrine was apparently adopted several centuries after Jesus. The question of whether or not the entire universe was created "out of nothing," however, is a different matter. Currently some physicists theorize that indeed the entire universe could have been a single quantum accident,[16] although such ideas are at present highly speculative.

Even without the doctrine of creation *ex nihilo*, any scientifically tenable system of theology must abandon the notion that the earth, complete with its rich layer of fossils and its intricate biological system, was organized a few thousand years ago. Similarly the notion that species are fixed and have not evolved with time must be abandoned. Such notions have not been tenable for at least fifty years. Interpreting the creation periods as literal days should have died with the Book of Abraham's substitution of the word *time* for *day* to describe each of the creation periods. Nonetheless the belief that the creation took place in either seven days or 7,000 years appears to be fairly widespread in the church and is occasionally suggested even by modern church leaders.[17]

Early church leaders apparently had much more progressive views of the age of the earth. W. W. Phelps wrote to Joseph Smith's brother on 1 January 1845: "Well, now, Brother William, when the house of Israel begin to come into the glorious mysteries of the kingdom, and find that Jesus Christ, whose goings forth, as the prophets said, have been from old, from eternity: and that eternity, agreeably to the records found in the catacombs of Egypt, has been going on in this system (not this world) almost two thousand five hundred and fifty five millions of years: and to know at the same time, that deists, geologists and others are trying to prove that matter must have existed hundreds of thousands of years; it almost tempts the flesh to fly to God, or muster faith like Enoch to be translated."[18]

The puzzling phrase "not this world" clouds this interesting statement. Duane Jeffrey has pointed out that the word "world" may have meant society or civilization, since Joseph Smith defined it that way.[19] In any event the context clearly indicates a belief in a physical system much older than a few thousand years. The figure 2.555 billion years implied in this quotation is particularly curious because it was not known until this century that the earth and the solar system are several billion years old. This figure by the way may be obtained by interpreting the seven periods of creation as 7,000 years, each day of each year equivalent to 1,000 years, which is a day in God's time according to the Book of Abraham.[20]

Many ideas have been proposed to reconcile LDS scripture with science. Some have hypothesized that the basic materials of the earth are perhaps ancient but that God assembled them together a few thousand years ago. Others speculate that the rocks and fossils are the remnants of a previous existence, and plants and animals currently on the earth were transported here recently. Such notions are in hopeless contradiction with scientific observations. There is no hint of a recent assemblage of the earth, and each of these theories fails to account for the progression of ancient species up to and including those currently on earth today. Others have suggested that God chose to create the earth (and the universe) with a great apparent age and with the appearance of an evolutionary development of living things in order to test the faith of mortals. Such a notion cannot be scientifically falsified, but it openly contradicts the belief that God works according to natural principles and implies that God has performed an incredible and intricate deception.

Two theories of the Creation permit the possibility of a divine hand altering the natural course of events. One is that evolution on earth was guided by a supreme being whose ultimate goal was to produce a species resembling himself. Nothing in current scientific knowledge would rule out this notion. Some would even argue that such divine intervention is a logical explanation of the sudden spurts and branches that are observed in the fossil record. The recently popular theory that asteroids or interstellar comets colliding with the ancient earth precipitated sharp evolutionary changes is a no less dramatic explanation of the sudden disappearances of previously successful species.

One stumbling block in reconciling LDS creation scriptures with scientific knowledge is Moses 3:7: "And I, the Lord God, formed man from the dust of the ground, and breathed into his nostrils the breath of life; and man became a living soul, the first flesh upon the earth, the first man also." Some have interpreted this passage as a definitive statement that there was no life of any sort on earth before Adam. However, others have pointed out that Adam is not explicitly named in the passage, and thus it might simply mean that humankind originated from the materials of this earth, which is certainly consistent with scientific knowledge. Still others have pointed out the phrase "living soul" and concluded that Adam was the first of the living organisms on earth to be joined with a previously created spirit. Some suggest that the statement applies only locally to the Garden of Eden. Perhaps the scriptural account of the creation of Adam and Eve is figurative, as was once suggested in the LDS temple endowment ceremony.

Recently some prominent church writers have begun to display a more open-minded approach than has prevailed during the last few decades. Hugh Nibley's "Before Adam"[21] argues that pre-Adamites are entirely acceptable. Nibley and others have also investigated the writings of early Christians, who believed in the creation of numerous other worlds with sentient beings and who emphatically rejected creation *ex nihilo*.[22] Perhaps the coming years will see a reopening of dialogue between LDS scientists and theologians on this topic.

Spirits, Bodies, and the Resurrection. Modern discoveries of DNA and molecular biology provide a highly tenable explanation of how the resurrection might occur. Scientists have known for years that each individual human cell contains encoded in its DNA sufficient information to in theory perfectly reconstruct the individual. However, they often overlook the fact that even DNA material is not required—only a record of this information which could be entered into a computer file.

A related issue—that we were created spiritually before coming to the earth and that our spirit personage exactly resembles our physical—poses a difficult problem for those seeking to reconcile theology and science. This notion appears to be at odds with known facts of biological heredity. The only way to explain this resemblance is to assume that God's foreknowledge is so great as to foresee every conjugal act and to foresee which of the millions of male sperm would unite with a particular ovum. Such a level of foreknowledge (and determinism) not only runs afoul of quantum physics but exceeds even that permitted by church authorities, who frequently counsel youth that there is no such thing as a unique predetermined marriage partner.

Perhaps the silence of LDS writers on this subject is due to the realization that it is difficult to reconcile this popularly held belief with known facts of genetics. Perhaps scholars and theologians need to re-examine this doctrine. Is it really necessary and scripturally well founded? Can it be moderated? Is the visual appearance of a spirit being merely a fluid quality that can assume the form of an assigned physical body?

Latter-day Saint theology, with its rich tradition of naturalism and open-minded attitudes toward science, is to many intellectually-minded members a major factor in their continued faith.[23] There is no question that its foundation of natural law and rationality permits a significantly cleaner accommodation of the principles of science than most other theological systems.

However, this tradition may be in danger as the LDS church continues to experience exponential growth, bringing in converts whose beliefs are deeply rooted in the theologies of traditional Christianity. Current church literature frequently includes statements about God's absolute omnipotence and ability to alter the laws of nature, even though these sectarian doctrines sharply conflict with traditional Mormon theology.[24] Similarly the conservatism that currently pervades creation beliefs in the modern church seems to have more in common with certain Christian fundamentalist sects than with the open-minded philosophies of the early Mormon church leaders.

Perhaps it is time for Latter-day Saints with scientific backgrounds to renew their efforts to establish dialogue with those of other disciplines in order to re-examine the philosophical roots of Mormon theology. This essay has been written in that spirit.

NOTES

1. Kenneth Hardy, "Social Origins of American Scientists and Scholars," *Science* 185 (9 Aug. 1974): 497-506.

2. Sterling M. McMurrin, *The Theological Foundations of the Mormon Religion* (Salt Lake City: University of Utah Press, 1965), 46.

3. Paul Davies, *The Accidental Universe* (New York: Cambridge University Press, 1982).

4. Armand L. Mauss, "Saints, Cities, and Secularism: Religious Attitudes and Behavior of Modern Urban Mormons," *Dialogue: A Journal of Mormon Thought* 7 (Summer 1972): 8-27.

5. James A. Hopson, "The Mammal-Like Reptiles: A Study of Transitional Fossils," *The American Biology Teacher* 49 (Jan. 1987): 16-26.

6. Thomas H. Jukes, "Molecular Evidence for Evolution," in *Scientists Confront Creationism*, ed. Laurie R. Godfrey (New York: Macmillan, 1962).

7. Robert Shapiro, *Origins: A Skeptic's Guide to the Creation of Life on Earth* (New York: Summit Books, 1986).

8. McMurrin, *Theological Foundations*; Blake T. Ostler, "The Mormon Concept of God," *Dialogue: A Journal of Mormon Thought* 17 (Summer 1984): 65-93.

9. Stan Larson, "The King Follett Discourse: A Newly Amalgamated Text," *Brigham Young University Studies* 18 (Winter 1978): 193-208.

10. Bruce R. McConkie, "The Seven Deadly Heresies," *BYU Speeches of the Year* (1980): 74-80.

11. Gary James Bergera, "The Orson Pratt-Brigham Young Controversies," *Dialogue: A Journal of Mormon Thought* 13 (Summer 1980): 7-49; James R. Clark, ed., *Messages of the First Presidency, Volume 2* (Salt Lake City: Bookcraft, 1965), 222-23; O. Kendall White, *Mormon Neo-Orthodoxy: A Crisis Theology* (Salt Lake City: Signature Books, 1987).

12. Keith E. Norman, "Mormon Cosmology: Can It Survive the Big Bang?" *Sunstone* 10 (Oct. 1985): 18-23.

13. Russell T. Pack, "Quantum Cosmology," *Sunstone* 11 (Jan. 1987): 2-4.

14. Paul Davies, *God and the New Physics* (New York: Touchstone, 1984).

15. Hugh Nibley, "Treasures in the Heavens: Some Early Christian Insights into the Organizing of Worlds," *Dialogue: A Journal of Mormon Thought* 8 (Autumn 1973): 76-98.

16. R. Brout, F. Englert, and E. Gunzin, "The Creation of the Universe as a Quantum Phenomenon," *Annals of Physics* 115 (15 Sept. 1978): 78-106.

17. Bruce R. McConkie, *Mormon Doctrine* (Salt Lake City: Bookcraft, 1966). McConkie subsequently backed away from this view.

18. *Times and Seasons* 5 (1 Jan. 1845): 758.

19. Duane E. Jeffrey, "Seers, Savants and Evolution: The Uncomfortable Interface," *Dialogue: A Journal of Mormon Thought* 8 (Autumn 1973): 41-75.

20. William Lee Stokes, "In the Beginning," *The Instructor* 100 (June 1965): 228-33.

21. Hugh Nibley, *Before Adam* (Provo, UT: FARMS, 1980).

22. Nibley, "Treasures in the Heavens."

23. Richard P. Smith, "Science: A Part of or Apart from Mormonism?" *Dialogue: A Journal of Mormon Thought* 19 (Spring 1986): 106-22.

24. See White, *Mormon Neo-Orthodoxy.*

2.
The New Biology and Mormon Theology

James L. Farmer, William S. Bradshaw, and F. Brent Johnson

EXEGETES AS WILLING AND CAPABLE AS EARLY MORMON APOSTLE AND intellectual Orson Pratt, who combined empirical and theological insights in sermons and pamphlets, have all but disappeared from the Mormon scene. His successors have retained the enthusiastic optimism of early Mormonism, but they have not replaced the empirical beliefs of the nineteenth century with more correct information which is available to us now. One can only wish that the discoveries of modern science had been available to Pratt and his contemporaries, for some of the discoveries open up new possibilities for theological discussion. The new biology has given us insights into the nature of life that bring into question many of the easy assumptions that were made about the nature of the soul (body and spirit). Recent developments raise interesting ethical and theological issues. In this essay we outline some of these without presuming to propose definitive answers.

Apostle Pratt believed that the spirits of human beings were created before the earth was formed, and that these spirits had the same dimensions and appearance as individual physical human bodies. It is now possible in laboratory experiments to remove cells from a human being and keep them alive indefinitely—long after the donor has died. Organs can be transplanted into another human being, where they function as part of the new body. Finally it is possible to keep a human body "alive" long after the brain is dead. Conversely there are organisms which begin life as single, independent cells, which at a certain time crawl together and form a new organism with specialized body parts and a new form of behavior. One wonders where the spirit is in these examples. Do new spirits inhabit the cultured cells? Does a "general" spirit quicken lower life forms?

It is also possible to fuse two or more mouse embryos to produce a single mouse (a chimera) with three, four, or more parents. As pointless as such a creation sounds it has great practicality for the study of biological processes. It is almost certainly possible to create human chimeras. If the spirit is present from the moment of conception or from very early embryonic development, how many spirits are housed in a chimera? Closely related to this question is the phenomenon of identical twinning. Identical twins begin as a single embryo which at some point in development splits into two. At what point are two spirits present?

Identical twins are clones. Another type of clone can be formed by removing a nucleus from an individual and implanting it into an enucleated egg. After the egg has developed into a many-celled embryo, several of the nuclei from the embryo can again be transferred to other enucleated eggs. These eggs develop into adults which are genetically identical to the original nucleus donor. This procedure proved to be valuable to stock breeders. If it can be applied to cattle, it can also be applied to humans. If human cloning is ever accomplished, what role will the spirit play—and at what stage of development?

The test tube baby is a reality. Ripe eggs in the ovary of infertile women are removed surgically and then fertilized by the husband's sperm. One or more healthy embryos are reimplanted into the woman's uterus. From this point on the pregnancy is not unusual. The unused embryos may be discarded or frozen. Are the discarded embryos human souls? What is the status of a frozen embryo? Mormons have a plethora of opinions but no clear doctrine on this point.

External fertilization offers several other new possibilities. Women have borne children without being pregnant, surrogate mothers having nurtured the embryos. It is possible that two women could have a child, since it seems possible to use one egg to fertilize another egg to produce an apparently healthy embryo. A woman who was totally incapable of producing eggs could bear children produced by external fertilization of a donated egg by her husband's sperm and the implantation of the embryo into her uterus. This last procedure is much like artificial insemination by a donor, a procedure accepted by the LDS church but not encouraged.

Stock breeders are perfecting techniques to allow them to maintain sperm, eggs, and embryo banks. Thus a mating which produces superior stock could be repeated thousands of times, with the embryos being implanted into surrogate mothers. If perfected, these techniques would allow humans to "custom order" their children from human embryo banks. For instance, a couple who wanted a superior athlete as their progeny could order an embryo produced from the sperm of a professional basketball player and the egg of a professional tennis player. The sex of the child could be controlled by discarding the embryos of the unwanted sex.

There do not seem to be any great technical obstacles to these procedures. The LDS church does not seem to be inordinately concerned with biological parentage, judging from its encouragement of adoption and its tolerance of artificial insemination. Perhaps then the crucial question would revolve around the fate of unused embryos.

The emotionally charged issue of abortion requires some comment. Spontaneous abortion is common in humans. Somewhere between 20 percent and well over half of all conceptions end in spontaneous abortion. Most of these happen in the first days or weeks of pregnancy, usually escaping the notice of physicians and even of the pregnant woman. When aborted fetuses are examined, a high percentage are found to be genetically defective. Thus abortion appears to be nature's way of eliminating most seriously defective fetuses. If one were to assume that every embryo is a human soul, the simplest conclusion would be that many (perhaps most) of our brothers and sisters never experience mortality in a meaningful way. There are more complicated assumptions—for instance, the nineteenth-century Mormon view that the spirit of the aborted fetus is reassigned to another body. The common belief that mothers will be allowed to raise a baby to adulthood after the resurrection should the child die early in this life is a variation on this theme. Scripture does not allow us to identify any of these assumptions as doctrine.

Amniocentesis is often (incorrectly) identified with abortion. This procedure, in which fluid and cells are removed from the amniotic sac for examination, can be used to determine whether or not a fetus is mature enough to survive outside the womb. It also allows the diagnosis and treatment in the womb of certain disorders such as methylmalonic acidemia and blood-type incompatibilities, conditions which are often lethal to the untreated fetus. Additionally it is possible to determine whether a high-risk fetus has a particular genetic disorder. These procedures allow couples who are known to carry defective genes or chromosomes and older women to have children without fear. These high-risk parents often forego having children altogether if such procedures are not available. Although there is still some risk of other birth defects, the overall risk is greatly reduced.

The ethical problem associated with clinical abortion of defective fetuses is fairly obvious. At one extreme are those who consider abortion synonymous with murder. Perhaps at the other extreme are those who believe that all considerations of abortion are private matters which are not the legitimate concern of society. The position of the LDS church is less clear. Although abortions are clearly forbidden in most cases, they are permitted under exceptional circumstances when the health of the mother is threatened or following rape. Abortion of defective fetuses has not been explicitly approved or disapproved, and it can be argued that clinical abortion is an extension of spontaneous abortion when defective fetuses are involved.

Recent discoveries raise other questions about the spirit-body relationship. At least two mental illnesses—manic-depressive syndrome and schizophrenia—seem to be genetically controlled. The new science of sociobiology—which has shown to be at least as controversial as the ideas of Darwin and his successors—argues that altruistic behavior is also genetic. If it indeed is true that much of human behavior is genetically controlled and is responsive to chemical modification and perhaps genetic engineering, what role should be ascribed to the spirit in overcoming sin?

Recombinant-DNA experiments (gene splicing) allow the

transfer of genes from any organism into bacteria. It is very likely that soon we will be able to place genes from any source into any organism, including human beings. This would allow the insertion of "good" genes in place of "bad" genes in some cases. Few people would argue that such gene therapy is unacceptable. However, if it should prove possible to alter behavior or some other socially sensitive trait, the impact on our ideas about the spirit-body relationship could be profound.

Some people believe that the moment of death is divinely determined. If this is so, why is death routinely interfered with by the use of antibiotics, surgery, and prayer? If the hour of death is determined, is it sinful to intervene or is it commendable because it demonstrates our love? A related issue is the phenomenon of faith healing. Physicians who are not necessarily religious use the techniques of psychosomatic medicine to achieve "faith" healings which are at least outwardly similar to those we see in the church. What is the relationship between the spirit and the body in these situations?

Many of these discoveries and techniques have worked together to create a paradoxical attitude in many people. On the one hand there is awe and admiration for the feats of science. On the other hand there is suspicion and fear that science is tampering with things that ought not to be interfered with. The resulting anxiety is sometimes relieved by a general feeling that "God would not let *that* happen." Perhaps there is a Murphy's Law of history: anything that can be used for evil will be. However, it seems that the appropriate response to a potential for evil is to seek to do good rather than attempt to set limits on science. Although the new biology may alter the way in which Mormons think about some ethical problems, it will not fundamentally change the need to live by faith in a world not fully comprehendable. The Lord may have placed very few constraints on us in our search for knowledge and understanding. Science moves inevitably toward synthesis of living things, as it has already achieved the ability to alter species. It is reassuring to know that Mormon theology offers the chance to eternal progression, not only in this life but in the life to come. As we discover more and more about the nature of God's universe, we are given the opportunity to use that knowledge to do good works.

3.
The 1911 Evolution Controversy at Brigham Young University

Gary James Bergera

Four years after assuming the presidency of Brigham Young University in 1903 George H. Brimhall embarked on an ambitious plan "to include in [his] faculty . . . the best scholars of the church."[1] LDS leaders had only recently upgraded their Provo, Utah, academy to university status, and the fifty-five-year-old Utah Valley educator was anxious to improve his school's largely home-spun faculty. Brimhall's initial coup was hiring in 1907 BYU's first Ph.D., Joseph Peterson, to oversee the psychology department. Brimhall also succeeded that year in recruiting Peterson's younger brother, Henry, who held a master's degree from Harvard, to supervise the school's College of Education.[2]

The following year, Brimhall convinced twenty-eight-year-old Ralph V. Chamberlin, chair of the University of Utah's biology department and dean of its medical school, to join the growing faculty. Upon his arrival Chamberlin was made head of the biology department, and in 1909 his brother, William Henry, was also hired. Trained in modern and ancient languages and theology, William taught classes in psychology, philosophy, and languages. In addition to their regular assignments, the Petersons and William Chamberlin, three of the most highly credentialed Utah academics of their day, were appointed to the part-time theology faculty.[3]

Academically superior to their colleagues, the Petersons and Chamberlins brought to BYU a contagious enthusiasm for the latest intellectual pursuits, and were, along with Brimhall and other members of the faculty, determined to counter persistent criticism that the rural Mormon school was "lacking in genuine scholarship" from its "farmer teachers."[4] In repeated attempts to upgrade the school's lackluster curriculum, subjects ranging from communism to eugenics were added and soon hotly debated both in and out of class.[5] "I recall one occasion in which there had been a good informal talk in a little group," Henry Peterson later wrote. Although less intellectually-oriented than his teachers, Brimhall himself reportedly "spoke up and said, '*I too am an evolutionist.*' That viewpoint [was] unavoidable."[6]

At services in 1909 commemorating the centennial of Charles Darwin's birth and semicentennial of his *Origin of the Species*, Ralph Chamberlin publicly pronounced the British biologist one of the greatest scientific minds of the era. BYU's student newspaper, the *White and Blue*, echoed: "Undoubtedly among the great men of the nineteenth century the foremost place should be given to the eminent scientist Charles Darwin." For Chamberlin, Darwin's theories of evolution explained both the origin of life and belief in God, while biblical scholarship unveiled "the progressive unfolding of the Divine." He subsequently published two lengthy articles in the *White and Blue* illustrating the aims of scriptural criticism. The Petersons and Chamberlins soon became well known for their support of organic evolution and scriptural exegesis. "How I enjoyed them!" remembered BYU alumna Annie Clark Tanner. "I had been a teacher of the Bible in several of the organizations of the church and now for the first time in my life I was learning some truths which made reasonable explanations of Bible difficulties."[7]

Seven months after the Darwin centennial, and perhaps in response to questions raised during the Darwin celebration, the First Presidency of the LDS church, consisting of life-long Mormon official Joseph F. Smith and counselors John R. Winder and Anthon H. Lund, asked Apostle Orson F. Whitney to draft an official statement on the "origin of the physical man." A special committee of apostles corrected Whitney's text, which was then read to the First Presidency and Quorum of Twelve Apostles, was "sanctioned by them" as "the official position of the church," and appeared in the November 1909 issue of the official *Improvement Era*. As published, the statement defended a spiritual and physical creation, the creation of man in the image of God, and Adam as the "primal parent of the race," without addressing the age of the earth, or, most importantly, the mutability of species. Still, the statement's anti-evolutionary sentiment was unmistakable, and many church members no doubt interpreted it as a refutation of Darwinism.[8]

Sketchy reports of the Chamberlins' and Petersons' "progressive" teachings had reached church headquarters and were referred to superintendent of church schools Horace Hall Cummings. Largely self-educated, Cummings had concluded from his own unsuccessful attempt to study in the East during the 1880s with church support that "previous faithfulness and good character [are] no assurance against" the loss of one's faith. Cummings's career in church education had been foretold by the widow of a church apostle who had blessed him in tongues that he "should visit the stakes of Zion, establishing and setting in order educational institutions in them." Like his mentor and career church educator, Karl G. Maeser, Cummings had remained within the ranks of the church school system, convinced that its value lay in spiritual and moral rather than intellectual development. Skeptical of secular teachings, he had instructed Brimhall in 1908: "The use of any text book on the New or Old Testament written by a non-member of our church [is] expressly forbidden, and the use of the outlines prepared for that purpose enjoined." Cummings viewed with alarm the growing popularity of evolution and scriptural criticism, which in his mind portended a move away from the religious simplicity he felt duty-bound to uphold.[9]

Reportedly responding to complaints from as far away as Mexico, Cummings visited BYU in late November 1910 to evaluate the situation. He subsequently reported to the LDS board of education that a number of teachers were "applying the evolutionary theory and other philosophical hypotheses to principles of the gospel and to the teachings of the church in such a way as to disturb, if not destroy the faith of the pupils." The board, alledgedly "thunderstruck" at the report, instructed Cummings to "make a thorough investigation of conditions there and bring them a written report of [his] findings." Cummings returned to Provo within the week and toured the school for nine days, "visiting classes, talking with teachers and students, and in the evenings visit[ing] some of the parents to see what they thought of the situation." Fearing a general condemnation of his faculty from church officials, Brimhall wrote a cautiously worded explanation to Joseph F. Smith a few days after Cummings's arrival. "While I believe [the Petersons and Chamberlins] are from their point of view perfectly right," he wrote, "still I think they are a little over-zealous in their desires to bring people to their point of view. As they look at it their teachings are in perfect harmony with the principles of the gospel, but there are certainly many who cannot perceive that harmony, and, therefore, it seems to me that a little [patience] will be in keeping with greater wisdom on their part."[10]

When news of Cummings's visit spread across campus, "the friendly, respectful spirit heretofore always shown me changed to one of opposition and fault-finding," he noted. Faculty and students alike "said I wanted to destroy the 'academic liberty' of some of their best teachers, and would kill the school." These defenders argued that "theological work had never been so interesting and well patronized. The 'new thought' was making a new school of the B.Y.U." Indeed, one Provo native observed that the teachings of the Petersons and the Chamberlins "seemed to meet a strong need in many students, as well as [in] some of the other faculty members." Their theology classes especially "were among the most popular on the campus and their status as well trained and highly competent men in their specialties attracted large followings." Thus among many upperclassmen Cummings became a "blue-nose kill-joy whose office was to detect and ferret out inrectitude [sic], waywardness and sin [and who] . . . was merely [tolerated], except by college graduates seeking teaching positions in church schools." Students began striking back with "semi-ribald yarns" regarding Cummings's "ultra piety and purity." Hoping to avoid "needless antagonisms," Cummings evidently hedged when he appeared before the faculty in early December and was asked what he would relay to the board. He reported evasively that "he was glad to learn through conversation with the [university] presidency that matters [had] been misrepresented."[11]

However, the report Cummings submitted six weeks later on 21 January 1911 did not mention misrepresentation. Cummings wrote that "when some of the most radical changes in theological views were first introduced" two years earlier, "it caused great disturbance in the minds of both pupils and the old style teachers." While most agreed that "interest in theological work had never been more universal or more intense in the school," and none expressed doubt "in the living oracles . . . and the ordinances of the gospel," still, Cummings reported, "there is a pronounced difference of opinion among both students and teachers upon many important points of doctrine and belief." Without mentioning names, he accused "four or five of the teachers" of championing organic evolution and biblical criticism. The theory of evolution, he alleged, was "treated as a demonstrated law and their applications of it to gospel truths [had given] rise to many curious and conflicting explanations of scripture." He described "the struggle [of] both teacher and student . . . when the new thought was being presented to them. . . . It was like the sorrow of the little child when first told there is no Santa Claus." "Conditions in Provo are unfavorable for . . . a solution [to this] difficulty," Cummings concluded. The number of teachers defending the new teachings "is sufficient to form a coterie having similar views, and the opposition they receive from others keeps them drawn together and determined to defend their views. . . . [They] have been warned by the presidency of the school and by myself, and even pleaded with, for the sake of the school, not to press their views with so much vigor. Even if they were right, conditions are not suitable; but their zeal overcomes all counsel and they seem even more determined, if not defiant, in pushing their beliefs upon the students. They seem to feel they have a mission to protect the young from the errors of their parents."[12]

One week later Cummings appeared before the faculty to summarize his report. Afterwards Brimhall, increasingly nervous, warned that "criticism of leaders should be kept in the background" and urged teachers to be loyal to "the heroes of Mormondom." "A general discussion" followed "in which a goodly number of teachers participated." Amos Merrill, an instructor of education, called for a resolution "invit[ing] the authorities of the church to appoint a committee to investigate the points of doctrine upon which [they had been] criticised." Brimhall, however, tabled the resolution, saying that it would be considered later at a "meeting called by the president for that purpose." Frustrated at the apparent lack of administrative support, Ralph Chamberlin alluded to Cummings's report in an

article appearing four days later in the *White and Blue*. "When we see
men so unhappily bound with prejudice and tradition," he wrote,
"that they are blind to the beauties and light of the grandest conception that science has yet won for man, we sorrow . . . Ultimate cause
and meaning," he concluded, "remain untouched and as impenetra-
ble as before. Evolution leaves the theistic argument from causality
in its essence untouched."[13]

Although members of the General Church Board of Education had received copies of Cummings's report nearly two weeks
earlier, they did not discuss its contents until 3 February. In his
presentation Cummings named the offending teachers as Henry and
Joseph Peterson and Ralph Chamberlin, "who, from an educational
standpoint," he conceded, were "perhaps the strongest men in the
institution, and they have a potent influence with the students, thus
making their theological teachings the more dangerous." In the
brewing confrontation, Brimhall aligned himself with Cummings,
telling board members that "the only thing he could see to do was to
get rid of these teachers." He reported that he had "patiently labored
with them in the hope that they would change their attitude, . . . but
it seemed that they were more determined than ever to teach theology according to their own ideas and theories, instead of according
to the revealed truth." Based on Cummings's and Brimhall's testimony, the board concluded that "immediate steps should be taken
[to investigate further] the three teachers named, and [to proceed
with] their removal if necessary." They also ruled that "other teachers
who may entertain the same ideas should be talked to very plainly
and given to understand that the teaching of such theories could not
be tolerated in the church schools." A special committee was appointed to meet with Chamberlin and the Petersons. Chaired by
Francis M. Lyman, president of the Quorum of the Twelve Apostles,
the committee included Heber J. Grant, Hyrum M. Smith, Charles
W. Penrose, George F. Richards, Anthony W. Ivins, as well as Brimhall and Cummings. Ivins, though suspicious of evolution himself,
soon resigned. "I will not . . . judge those men," he reportedly
protested. "We are not qualified."[14]

One week later to the day the three professors were sum-
moned to Salt Lake City. "We suddenly were brought out into a
room," wrote Chamberlin, "with six of the top dignitaries of the

church there to try us. We were, as they say, flabbergasted." Chamberlin was charged with "teaching evolution," which he did not deny. The three men asked for a copy of the charges against them but were refused. They were, however, aware of the substance of Cummings's report and the broad issues under discussion. All "frankly acknowledged" belief in biblical criticism and "absolute certainty as to the truth of evolution." More seriously, they evidently balked at recognizing the authority of the university president or Board of Trustees to rule on questions of science. The committee remained in session nearly five hours. "Many questions [were] asked" and answered, Apostle Charles Penrose recorded, "some directly, others evasively." But, Elder Heber Grant added, the three men "manifested a very good spirit." The committee met again the following morning and, according to Penrose, "all agreed that the ideas and belief expressed by the professors under fire ought not to be taught in church schools but that the men were sincere and good." They then resolved to "report accordingly and to recommend that their service be dispensed with unless they conform[ed] to the decisions and instructions of the Board of Education." Grant's account, however, is less generously phrased: "We were of a unanimous opinion that it would be unsafe for them to continue teaching at the Brigham Young University." In their report, submitted later that day, the committee recommended that "the services of those three teachers in the B.Y. University be dispensed with unless they change their teachings to conform to the decision and instructions of the Board." The following week BYU board members adopted a nearly identical resolution, while William Chamberlin, whose teachings had not come under board review, published a four-page defense of evolution as an "Aid to Faith in God and Belief in the Resurrection" in the *White and Blue*.[15]

Again Brimhall pleaded with the professors to conform to the board's decisions. Ralph Chamberlin responded defensively, "If you can bring me one student whose faith I have injured in Mormonism, I will bring you five that you, through your narrowness, have driven out of the church. . . . I never gave a public lecture on evolution until I had consulted you as to whether it would be all right. You urged me to do it. Now, why have you changed suddenly?" Brimhall could only feebly joke, "Well, I'll tell you, Brother Chamberlin, I know which side my bread's buttered on."[16]

BYU trustees were to communicate their charges to the three men on 21 February. Unfortunately, the professors first learned of the board's position when they read an editorial attacking higher criticism in the evening's *Deseret News*. Peterson publicly denied that he had taught anything contrary to the gospel and added that, in view of the accusations, he doubted there was much he or the others could do. On 24 February, the board finally issued its ultimatum to Peterson that he modify his teachings or be dismissed. Board members stressed that "from their point of view" he "was out of harmony with his brethren."[17]

Conditions deteriorated rapidly at BYU. When Joseph Peterson received a similar ultimatum, he promptly resigned. News of the development spread throughout faculty and students. Brimhall sent a lengthy letter to BYU trustee Reed Smoot. With forced optimism, Brimhall wrote of probable repercussions to the school and of his resolve to protect the church:

"We are having some little out-of-harmony conditions here. I do not look for a safe reconciliation. I have been hoping for a year or two past that harmony could be secured by waiting, but the delays have been [fraught] with increased danger. There is a possibility yet, but not a probability of adjustment. The school cannot go off and leave the church in any line of activity without *perishing in the desert*. . . . There are some people who predict the death of the college if these men go. I am ready to say that if the life of the college depends upon any number of men out of harmony with the brethren who preside over the church, then it is time for the college to die. I would rather the Maeser Memorial remain a sealed tomb containing our college hopes and ambitions until the day of a new educational resurrection than to have its doors thrown open to influences antagonistic to the heroism, inspiration and revelation of those who have made the school and who have the right to say, 'Thus far shalt thou go and no farther.' The school follows the church, or it ought to stop."[18]

On 11 March, the *Deseret News*, attempting to answer criticisms that it had been less than objective in its coverage of the controversy, published a letter by William Chamberlin defending evolution together with an editorial attacking Chamberlin's position.

The next morning the *Salt Lake Tribune* carried a detailed account of the controversy, claiming that as many as 80 percent of the faculty sympathized with the Petersons and Chamberlin. When Joseph F. Smith was told that "a number of [Provo] merchants and others favoring the . . . teachers had withdrawn their patronage from the [*White and Blue*]," he "spoke up immediately and said that the First Presidency wanted no change in the paper's policy and . . . [said] he would instruct [Zion's Savings Bank] to keep the paper out of financial difficulties." Smith also admonished his son, Andrew, a student at the high school adjoining BYU: "For my sake, my son, as well as your own[,] eschew the Petersons' and Chamberlin's evolution and all such things." On 13 March over 100 undergraduates assembled on campus in a mass rally to "stand by their teachers." The students distributed a petition "ratifying and endorsing the teaching of the professors, and praying for their retention by the Board of Trustees." Of a total college enrollment of 114 undergraduates, as well as a handful of professors, over 90 students and faculty signed the statement, which both the *Tribune* and the *Herald-Republican* printed. Predictably, the *Deseret News* chastised the students for airing their criticisms in print, especially in the *Tribune*, while Brimhall publicly scolded them for "dictating" to the "prophets."[19]

The following afternoon Brimhall met privately with Henry Peterson. Brimhall reported to Joseph F. Smith that they talked "for hours . . . and until away long in the night, but to no avail." "All that I needed to do," Peterson later wrote, "was to be a good boy, teach the permitted doctrine only, and I could stay with them. Think of it! I was invited to stay as a hypocrite teaching one thing to my students and believing and feeling another!" The next day, Brimhall wrote Peterson that he was being dismissed: "Under existing conditions, we cannot see our way clear to recommend you to the Board of Trustees as a member of the faculty of the Brigham Young University for the academic year 1911-12." Brimhall forwarded a copy of the letter to Smith, informing him, "This is the first time during our administration that we have had occasion to handle a teacher and the necessity is very, very painful to us." He reminded the church president that Peterson's brother, Joseph, had "tendered his resignation some time ago." That evening, an open letter from Henry Peterson appeared in the *Provo Herald*, advising readers: "Don't let people tell you from the pulpit or otherwise that to accept evolution means to foresake your faith or deny God." Within the week, Brimhall faced his faculty and "gave a brief history of recent events pertaining to the criticism of the work of the school, and impressed upon [them] the necessity of all members heartily supporting the school and the church." Two days later he warned a prospective teacher, "While the church does not presume to decide scientific questions, it does claim the right to decide as to what of science, or of anything else, is suited to the schools under its creation, and under its direction." "Your only safety," Reed Smoot counseled Brimhall, "lies in having the school follow strictly the policy mapped out by the teachers of the church."[20]

Previously silent on the issue, Joseph F. Smith published statements in the April issues of both the *Juvenile Instructor* and *Improvement Era*. In the *Instructor*, he wrote: "Some of our teachers are anxious to explain how much of the theory of evolution, in their judgment, is true, and what is false, but that only leaves their students in an unsettled frame of mind. They are not old enough and learned enough to discriminate, or put proper limitations upon a theory which we believe is more or less a fallacy. In reaching the conclusion that evolution would be best left out of discussions in our church schools we are deciding a question of propriety and are not undertaking to say how much of evolution is true, or how much is false." In an earlier draft, Smith had added, "Without undertaking to say who has the best of the argument, the school authorities have thought it wise to ask our church school teachers to modify their instructions so as to eliminate dissension. If prudence had characterized these discussions, and our teachers who know the doctrines of the church had been more conservative, much of the sensation which has been created might have been avoided." The *Improvement Era* carried a statement expressing much the same sentiment, with an appended overview of the preceding three months' events.[21]

Also in April the *Utah Educational Review* printed a thoughtful dissenting critique of the controversy. Milton Bennion, *Review* editor and professor of philosophy and education at the University of Utah, argued that while church leaders emphasized their commitment to an absolute truth, the ability to understand that truth could be hampered by unchecked dogmatism. While agreeing that church leaders enjoy the right to supervise—even restrict—certain teachings,

Bennion reminded readers that earlier scientific theories had once been branded heretical by the governing church. He urged church educational administrators to "grant the utmost liberty of belief in respect to the non-essentials [of faith] without questioning the fellowship of members who exercise this liberty," since "serious attempt on the part of church officials to dictate the methods and results of science in church schools" could "mean the death of higher education" in the church school system.[22]

In early April, Henry Peterson unsuccessfully petitioned Joseph F. Smith to reconsider the three professors' case. "I have found on direct statements from some members of the board," he wrote, "that they voted for the resolution that puts us out of the church school service on a misunderstanding. I thought I should like to have such corrected." Peterson evidently believed that their espousal of evolution and higher criticism had been taken as evidence of apostasy, and he assured Smith of their belief "in God and inspiration." In order that "the cause of education may be saved from further misunderstanding," he also asked that the church issue an official statement which "would quiet the fears of people instead of . . . further arousing them." He alleged that many "are already so fearful and supersensitive that [they] hardly dare to send their children to their own town schools for fear they will hear of evolution." Yet "every text book is written [with evolution] as the basic principle. Contrary to what some people say, the general principles of evolution are almost universally accepted."[23]

Throughout the following weeks, Brimhall was left to deal as best he could with dissatisfied faculty and students. In mid-May, he wrote again to Smoot, "I would be in perfect misery if I were not in harmony with those over me—I can stand it to be out of harmony with others. My policy has been to follow the interests of our faculty and also follow the interests of the student body, [but] I cannot be expected to follow either of the latter unless they are in perfect harmony with those above me." Smoot replied supportively, "If the time ever comes that it is impossible for me to be in harmony with my presiding officer, I will quickly resign, if it involves any great principle affecting my conscience or my religious beliefs."[24]

About this same time, Ralph Chamberlin, who had contemplated resigning, was asked to meet with Susa Young Gates, a member

of the Board of Trustees. She told Chamberlin that she understood
he had "recanted on the things [he] had been teaching." Chamberlin
denied this and told her he would also resign. "I have an obligation
to the students, and I'll teach them what I honestly believe can be
supported by evidence." Joseph Keeler (a counselor to Brimhall in
the BYU presidency) later asked, "Brother Chamberlin, why can't you
teach this subject the way we want it taught, [instead of] the way you're
teaching it?" Chamberlin replied, "I'm so constituted that I can't
teach what I don't believe." Despite the Board of Education's ultimatum, Brimhall evidently promised Chamberlin he would not be
required to modify his teaching if he remained. According to Chamberlin, Brimhall pleaded, "We want you to stay. . . . If you'll stay and
work with us there isn't anything in the gifts of the church you can't
have." Chamberlin refused because "these other men [had been]
compelled to leave." Brimhall informed Joseph F. Smith of Chamberlin's resignation on 12 June.[25] Chamberlin's brother, William, would
remain at BYU for another five years before finally resigning.

Christen Jensen, professor of history and political science,
and his wife, Juliaetta, had hosted a party on 25 May honoring Joseph
Peterson and his wife. Also in attendance were the Henry Petersons,
the Chamberlins, and eleven other faculty and their wives. "The
company was much of the 'insurgent' type," Mrs. Jensen wrote, "but
we cared to have only those who are in sympathy with the three men
who are to be dismissed at the close of school." She continued, "This
fight has been extremely bitter in many ways. President Brimhall has
talked to his faculty in the most insulting, uncultured manner such
as no truly educated president would do to his faculty, many of whom
are far, far superior to him in scholarship, and in everything else. I
have lost all my respect for him. . . . If the school is not injured I shall
miss my guess." Within two weeks, Brimhall optimistically assured
the faculty that "matters have been rectified. These particular difficulties will not recur."[26]

Ralph Chamberlin remained in Provo for one year before
returning to the University of Utah and then to an appointment at
Harvard. In early 1922, shortly after Franklin S. Harris's appointment
as Brimhall's successor, Chamberlin applied to teach again but was
told that "our funds will be very restricted this year." Harris explained
that while he hoped Chamberlin could become "affiliated with the

faculty here," he doubted that the school could offer a suitable salary for "a man of his training" and admitted that there was still "a little prejudice that needs to be overcome among some of the board."[27]

Henry Peterson had planned to run for Utah State Inspector of High Schools but was opposed by church authorities because of his "mode of thinking and causing doubt in the hearts of the children." He later moved to northern Utah where he taught in the Box Elder County School System and then at Utah State Agricultural College. When Peterson left BYU he sold his home, which he had built in 1911. Twelve years later the house was sold to the university. In 1927 the structure was renovated and has since served as the official residence of the university president.[28]

When Joseph Peterson left BYU he transferred to the psychology department of the University of Utah. In 1915, together with fourteen other faculty members, he resigned in protest when four professors were dismissed during a struggle over church influence at the school. He then taught at the University of Minnesota, where he was appointed chair of the psychology department in 1918. He later moved to the George Peabody College for Teachers in Nashville, Tennessee. In 1934, he was named president of the American Psychological Association. He died the following year.[29]

The impact upon BYU of the three men's departure was profound. Although some patrons were reassured at the realignment of church and school, others feared that the university had been irreconcilably compromised. One student remembered: "It seems tragic that these men had to go. I am satisfied they were undermining no one's faith in God as he is defined in Mormon thought. They were good men in every sense of the word and had the students' best interests at heart." Thomas L. Martin, BYU dean of applied sciences, later lamented, "We lost much when [they] left us. If some of the narrowness which caused the upheaval in 1911 could have been prevented from exercising its power, I believe the vision that George Brimhall had in mind would have been accomplished; and if we could have had a free hand in dealing with these men and their associates, people would be singing our praises all over the country at the present time."[30]

Following the controversy, many faculty and students were reluctant to discuss some "matters of scientific and sociological value for fear of losing their positions and receiving the boycott of the church." Others began asking if there were "any [other] doctrines of the church which [were] inconsistent with the commonly accepted conclusions of science." School trustees approved a new teaching contract in October 1911 which required loyalty to church authorities as a condition of employment. Brimhall gradually eliminated classes in philosophy, ethics, and psychology, in favor of additional courses in religion, theology, and teacher training. Special summer school conferences stressed the importance of revelation, "which the 'evolution' and 'higher criticism' wave tends to obliterate." "I am more and more convinced," Brimhall wrote, "that while philosophy is valuable, there are so many more things of more importance to our young men and women that we shall be justified in eliminating some of our courses in philosophy and instituting other things that bear more directly on our practical lives, because I believe that a course in our theology and religion is wider and deeper than any course of ethics within our reach."[31]

In September 1911, Harvey Fletcher joined the BYU faculty with a doctorate in physics from the University of Chicago. Initially, he remembered, "they wouldn't let me teach theology . . . because I had a Ph.D." When William Chamberlin learned in mid-1916 that "most of [his crowded] courses had been cut out for [the] next year and that what [was] left had been put in the Department of Education," he resigned. One student later wrote, "William H. Chamberlin was a meek, humble, gentle, non-assertive man. . . . By force of his thinking and ideas . . . he had a tremendous influence with the upper classmen of the university." Another added, "He helped many students whose faith was disturbed by the impact of scientific and philosophical thought to achieve a more mature religious and intellectual perspective." William died five years later in Logan, Utah; a biography, authored by his brother, appeared in 1925.[32]

Other faculty losses after 1911 included James L. Barker, Edwin S. Hinckley, Earl Glade, Christen Jensen, and Harvey Fletcher. When Fletcher accepted a position at Western Electric, Brimhall told him that he was "being disloyal to the church" and asked him to talk with Joseph F. Smith. Smith gave Fletcher his blessing on Fletcher's promise that he would "keep [his] testimony strong and keep up [his] church activities." From 1911 to 1921, when Brimhall retired, the number of full-time faculty decreased some 30 percent. During this same period, the number of undergraduates jumped nearly three-fold, but baccalaureate degrees declined over 63 percent and only two master's degrees were conferred. In efforts to counter predictions that the school could not weather the faculty losses, church appropriations were increased 50 percent beginning in 1912.[33]

The departure of Joseph and Henry Peterson, Ralph and William Chamberlin, and colleagues leveled a serious blow to the academic reputation of Brigham Young University—one from which the Mormon school did not fully recover until successive presidential administrations. At issue in the spring of 1911 was not only the question of a literalistic approach to religion, but the role of a church and its administrators to intervene in the daily curricula of an institution of higher secular learning. If science lost and religion won in 1911, defeat and victory would prove short-lived, even illusory, for such tension still exists at Brigham Young University[34]—more than eighty years after the Petersons and the Chamberlins left—suggesting, as Albert Einstein once observed, that "religion without science is blind, while science without religion is lame."[35]

NOTES

1. Ralph V. Chamberlin, *Life and Philosophy of W. H. Chamberlin* (Salt Lake City: Deseret News Press, 1925), 137. For example, Joseph Peterson graduated from Brigham Young Academy in 1902, had taught LDS seminary in Idaho, and had just earned at doctorate degree from the University of Chicago, where he studied under pioneer behaviorial psychologist John B. Watson. See Ernest L. Wikinson, ed., *Brigham Young University: The First One Hundred Years*, 4 vols. (Provo, UT: Brigham Young University Press, 1975-76), 1:409-10, hereafter BYU; also Richard Sherlock, "Campus in Crisis—BYU, 1911," *Sunstone*, Jan./Feb. 1979, 11.

2. *Henry Peterson: Educator, 1868-1957* (n.p., 1982). Shortly after his arrival in Provo, Henry was called to serve on the LDS religion classes and general Sunday school boards. He was later appointed a member of an ad hoc committee to study the problems of church youth. See Sunday School General Board Minutes, 26 June 1907, 19 July 1909, archives, Historical Department, Church of Jesus Christ of Latter-day Saints, Salt Lake City, Utah, hereafter LDS archives; Religion Class General Board Minutes, 22 June 1910, 4 Apr. 1908, LDS archives.

3. BYU, 409-10, 503; Sherlock, 11. A graduate of the University of

Utah, Ralph Chamberlin had earlier taught math, science, language, and biology at the LDS College in Salt Lake City before continuing graduate studies at Stanford and Cornell, where he received a Ph.D. in 1905.

4. Joseph Peterson to Brimhall, 30 Aug. 1910, Brimhall Papers, Brigham Young University Archives, Harold B. Lee Library, Brigham Young University, Provo, Utah, hereafter BYUA; Ralph V. Chamberlin to Brimhall, 3 Sept. 1910, Brimhall Papers.

5. Ralph V. Chamberlin, "Darwin Centennial Speech," 12 Feb. 1909, Chamberlin Papers, Utah State Historical Society, Salt Lake City, Utah; see the articles in the *White and Blue*, 16 Feb., 12 Nov., 24 Dec. 1909, 29 Apr. 1910, 31 Jan. 1911

6. *Henry Peterson: Educator*, 118-19.

7. Annie Clark Tanner, *A Mormon Mother* (Salt Lake City: Tanner Trust Fund, University of Utah, 1976), 216-17. See Edward J. Johnson, "George H. Brimhall Biography," BYUA.

8. BYU Faculty Minutes, 25 Sept. 1909, BYUA; George F. Richards Journal, 27 Sept. 1909, 22, 30 Oct. 1921, LDS archives; James E. Talmage Journal, 27, 30 Sept. 1909, Special Collections, Harold B. Lee Library, Brigham Young University; Anthon H. Lund Journal, 14, 15, 20 Oct. 1909, LDS archives; "The Origin of Man," *Improvement Era*, Nov. 1909, 75-81; *Divine Mission of the Savior*, Course of Study for the Priests (2d Year), Prepared and Issued under the Direction of the General Authorities of the Church (Church of Jesus Christ of Latter-day Saints, 1910), 35; Duane E. Jeffery, "Seers, Savants and Evolution: The Uncomfortable Interface," *Dialogue: A Journal of Mormon Thought*, Fall/Winter 1973, 61; cf. John A. Widtsoe, *Joseph Smith As Scientist, A Contribution to Mormon Philosophy* (General Church Board, Young Men's Mutual Improvement Associations, Church of Jesus Christ of Latter-day Saints, 1908); "Editor's Table," *Improvement Era*, Apr. 1909, 489-94, and May 1909, 505-09. For Whitney's earlier views on evolution, see "Man's Origin and Destiny," *The Contributor*, June 1882, 268-70.

9. Cummings, "Autobiography," chap. 41, 2, LDS archives (cf. Cummings Journal, 22 Sept. 1917, LDS archives); Cummings to Brimhall, 27 Feb. 1908, Brimhall Papers.

10. Cummings, "Autobiography," chapter 41, 2-3; *Henry Peterson: Educator*, 123; General Church Board of Education Minutes, 2 Dec. 1909; Brimhall to Smith, 3 Dec. 1910, Brimhall Papers.

11. Cummings, "Autobiography," chap. 41, 5; Mark K. Allen, "The History of Psychology at Brigham Young University," 63, BYUA; Tanner, 216-17; Johnson; Faculty Minutes, 7 Dec. 1910.

12. Cummings to Smith and Members of the General Church Board of Education, 21 Jan. 1911, BYUA.

13. *White and Blue*, 31 Jan. 1911; Faculty Minutes, 28 Jan. 1911; Ralph V. Chamberlin, "Evolution and Theological Belief," *White and Blue*, 31

Jan. 1911, a four-page supplement, reprinted in Chamberlin, *The Meaning of Organic Evolution* (Provo, UT: the Author, 1911), chap. 4.

14. General Church Board of Education Minutes, 3 Feb. 1911; Ivins, in Chamberlin, Oral History, 11, BYUA. See Ivins, "A Study of Evolution," *Improvement Era*, Dec. 1917, 161-66.

15. Chamberlin, Oral History, 6, 9-11; Penrose Journal, 10, 11 Feb. 1911, Utah State Historical Society; Grant Journal, 10, 11 Feb. 1911, LDS archives. Grant reported that Joseph B. Keeler also attended the first of the two meetings. Richards Journal, 10, 11 Feb. 1911; Francis M. Lyman et al. to Smith and Members of the Board of Trustees of the Brigham Young University, 11 Feb. 1911, BYUA (cf. Board of Trustees Minutes, 11 Feb. 1911); William H. Chamberlin, "The Theory of Evolution as an Aid to Faith in God and Belief in the Resurrection," *White and Blue*, 14 Feb. 1911.

16. Chamberlin, Oral History, 7-9.

17. Board of Trustees to Smith, 25 Feb. 1911, Brimhall Papers. See articles in *Salt Lake Tribune*, 23 Feb. 1911 (cf. 19 Feb. 1911); *Deseret News*, 21 Feb. 1911; and *Salt Lake Telegram*, 23 Feb. 1911.

18. See Brimhall to Cummings, 17 Mar. 1911; Brimhall to Smith, 17 Mar. 1911; Brimhall to Smoot, 8 Mar. 1911; all in Brimhall Papers.

19. *Deseret News*, 11 Mar. 1911; *Salt Lake Tribune*, 12 Mar. 1911 (cf. Chamberlin, Oral History, 8, and Edwin S. Hinckley to Brimhall, 24 Feb. 1911, Brimhall Papers); Heber Charles Hicks, "The Life Story of Heber Charles Hicks," 40-41, BYUA; Smith to Andrew K. Smith, 25 Feb. 1911, LDS archives (Smith evidently left school because of poor grades and excessive absences); *Daily Herald*, 14 Mar. 1911; *Salt Lake Tribune*, 15, 16 Mar. 1911; *Salt Lake Herald Republican*, 15 Mar. 1911; *Deseret News*, 16 Mar. 1911. For copies of the student petition, see Brimhall Papers and Chamberlin, *W. H. Chamberlin*, 149-51. Brimhall, in "Devotional Remarks," 16 Mar. 1911, BYUA, reprinted in *Deseret News*, 16 Mar. 1911.

20. Brimhall to Smith, 17 Mar. 1911, Brimhall Papers; Brimhall to Peterson, 16 Mar. 1911, Brimhall Papers (cf. *Henry Peterson: Educator*, 131-32); *Daily Herald*, 17 Mar. 1911; Faculty Minutes, 23 Mar. 1911; Brimhall to Ericksen, 25 Mar. 1911, Brimhall Papers; Smoot to Brimhall, 26 Mar. 1911, Brimhall Papers.

21. Smith, "Philosophy and the Church Schools," *Juvenile Instructor*, Apr. 1911, 208-209; Smith, "The Church and Science," Smith Papers; Smith, "Theory and Divine Revelation," *Improvement Era*, Apr. 1911, 548-51.

22. Bennion, "The 'Evolution' and 'Higher Criticism' Controversy at the Brigham Young University," *Utah Educational Review*, Apr. 1911 (cf. Joseph Peterson, "The Blessings of Science and Evils of Pseudo Science," *Utah Educational Review*, May 1911). Nine years later, the First Presidency considered Bennion as Cummings's replacement as superintendent of church schools and also as Brimhall's successor as BYU president. They

decided, however, that the church needed a "Mormon spokesman" at the University of Utah and instead called his brother, Adam, as superintendent and Franklin Harris as president (see BYU, 233-34).

23. Peterson to Smith, 3 Apr. 1911, LDS archives.

24. Brimhall to Smoot, 11 May 1911; Smoot to Brimhall, 21 May 1911; both in Brimhall Papers.

25. Chamberlin, Oral History, 7; Brimhall to Smith, 12 June 1911, Brimhall Papers.

26. Juliaetta B. Jensen Journal, 25 May 1911, in Allen, 72; Faculty Minutes, 2 June 1911.

27. BYU, 428; Allen, 72-74; Chamberlin to Franklin S. Harris, 3 Jan. 1922, Harris Papers, BYUA; Harris to Chamberlin, 14 Mar. 1922, Harris Papers; Chamberlin to Harris, 29 Sept. 1923, Harris Papers; Harris to Chamberlin, 10 Oct. 1923, Harris Papers; Harris to Richard R. Lyman, 1 Oct. 1923, Harris Papers.

28. Anthon H. Lund Journal, 23 Apr. 1912; Ephraim Hatch, "History of the Brigham Young University Campus and the Department of the Physical Plant," 4:8-9, BYUA; BYU, 428; Allen, 72-74.

29. For the 1915 controversy at the University of Utah, see Joseph H. Jeppson, "The Secularization of the University of Utah, to 1920," Ph.D. diss., University of California, 1973, 180. For Peterson's later work, see Lyle Lanier, ed., *Psychological Monographs*, 1938, i-v, 1-237; and Peterson, "Completeness of Response as an Explanation Principle in Learning," *Psychological Review*, 1916, 153-62, "Aspects of Learning," *Psychological Review*, 1935, 1-27, *Early Conceptions and Tests of Intelligence* (Yonkers: World Book Company, 1924), and "The Scientific Study of Human Behavior," *Brigham Young University Alumnus*, 1927, 4-5.

30. Johnson; Martin to Heber C. Snell, 16 Mar. 1942, Snell Papers, Archives and Manuscripts, Utah State University, Logan, Utah.

31. E. E. Ericksen, *The Psychological and Ethical Aspects of Mormon Group Life* (Salt Lake City: University of Utah, 1975), 65; Tanner, 216; Board of Trustees Minutes, 25 Oct. 1911; *Daily Herald*, 6 Oct. 1913 (cf. Board of Education Minutes, 29 Dec. 1913); Brimhall to Joseph Fielding Smith, 11 Mar. 1916, Brimhall Papers.

32. Fletcher, Oral History, 19 Sept. 1968, 43, BYUA; Fletcher, "Autobiography," 38, 42-43, BYUA; Chamberlin, *W. H. Chamberlin*, 211; "A Sentiment," *White and Blue*, 31 May 1916; Russel B. Swensen, "Mormons at the University of Chicago Divinity School: A Personal Reminiscence," *Dialogue: A Journal of Mormon Thought*, Summer 1972, 38.

33. Fletcher, "Autobiography," 42-43; "A Brief Survey of the Work of Brigham Young University From the Beginning of the School Year 1906-07 to the Close of the School Year 1913-14—Eight Years," Printed Material 34, e-2, BYUA.

34. For organic evolution and science at BYU after 1911, see Gary James Bergera and Ronald Priddis, *Brigham Young University: A House of Faith* (Salt Lake City: Signature Books, 1985), 148-71.

35. In Stanley L. Jaki, *The Relevance of Physics* (Chicago: Univeristy of Chicago Press, 1966), 345.

4.
Inner Dialogue: James Talmage's Choice of Science as a Career, 1876-84

Dennis Rowley

JAMES E. TALMAGE'S INTEREST IN SCIENCE WAS FIRST AWAKENED BY HIS grandfather, James Edward Talmage, an herbal doctor in the village of Ramsbury, Wiltshire, England.[1] Young James lived with his grandfather from age three to five while attending infant school and visited him often in later years, sometimes just to walk in the woods and visit, sometimes for weeks and months while attending school in Ramsbury.[2] Occasionally he traveled with the older man.[3] In 1874, shortly after graduating from the National School in Hungerford, Talmage and his grandfather toured Wiltshire and Berkshire. As they tramped the woods and streams looking for herbs, the elder James taught young James his first simple botany lessons, awakening a love for nature that never died.[4] Talmage gathered, identified, and labeled a collection of botanical and mineralogical specimens which he took with him to Utah two years after his grandfather's death in 1874.[5]

Talmage's English schooling appears to have contributed little to directly stimulate his interest in science or to add to his grandfather's teachings. He was taught religion, geography, English history, reading, writing, arithmetic, and singing. History and geography stressed the greatness of English accomplishments and were designed to instill pride in the empire and its heroes. Geography students were required to know the minerals and principal coal fields of England, but that was as close to science as any part of the basic

43

curriculum came. The daily regimen at all levels above infant school was prescribed and strict. Memorization and recitation were emphasized. Examination questions asked for description or simple recall rather than analysis or independent thinking.[6] It is possible, though unlikely, that James also took courses in algebra, geometry, natural philosophy, natural sciences, political economy, English literature, French, Latin, or German.[7]

This education taught him the indispensable skills of hard work, a sense of order, and self-discipline. He became precise in the use of language and developed a retentive memory. Some of these traits were reinforced at home where he helped his parents manage the Bell Inn. Hungerford was a prosperous resort and market town on the main east-west thoroughfare between London and Bristol, about an hour away from London by train. In its shops, lecture hall, and library, and from the passage of travelers in and out of the Bell and other inns, there was much activity to develop the powers of observation and the curiosity necessary to a successful scientist. Thus, when young James left England, although he had not yet consciously chosen to devote his life to science, the seeds for a future decision had been planted.

The chief nurturer of these seeds was Brigham Young Academy's principal, Karl G. Maeser. When Talmage arrived in Utah in 1876 at the age of fourteen, he was attending the academy within a few weeks. During the next eight years, he finished the complete course of the academy, taking virtually every grammar, academic, normal, and scientific class offered and receiving every certificate and diploma awarded. Between August 1876 and June 1879, he took about forty ten-week classes from Maeser ranging from arithmetic, rhetoric, and composition to natural philosophy, chemistry, and geology.[8]

Maeser's first love was the art of teaching. His greatest expertise was in the classics. But, he also had an adequate knowledge of the sciences and with the proper textbook he taught all of them at an elementary level.[9] In each class Maeser did his best to carry out Brigham Young's admonition to teach nothing without the spirit of God. Thus he told his students in the "Theory of Teaching" that they must "introduce the subject [of religion] . . . wherever the opportunity offers; . . . For instance, in the geography of South America the wide-awake teacher could instruct in regard to the history and travels of the Nephites and Lamanites. In the geography of the eastern states, the site of the burial of the plates etc."[10]

In that spirit, Maeser taught Talmage about science and made science more attractive because he reinforced the spiritual mind-set Talmage had acquired in England.[11] Talmage's 1876 geography notes capture Maeser's typical mix of Mormon teachings and science and his tendency to oversimplify when teaching without a text (as he was in this instance):

THE CREATION

We have two sources by which we gain a knowledge of the creation viz. 1st Revelations in Scripture and 2nd by Geological discoveries. The 1st source viz Revelations in Scripture will be found in Genesis (See Bible). We find there that God showed Moses six visions—I. He saw only mists huricanes & fearful commotion. II. Saw that the huricanes had ceased & also the waters had separated from the clouds, and rocks peeping out from the Oceans. III. He saw the rocks had been washed, powdered and decomposed which formed soil, which was green with small plants, & the waters had cooled off & had in them some small animals, IV. appeared as trees on the land with great animals in the water & the air. V. He saw all kinds of monsters on land in water & in the air. VI. appeared to him in its perfect state with man in Garden of Eden. We cannot say how long a time elapsed between these great changes, but must have been millions of years. The Bible says God created the world in six days, but this does not mean the time which we call days now, viz 24 hours it means simply 6 great periods. We also read of two creations spiritual & temporal. Whenever any Geological discoveries are made they verify the statements of the Bible though we must not take the Bible as a History it was never meant for it.[12]

To students planning to be teachers, Maeser stated that the aims of natural science were: "1. To become acquainted with Nature. 2. To learn to utilize the elements of nature for the use and benefit of self and others. 3. To demonstrate the wisdom and goodness of the Creator."[13] Following his own advice, Maeser depended heavily upon "Steele's Series in the Natural Sciences"[14] in his lectures and examinations. Each volume reprinted a verse of scripture or a poetic verse about the Creator on the title page, and there were abundant references to the "work of the Creator" throughout the text.

Maeser also encouraged interest in science outside the class room. The earliest circulars of the academy spelled out plans for a museum and a laboratory. The museum (or cabinet) was established in October 1876, the result of student/citizen donations and faculty-led field trips to gather specimens.[15] In his term report of June 1877 Maeser reported on growth in the museum's botanical and mineral specimens, lamenting their lack of organization and the lack of a chemical laboratory and astronomical apparata.[16] On 21 August 1878 Maeser appointed Talmage the first curator of the museum and the laboratory, the latter only a few pieces of equipment without a place to use them until Oct. 1880. The appointment probably reflected Talmage's interest, enthusiasm, as well as the donation of his personal collection.

During those first three years, Talmage learned a great deal of elementary science and developed increasing enthusiasm for it. By June 1879 he had taken courses in natural philosophy (physics), chemistry, physiology, astronomy, geology, and electricity. His examination answers in the sciences were longer (including detailed drawings) and more exact than in other subjects. Test responses in other courses tended to be merely adequate or very brief.[17] An algebra examination contains this response to two problems: "Absent when information covered."[18]

After he received his normal diploma in June 1879, Talmage began to teach full-time at the academy. His intellectual pace quickened and the pressures and influences in his life multiplied until he felt propelled toward a decision about his future in science. He taught his first science course, elementary physiology, in the spring of 1880. At that point Maeser had sufficient confidence in his student to recommend to a bishop and his wife that seventeen-year-old Talmage operate on their son, who had a bullet lodged in his thigh as a result of a hunting accident. Talmage and Maeser were boarding with the boy's parents at the time on a tour of schools in southern Idaho, far from a doctor. Maeser's confidence was not misplaced. Talmage removed the bullet, the boy recovered nicely, and Talmage's self-confidence and interest in things scientific grew correspondingly.[19]

When Maeser informed Talmage that he would be teaching chemistry along with two other science courses in the fall of 1880, Talmage took a three-week intensive course in qualitative analysis from Professor Thomas Hadley of Ogden. Hadley, an assayer, was an old friend of the Talmages who had studied chemistry in England. He taught Talmage fundamental chemical analysis procedures and formulae. Neither Maeser nor George Coray, who had taught Talmage elementary chemistry during 1879-80, had sufficient background to supply this information. Maeser supported Talmage's request to draw an advance on academy funds to complete the course.[20]

In the next two years, Talmage taught virtually every science course offered at the academy. He also continued to teach penmanship, reading, grammar, Latin, and drawing—a total of eight classes during the first term in 1880 and ten during the second. In addition he was still taking classes as well. Apparently Maeser was not totally sympathetic with Talmage's desire to continue taking science classes while teaching full time. Although he arranged Talmage's teaching schedule so his free periods coincided with the times the science classes were offered,[21] he did not reduce his teaching load or increase his salary despite Talmage's regular complaints that he was worth more money.[22]

But to his credit, especially in light of financial difficulties experienced by the academy in its early years, Maeser supported Talmage's growing demands for chemicals and scientific apparata. Talmage records happily in his journal on 15 December 1881 that Maeser agreed to replace a new microscope because its magnification was not powerful enough for their needs. On 21-22 January 1882 after a successful public experiment by some of his students, Talmage promptly requested another $150 worth of supplies while, as he put it in his journal, there was an "excess of good feeling" from Maeser and the board.

Without any lessening of the love and respect they felt for each other, the role shift from student to colleague caused inevitable differences to surface. For example, to Maeser education meant drawing out and cultivating "that contained in the mind, more than crowding new subjects continually into the mind."[23] In contrast Talmage tried to learn everything he could about every subject he could with an emphasis on science. By early 1882 he proposed taking his insatiable appetite to the infidel and anti-Mormon east coast—specifically to Lehigh College in South Bethlehem, Pennsylvania, and Johns Hopkins University in Baltimore, Maryland. Maeser could not approve. His aversion to eastern education was profound.[24] His concern for the spiritual safety of a beloved student must have been intensified by the academy's financial problems and his concern over the added cost of Talmage's present and proposed activities.

However, Talmage found encouragement and financial support from other friends—probably George Coray and Joseph M. Tanner, who encouraged him strongly after he was in the east and presumably earlier. Tanner, who wrote him regularly after he went east, was Talmage's immediate supervisor at the academy and was a man with an open and inquiring mind and a devotion to learning. Coray, the first person to teach and examine Talmage in the results of specific experiments, shared his interest in experimental science. Both Tanner and Coray would follow Talmage east, Coray to Cornell in 1883 and Tanner to Harvard in 1891.[25] Their combined financial support amounted to over half the cost of Talmage's year of study at Johns Hopkins University.[26]

J. L. Townsend, a Payson, Utah, pharmacist and taxidermist who also composed music and poetry, gave Talmage a one-day course in taxidermy in April 1881. Richard A. Proctor, a famous English astronomer, gave public lectures in Salt Lake City, 7-8 February 1881, from which Talmage learned of the controversial theory of the birth, growth, decay, and death of worlds. On both occasions he described the teacher's personality in his journal. He disliked Townsend's conceited nature (because it reminded him of his own conceit) and observed "that, though Prof. Proctor's theory is logical and fascinating, I am able clearly to see how he lacks that firmness, which one who has just claim by his Priesthood on the spirit of God will possess. Proctor says that the theory of the winding up scene being at hand is without foundation; that it is the 'Cracked-brain project of the nineteenth century'; as every century has been characterized by some such alarm. Prof. Proctor with us all will find out."

Talmage had felt insecure and inadequate when he began teaching science, though his classroom poise, dignity, and self-assurance masked such feelings. He completely reworked his class notes, rereading the texts, taking additional notes, and working at least partially through their bibliographies.[27] In the process he first read British natural philosopher John Tyndall on sound and light and the *Manual of Geology* of American geologist James Dwight Dana.[28] He rewrote his notes every night in preparation for the next day's lectures, getting by on four to five hours of sleep a night. Later he would confess that he had no inherent love for teaching,[29] a condition his feelings of inadequacy no doubt exacerbated.

His efforts in the classroom seemed unappreciated. In late 1881 after a full year of teaching science he lamented that the students seemed "to care for science but little" and that to many the very word was a "revolting name."[30] Not only did he feel wounded because of his love for the subject, but his continued teaching depended on student enrollment. Science courses were listed as optional and were not always well attended. If any of his courses were dropped, he would have been assigned to teach courses in other areas thus losing in addition, preparation time in the sciences. Also, he needed the the practical experience to obtain an advanced certificate, necessary for his admission to Lehigh University. He turned increasingly to classroom experimentation since his first year had taught him that "only experiments hold [the students'] attention."[31] Although he loved experimentation and his Pestalozzian training from Maeser emphasized object-teaching, he seemed to resent the students' unwillingness to perform the mental labor of understanding a scientific principle without experimentation.

Although a laboratory had been established in October 1880, the equipment was inadequate. His brief sessions with Hadley and Coray in chemistry had left him on his own for any other subject. Presumably, his usual (and the safest) procedure was to unpack any newly acquired apparatus, set it up, and try the experiment himself prior to attempting to demonstrate it in the classroom. However, in a journal entry on 22 August 1881 he characterized himself as "impetuous, rushing and energetic," which may have resulted in some of his more colorful classroom experiments. On one occasion he and his assistant Daniel Harrington prepared to demonstrate the functioning of the lungs of a small animal to a physiology class. Harrington recorded, "Of course, before these things could be shown, the cat must be killed. Talmage held the gunny sack securely, as he thought, while I had the axe in the air. At this moment a small hole in the sack tore open and the cat broke out and ran wildly off into the lot." The cat was recaptured, the necessary organ removed, and Talmage demonstrated the expandibility of the lungs by inflating them with a small tube.[32]

A more spectacular experiment which went awry had potentially more serious consequences:

I was lecturing upon the "Composition of Water" and demonstrating the various properties of Oxygen and Hydrogen. While exploding a mixture of the gases in a cylinder, the latter burst with such a concussion as to extinguish all lamps in the room excepting those held in the chandeliers.

My feelings were difficult to describe as I realized the probable extent of the consequences. A scare ensued among the audience, but soon abated. One young lady was struck on the left side of the forehead by a flying fragment of glass; when she discovered traces of blood she fainted very nicely and I changed at once my occupation from that of a public lecturer to an attendant physician. She recovered, however, when 'twas found that the large amount of blood filling the bowl from which I was bathing her head came from my own hand. Two pieces of glass had struck the index finger of my right hand, one fragment burying itself in the knuckle joint. Another young lady had been struck on the left shoulder, the fragment piercing the clothes and inflicting a severe gash. Beside these, four or five were robbed of traces of skin, and all were severely scared.

After the circumstance I went back and completed the lecture, which act, I believe, did much to lessen the fear of the audience. . . . Fatal results may have followed. . . . I chide myself for one thing: that I did not insist on all keeping the back seats.[33]

Still other experiments robbed him of time and money, while adding to his frustrations. Between April 1 and 11, 1882, while studying electricity, he tried eight times on as many days to partially duplicate Franklin's experiment "to test the results of the electricity of the atmosphere." He procured or built and subsequently lost or ruined a total of six kites and one balloon before giving up.[34]

Six months after his first classroom explosion, when he had

learned to take a few precautions, he described the following experiment in his journal.

> June 6, 1882. Experienced another accident in the course of experimenting. A small wooden powder mortar, to be fired by the passage of electricity called an "Electric Bomb," had recently been procured by the Academy; and as I was demonstrating before the Physics class in the small Laboratory the bomb burst with terrific force, demolishing the Leyden Jars placed alongside to accomplish the experiment, and shattering the whole instrument into splinters. Luckily I had opened the window & placed the whole on a board shelf on the outside. The force of course was directed right and left, and no one was hurt.

Such dramatic and unpredictable lectures, not unnaturally, increased attendance. One week after the oxygen explosion on 14 December, he noted in his journal: "The room became so crowded as hardly to afford standing room, and the rostrum upon which I had placed my apparatus was literally besieged. Such a crowded room interfered with my machine to a certain extent. This is my usual luck, my experiments are generally highly satisfactory when I perform them alone."

His expanding reputation as an expert—fueled by dozens of invitations to lecture from bishops and youth groups in Utah Valley and beyond—also brought mixed feelings. He liked the attention and publicity but also knew that few Utahns knew enough science to recognize an expert. Even more unsettling than the flattery were occasional questions about his competence to teach some of the science courses. To stem such criticism, he had passed examinations for an advanced normal certificate in the natural sciences in 1881. The certificate attested to his theoretical knowledge and practical ability to teach. On 13 November 1881 he recorded his intention of spending three hours every evening in his tiny laboratory. He was nineteen years old.[35]

The encouragement of key individuals, the expectations of students and public, occasional criticism, his desire to know, and the diminishing opportunities to learn more at the academy made up a complex mixture pressuring him toward further academic study. But the decision to leave Utah did not come easily. Beginning in the fall of 1880 his journal entries became increasingly introspective and occasionally, confused. The alluring but unshaped future was a consistent theme.

> Sept. 1, 1880. I really do not approve of the plan of saying before-hand what one intends doing, . . .
> Nov. 6, 1880. I do not like the vocation of teaching, that is, as a District School teacher, . . . Here in the Academy I am teaching all higher, scientific or philological branches; in order to do which I am necessitated to work up on the subjects myself, thereby opening up to me a field of research which is almost as beneficial as regularly attending school. . . . I can see plainly that I will not be enabled to save the least means for a start in life. In fact cannot see my way clear for my future course.
> June 17, 1881. . . . if I would give way to selfish feelings I would today almost register a vow that I would not serve in the B. Y. Academy again unless I were well paid. . . . Then again I think and realize that the training I am receiving in teaching these higher branches benefits me as much, if not more than regular attendance at school would.
> Nov. 13, 1881. I began to consider how my labors may be laid to greatest advantage during the coming winter months. . . . opportu-nities for study and research will not last long. I may be sent on a mission before winter or my occupation may be varied as to admit of but little time for private study.
> Dec. 12, 1881. I want to do good among the young—probably lecture amongst the Improvement Associations, and encourage the study of nature. I have to give a first lecture on the subject of harmony between Geology and the Bible—a subject upon which so many of our people have mistaken ideas.[36]

On 23 January 1882 he took a firmer but still tentative stand: "I have for myself harbored a vague idea of making an effort to raise sufficient means to pass a year in a prominent science school or college. . . . I may be counseled however to remain among my own people and as I hold myself as on neutral ground willing to following counsel implicitly in this important step, I can only refer to such as a vague idea." On 8 and 14 March his future at the academy was cast in the conditional: "If I remain in charge of the Scientific Department," and "if I retain my position in the academy another year . . . " Finally on 31 March, he wrote: "My desire to attend some leading institution for a time to train myself in scientific pursuits has been growing with me. A conversation with Bro. Maeser on the subject resulted in his heartily seconding my desires, and saying that he expected the project to be given me as a mission."[37]

Maeser's enthusiasm was probably sincere (although short-lived), despite his animosity toward eastern education. His suggestion that Talmage be called on a mission was customary for the time. He had been quite insistent that Talmage accompany him on his tour of northern Utah and southern Idaho schools in the summer of 1880 and again in 1881 through southern Utah, despite Talmage's reluctance. He would have much preferred to remain in Provo and conduct experiments and study, but Maeser had extended the invitation in the form of a mission.[38] However, he made the best of both trips, taking notes, collecting specimens, making new friends with whom to exchange specimens, and cultivating his speaking ability. Maeser probably intended Talmage to see the relative comfort of his position at BYA. Indeed, Talmage came away convinced he did not want to teach in the district schools and haunted by the education needs of "his people." However, he saw increasingly the mastery of higher science as his way of meeting those needs.

A key event in convincing Maeser that Talmage's faith could withstand an eastern education occurred on 8 March 1882, when Talmage used a newly acquired optical lantern and stereopticon slides to deliver an illustrated lecture to the Polysophical Society on "The History of the Earth." According to his script-like notes for the lecture (partially in shorthand), nineteen-year-old Talmage spoke warmly of the correctness and utility of the principle of uniformitarianism and proclaimed that studying the history of the earth as written in the rocks "cannot but lead us nearer the platform of God." Using time periods of undetermined length in place of days as Maeser had taught him, he matched the biblical account of the Creation with the geological time scale, traced the history of the earth from its origins according to the nebular theory of Laplace up through the long pre-human period to the destructive glacial period which God had sent to bring "great and pleasing variety" to an earth that had known "comparative perfection" prior to that time. Then came mankind, "a new creation," being among other things the first among God's creatures who "reached toward the knowledge of himself and of his God." In ringing tones Talmage declared the reality of evolution which even "a glance at the past" will show and according to which "the simple forms have ever preceded the more complex." However, he noted that "the missing link between the form of man and that of the highest animal forms has never as yet been found." He closed by a reiteration of his central theme that science and religion were but separate paths of truth to the same God and that they were not in conflict: "This earth is but a great record, each continent but a page, each community but a paragraph, and each human being's body but a sentence."[39]

Maeser and members of the academy board were so pleased that they asked Talmage to repeat the lecture on 15 March, which he did before a large and enthusiastic crowd. The views Talmage expressed were certainly not uncommon among the educated and the leaders of Mormon society at that time.[40] Although Maeser would make a strong public statement against evolution in 1893, on that spring evening in 1882 he seems to have been at least partially convinced by the vision, eloquence, and stereopticon lantern of young James Talmage. It was only two weeks later that Talmage had his conversation with Maeser about further study.

While Talmage awaited the arrival of the first school catalogs to see if he had admission deficiencies, he cautiously wrote that he was training an assistant and a teacher to take his place, if he left. He later resolved, "Shall begin at once," when he learned he had deficiencies in algebra and German.[41] He firmly turned down two job offers, one on 20 April as principal of the St. George schools with a provision of special attention to the scientific branches, and another on 25 April when the Gunnison Sugar Committee tried to hire him for its chemical plant during the approaching sugar season.

On 15 May Talmage had an interview with LDS Church President John Taylor: "Visited Prest. Taylor at his residence; explained to him my desires. He kept me in a long consultation, asking many questions as to the purposes of my desired trip, and closed by giving his decided advice that I proceed to some leading institution there to pursue a course of study in the Sciences. Returned to Provo in afternoon and reported at once my intended withdrawal to the Principal." This meeting was significant in determining the future course of Talmage's life and career. Even though he was seeking confirmation for his tentative decision rather than open advice on the best course of action, President Taylor's disapproval would have been a nearly insurmountable obstacle, given Talmage's devotion to the church.

As spring wore into summer, Maeser's encouragement seemed to wane. On 16 June Talmage recorded in his journal: "My intended withdrawal as reported to the Faculty and Board, was kept very quiet, no public notice of the same in any report being made. The Principal informed me that such were his instructions, but declined to give me his reasons." On 23 June Talmage recorded that "the Principal still informs me that I am expected back at the Academy when I conclude my studies in the East." And finally, on behalf of the board and the faculty, Maeser wrote a testimonial of Talmage's service and gave it to Talmage on 25 August just prior to his departure. In it he stated that they had yielded "only reluctantly" to Talmage's request for release and that they hoped he would return to them "in due time still more qualified to assist . . . in the advancement of the educational interests of . . . [their] Mountain Home."[42]

Talmage spent a hectic summer of experimentation and study in preparation for school, taking time out only to help his father hay and to dig up another human skeleton from a nearby canyon to add to one he already had transferred from the lake shore to the laboratory.[43] He spent his time studying so he would reap the greatest possible return for the time he spent in the east. Apparently he already had enough money, for he recorded in his journal on 4 September 1882 that he arrived at Lehigh with $420 from his savings after paying for the trip, a remarkable feat considering that his teaching salary for the previous three years had been $1200 out of which he had to live and buy chemicals, apparata, and books. He also paid his father $40 per term beginning in 1880 to help pay back money advanced for school expenses.

Talmage rejected urgings that he attend medical school and felt relief when his stake president counseled him to stick with science. "Such meets my wishes," he recorded, and added:

> I have many times contemplated my probable destiny and mission in life without obtaining a satisfactory conclusion; but I have for

some time past felt an intense desire to become familiar with the
walks of Science for the Sciences have to be redeemed from their
present position of infidelity & skepticism. The idea has been a
favorite one for my meditations of late, and has formed the theme
of my public speaking. I conclude that this great mission has to be
performed by the Priesthood of God, and to lay a single stone in
such a work *is perhaps my mission in life*.[44]

Talmage arrived at Lehigh College in South Bethlehem,
Pennsylvania, on 4 September 1882, and like a man possessed, threw
himself into his courses.[45] At both Lehigh and Johns Hopkins University where he enrolled the following year, he took classes from
leading men in their fields, copied the notes of professors and
students for classes he could not take, and reviewed, studied, and
audited classes so he could challenge lower-level courses by examination. He also spent long hours in the library reading Herbert Spencer
and Charles Darwin, among others, and even longer hours in laboratories exhilarated at performing virtually every experiment and analysis he had read about. In addition he used every available opportunity
to visit sites of scientific, cultural, and economic interest, collecting
abundant specimens and on occasion conducting an experiment or
two. Though he concentrated on chemistry, physiology and biology
were also priorities. He took courses in geology, physics, mineralogy,
metallurgy, astronomy, and botany, as well.

In chemistry his interests ranged widely, benefiting from the
industrial and agricultural emphasis at Lehigh and the organic and
medical emphasis at Johns Hopkins. At Lehigh he took courses in
agricultural and manufacturing chemistry, assaying, toxicology, and
medical chemistry. At Johns Hopkins he took chemical physics,
analytical chemistry, medical chemistry, the chemistry of the compounds of carbon, organic chemistry, and quantitative analysis. Students had to keep current with *Chemical News* and *The American
Chemist*. The latter was co-edited by William H. Chandler of Lehigh,
a man from whom Talmage heard a few lectures. At Johns Hopkins
Talmage records an invitation on 9 October 1883 to the regular
meetings of the *Chemistry Journal*, a group organized to keep the
faculty and upper level students aware of current research and
writing. Both institutions were also interested in applied science and

in the university's relationship with the industrial community. This concern led to some contract work and employment opportunities, both temporary and permanent, for students and graduates, some of which were offered to Talmage.

Laboratory work was his first and permanent love. After George Coray arrived in the east, he wrote to Talmage suggesting that they return to Utah after their schooling, pay off their debts, and "proceed to establish and build up a laboratory." Talmage replied that he could "make no promises for the future, though my heart's desire is to see a laboratory in Utah."[46]

At Lehigh Talmage gave a lecture entitled "Chemistry and Life" based in part on his own laboratory research. In it he made the point that the term "organic chemistry" was a misnomer because any substance ceased to live when experimentation began. He reminded his audience that sometimes life must be sacrificed for the interests of science. Included in the lecture was a report on the amazing resistance of some animals, especially cats, to certain poisons that are deadly to man. Earlier in his Toxical Analysis notebook he had entered the following:

Full-grown male cat
Administered 0.3 grams white Arsenic (As_2O_3) April 10/'83 at 7:30 p.m.
Second dose of 0.3 grm. at 9 p.m.
Third dose, next morning at 10.
Killed by force at 12:30.

Subsequently he removed every organ for weighing, measuring, dissecting, and analyzing, recording the information in twelve pages of notes.[47]

During the summer of 1883, when he was preparing for John Hopkins by reading biology in the Lehigh library (including Herbert Spencer's *First Principles*) and gathering specimens, he went

... fishing for frogs; caught a very large specimen and was anxious to preserve it for its skeleton entire. Did not know how to kill it there on the ground without torture, unless by cutting off [its] head which would have spoiled the bones. So at a sudden gash I cut out its heart, liver, etc. The friend with me picked up the heart which was beating strongly; but as soon as I released the "heartless" frog it turned off its back and took vigorous jumps for the water. Its leaps were 3-4 feet as measured. It saw us and tried to avoid us whenever we approached it; seemed entirely unhurt and continued its strong demonstrations for 1-1/2 minutes; having taken no less than 15 leaps in all directions; when I picked it up to prevent its getting into water; then it died suddenly.[48]

Such incidents reveal the depth of Talmage's commitment to laboratory work and his general fascination with science. For every student who has performed dissections in a biology course, an animal or amphibian had to die. Since Talmage was a student in a time and place when fully supplied laboratories were a luxury, he early developed the habit of supplying his own specimens. Perhaps the most telling example of the depth of his scientific curiosity and his commitment to experimentation occurred in the spring of 1884 while he was studying narcotics at Johns Hopkins. He recorded the following entries in his journal:

> March 17. I have been engaged some time in the study of the effects of Narcotics upon the system, i.e. studying the same theoretically only. Today I found a gentleman who works in the same Laboratory as I, and who has for 2 years been addicted to the habit of eating Haschich or extract of *Cannabis Indica*. He was very willing to give me any data from his own experience; and gave me such.
> March 18 . . . Three of us in the University have entered upon the study of the Narcotics in use.
> March 21. The result of our work in research upon Narcotics has been tolerably satisfactory. We utilize my friend referred to above, with his Haschich eating experience—and find four or five others whom he knows have also an experience upon the subject. But the effects experienced by the different ones are so widely different that we can scarcely draw a conclusion. The opium habit is well explained by books, and the bad after effects of the same are sufficiently appalling to keep down experimentation upon the subject. But, the ill effects are reported very low in the Haschich or Hemp administration; and we have concluded to try effect of small dose upon ourselves.
> Of course, such a course is the proper one for the study of the effects of the drug, though I very much disliked the idea of doing

such a thing, for as yet I have never known what it is to be narcotized either by tobacco, alcohol, or any drug. . . .

March 22. This being Saturday, was the day I selected to study practically the effects of Haschisch. This evening, after work and all was over, I took at 3 doses each an hour after the preceeding, 5 grains solid extract Cannabis Indica. At this writing—midnight—5 hours since last dose, I have experienced no effect whatever. The effect is said to be widely different in different people.

March 23. Sunday. Spent quietly. Have had no result to be noted of my physiological experiment yesterday. . . .

April 5 . . . Took in all 15 grains. No effects.

April 6. Sunday . . . Continued my experiment by taking 20 grains *Cannabis Indica* and the effect was felt in a not very agreeable way.

Talmage would lecture to the Brigham Young Academy faculty in September 1884 on "The Effects of the Narcotic Hashish on the Human System," but the Faculty Minute Book does not record whether he mentioned the source of his information.

With an eye to the future, Talmage shipped specimens home by the crateful. His journal records an incredible variety, including examples of: "the processes in the manufacture of tin cans," "the process of oil refining," fossilized shark teeth, tobacco leaves, phosphates, lead, asbestos, zinc, iron, steel, chocolate, cork, fertilizer, rubber, ferns, minerals, vinegar, fossil shells and bones, pottery, paraffin, soap, candles, illuminating oil, iron ore, and even the complete skeleton of a monkey from the zoo in Druid Hill Park.

He also obtained an articulated human forearm, finger, some other bones, and a large piece of skin from the university dissecting rooms with the aid of a student and the janitor. Although he disapproved of the callousness of the medical students and even the janitor, who apparently sold bones to the students regularly, he was even more surprised on 14 January 1884 when he was scraping the finger bones and preparing the skin for preservation. "A young gentleman of the University came to my room. . . . He is a classical scholar and I believe intends to study to become a Minister. Oh! the utter horror he expressed at what he saw me engaged in, was something intense. In fact, he could not rest in the room—was terrified. . . . He is 29 years of age and a fine scholar. What will not use and habit cause one to be?"

Perhaps most significant in its impact on Talmage was his opportunity to participate in original research at Johns Hopkins under the direction of Ira Remsen and Harmon N. Morse, both on the cutting edge of research in their fields. From 1872 on Remsen wrote numerous books and papers covering a wide field of chemistry and was founding editor of the *American Chemical Journal*, 1879-1913.

Harmon Northrop Morse, professor of inorganic chemistry, published ten papers in the *American Chemical Journal* between 1880 and 1892 based on investigations in his laboratory, some of which were conducted when Talmage was working there. In addition Morse invented equipment for reading gas volumes over water, determining the equivalents of metals, grading and calibrating liquid measuring apparatus, an electric furnace, and electric laboratory heating devices. Between Remsen and Morse many original discoveries came out of the Johns Hopkins labs, including white phosphorous, saccharin, and a phenomenon that became known in the chemical world as Remsen's Law. Shortly before Talmage left Baltimore to return to Utah he dejectedly described the work he had been doing with them: "May 9 [1884]. . . For nearly 3 months I have been engaged on a piece of original work in Chemistry—'on the *oxidation of Cymene Sulphamide in alkaline solution*'. The labor has not been easy—great difficulty having been met in purifying the substances fit for analysis. Another line of investigation will have to be pursued: and the Professors told me today it would be impossible to do anything in less than another 3 months, and as the college closes in a month the subject would be better given up. I shall be unable to continue the labor at home for lack of material."

Despite Talmage's absorption in his studies and research, an odd theme of self-justification runs through his journals, a determination to prove that his choice was correct and that Mormons could study in the east without losing their faith. Because his religious commitments meant that he was never totally free to follow his "selfish" interests in science, he frequently pondered how far he could go without being disloyal to his faith.[49]

Had Talmage been more free to choose, he may have remained in the east until he finished a degree. From a practical standpoint, he was out of money by the spring of 1884, but he could easily have earned more in the east working as a chemist and, in fact, refused several job offers, one from the College of Western Maryland as a professor of chemistry which included an all-expense-paid year in residence as a student, to earn the necessary degree. At first he was tempted, even though chemistry was "but a minor study there anyway." Ultimately he declined, confiding in his journal that he did not value a degree so highly that he was willing to pay such a price in time. But, he did value a degree and had been willing to accept one from Western Maryland if they would confer it on the basis of June examinations.[50]

Another offer had come in the late summer of 1883, when Talmage was deciding whether to go to Johns Hopkins or stay at Lehigh. As money began to arrive for the next year of study from J. M. Tanner, George Coray, and members of the academy board, his mind turned strongly to home and his obligations there. Had Coray joined him at Lehigh, Talmage would almost surely have completed his degree there. When Coray went to Cornell instead and Maeser responded to Talmage's appeal for advice by telling him to make up his own mind after prayerful consideration, he made his final decision for Johns Hopkins, but he felt "sadly alone" in the decision.[51] While he waited for classes to begin in Baltimore, he wrote three essays for Utah audiences, apparently to be used later and perhaps partly out of homesickness. In "Good for Nothing," he described how to the chemist there is no such thing as "dirt." It includes a moving passage about Adam being a great philosopher even though he lacked a college degree.[52]

Talmage immersed himself as thoroughly in his studies at Johns Hopkins as he had at Lehigh. Then on 30 January 1884 he received word that Brigham Young Academy had burned to the ground. He was ready to begin his last term of schooling, but he was willing to leave for home immediately if called. Despite his prompt response, there were hints of ambiguity. A few weeks earlier he had written George Coray that "I . . . hope to come East again, when the cloud of debt will have passed off me." One month after hearing about the fire, he mentions "if" in connection with teaching again.[53]

Apparently, however, Talmage never seriously considered staying longer. The Utah question—meaning the Mormon question of plural marriage—was a current issue. Talmage responded to dozens of inquiries about the Utah question, including at least two letters prompted by public lectures, each time defending his people and religion. He was offended in Baltimore by crime, drunkenness, poverty, and the practices of other churches. All of the above plus the constant influence of letters from home telling of sick family members, giving him advice, sending news of the academy, and requesting assistance in procuring scientific apparata, made it nearly inevitable that he return home on schedule.

He could return home with the assurance that he had tested his choice in the big leagues of American science and that Mormons had nothing to fear from science. With rare exceptions, his professors had been warm, encouraging, and focused on the specific detailed facts of their science. He mentions Darwin only twice in the two years, on both occasions complaining about recent lectures on the subject by ignorant clergymen who misrepresented Darwin in particular and science in general.[54] He returned as he had been instructed, "like a bee to the hive,"[55] but he re-entered with the firm intention of returning to the blossoms and nectar of science at his earliest opportunity.

NOTES

1. See *The Contributor* 16 (Feb. 1895): 229, based on an interview with James E. Talmage. He also said that his father followed the herbal profession "afterward." According to his son, Talmage frequently told his children stories of the elder James's influence. John R. Talmage, *The Talmage Story* (Salt Lake City: Bookcraft, 1972), 1-2, hereafter cited as *Talmage Story*.

2. Most biographical accounts refer only to his attending infant school in Ramsbury. His "Notes on English History," however, carry the clear label, "Ramsbury, Wilts, 1872," and corroborate his journal statement that he attended the National School in Hungerford only intermittently between the ages of five and twelve. Talmage Papers, box 9, folder 1, Archives and Manuscripts, Harold B. Lee Library, Brigham Young University, Provo, Utah; hereafter cited as Papers.

3. *The Contributor* 16 (Feb. 1895): 229.

4. See James E. Talmage Journal, Vol. 2, 4 Apr. and 12 Dec. 1881, in Papers and hereafter cited as Journal and the preface to *First Book of Nature* (Salt Lake City: Geo. Q. Cannon & Sons Co., 1888).

5. Later as the first curator of the museum collections of the Brigham Young Academy, he added his personal collection to the holdings. Ernest L. Wilkinson, ed., *Brigham Young University. The First One Hundred*

Years (Provo, Utah: Brigham Young University Press, 1975), 1:169, hereafter cited as *BYU Centennial History*.

6. See Examination Paper for Standard VI, Papers, box 9, folder 1.

7. The decision to add any subject beyond religion, the three R's, singing and sewing for the girls was made by each local school.

8. For the number of classes Maeser taught, see Brigham Young University Archives, hereafter cited as UA, Register of Studies, which is not extant for the period of 1877-79, the Circulars, and the notes and examinations of Talmage in Papers, boxes 9 and 10.

9. *BYU Centennial History* 1:159; Douglas F. Tobler, "Karl G. Maeser's German Background, 1828-56; The Making of Zion's Teacher," *BYU Studies* 17 (Winter 1977): 155-75. Maeser taught his students that the teacher of primary and intermediate grades must have a thorough understanding of all the natural sciences even though "formally, in a common school these can claim no place." See Papers, box 9, folder 4, "Theory of Teaching," 93.

10. Papers, box 9, folder 4, "Theory of Teaching," 41.

11. *Talmage Story*, Ch. 1.

12. Papers, box 10, folder 6, Geography Notes. Allowances must be made, of course, for any distortion of Maeser's teachings as they passed through Talmage's mind; however, all of Talmage's BYA notes are a valuable source for the content of what Maeser actually taught in the early years in contrast to what he said ought to be taught in his 1898 *School and Fireside*.

13. Papers, box 9, folder 4, "Theory of Teaching," 132.

14. J. Dorman Steel, *Fourteen Weeks in Physics* (New York: A. S. Barnes & Company, 1878). Other titles in the series were physiology, zoology, chemistry, astronomy, and geology. Steele was an educator who achieved great success as a popularizer of science.

15. UA 186, Folder M50, Vol. 1, 19.

16. UA, Register of Studies, June 1877.

17. For example, compare the essay entitled, "What arguments have we that Joseph Smith was sent of God?" in Papers, box 9, folder 2, with "The Cotton Gin" and "The Microscope" in Papers, box 9, folder 3.

18. Papers, box 9, folder 7.

19. Journal, 28 July 1880.

20. Journal, Aug. 1880; *Ogden Daily Junction*, 23-24 Aug. 1880; Maeser to John Taylor, 23 July 1880, UA. Maeser correspondence, box 1, folder 2; U.S. Census for 1900, Utah, Salt Lake, 3rd Precinct, Roll #1241684, 12 June, District 273, Sheet 12, page A; and Papers: Scientific Analysis in box 10, folder 2, Chemistry Tables in box 9, folder 8, and "Scraps" in box 10, folder 6.

21. UA, Register of Studies, 1880-81.

22. Journal, regular entries 1879-82, see e.g., 6 Nov. 1880, 17 June 1881, 25 Aug. 1881.

23. Papers, box 9, folder 4, "Theory of Teaching," 7.

24. BYU Centennial History 1:215, 224.

25. UA, biographical files for both men.

26. Journal, 27 June 1884. Other supporters were Thomas Hadley and Joseph L. Barfoot, long-time curator of the Deseret Museum whom Talmage had met at the museum in February 1881. Thereafter they exchanged specimens and Barfoot helped Talmage with specimens at the BYA Museum. Talmage credited Hadley and Barfoot with awakening his interest in nature. See The Contributor 16 (Feb. 1895): 231.

27. Papers, box 10, folder 3. See also Journal, 1 Sept. and 6 Nov. 1880; 17 June 1881.

28. Papers, box 9, folder 5, and box 10, folder 3. It is not known which edition of Dana's manual Talmage used. If it was the 1874 edition, in which Dana began to give qualified support to evolution in much the same way Talmage subsequently did, then the likelihood of Dana having been an influence in helping to formulate the details of Talmage's stand is increased. See Bert James Loewenberg, "The Reaction of American Scientists to Darwinism," American Historical Review 38 (1932-33): 698-701.

29. The Contributor 16 (Feb. 1895): 230.

30. Journal, 14 Nov., 14 Dec. 1881.

31. Journal, 14 Nov. 1881.

32. UA 317, Papers, box 9, folder 5.

33. Journal, 7 Dec. 1881.

34. Journal, 1 Apr. 1882.

35. Journal, 13 Nov. 1881.

36. Journal, dates given.

37. Journal, dates given.

38. Journal, 17 and 28 June and 22 Aug. 1881.

39. See original notes, partially in Pitman shorthand, in Papers, box 10, folder 5. I am indebted to LaJean Purcell for the transcription of these notes.

40. Davis Bitton, "Anti-Intellectualism in Mormon History," Dialogue: A Journal of Mormon Thought 1 (Autumn 1966): 111-33, and John A. Widtsoe, Joseph Smith as Scientist (Salt Lake City: YMMIA General Board, 1908).

41. Journal, April-May, 1882.

42. Journal, 25 Aug. 1882. Compare Maeser's advice to Talmage to remain at Johns Hopkins if he could (Journal, 13 Feb. 1884) after the academy fire. Perhaps Maeser was less concerned about Talmage losing his faith after having corresponded with him for almost two years.

43. Journal, 3 July and 7 Aug. 1882, 26 Oct. 1881.

44. Journal, 17 June 1882. Talmage's father is seldom mentioned in the journals, but he was among those who argued for medical school and

urged him to spend the summer studying.

45. Information on Talmage's courses is drawn from journal entries and class notes. In general see Papers, box 10, folder 5, through box 13, folder 7, and box 1, folders 1-2.

46. Journal, 24 Dec. 1883.

47. Journal, 26 Apr. 1883; and Papers, box 10, folder 5, box 11, folder 6, "Analyses," 3-15. Again I am indebted to LaJean Purcell for transcribing the Pitman shorthand. See also earlier references to toxicology in Journal, 3 and 10 Apr. 1883.

48. Papers, box 13, folder 1; Journal, 1 Aug. 1883.

49. Journal, see e.g., 9 Sept. 1883.

50. Journal, 23 June and 8 July 1883; 28 Mar. 1884. He also considered the possibility of approaching a North Carolina institution that would award a degree by academic record and examination; 2 May 1884.

51. Journal, 17 Aug. 1883. See also 9 Sept. 1883.

52. Papers, box 12, folder 9.

53. Journal, 24 Dec. 1883, 29 Feb. 1884.

54. Journal, 4 May and 16 Mar. 1884.

55. Journal, 9 Sept. 1882; 9 Sept. 1883.

5.
A Turbulent Spectrum: Mormon Reactions to the Darwinist Legacy

Richard Sherlock

IN LATE 1930 B. H. ROBERTS OF THE FIRST COUNCIL OF SEVENTY wrote to Rudger Clawson, president of the Council of Twelve Apostles, protesting a speech given by Elder Joseph Fielding Smith published the previous October. Smith's speech had attacked one of the pillars of evolutionary theory, the paleontological record of life and death stretching back hundreds of millions of years. In his letter Roberts wrote: "I call in question the accuracy of Elder Smith's position in reference to the whole doctrine of his discourse, as being contrary to a great volume of well-developed and ascertained truth, established by the researches of scientists of highest character, of profoundest learning, and world wide research. I hold his doctrine contrary at least to the plain implications of scripture; as tending also to reduce the church of the New Dispensation to the character of a narrow, bigoted sect, forsaking the God-given world movement idea of it; and as injurious to the continued faith in the adherence to the teachings of the Church not by a 'scattered few' but by a very great number of its membership."[1]

In a paper presented to the council on 14 January 1931 in defense of his position, Smith wrote, "Any doctrine whether it comes in the name of religion, science, philosophy or whatever it may be, that is in conflict with the revelations of the Lord will fail. . . . you will find that every doctrine, theory, principle no matter how great it may appear, no matter how universally it may be believed, if it is not in accord with the word of the Lord it will perish."[2]

Here were two pillars of twentieth-century Mormonism wrestling with the modern understanding of nature and history. Roberts had been a member of the First Council of Seventy for over forty years, a defender of the faith in innumerable situations, and a prolific author of works in explanation and defense of the church. Smith had been an apostle for twenty years, the son of a church president, and destined for that office. The issue on which these men collided was ostensibly the paleontological record of life and death that supported the evolutionary superstructure of modern biology. But there was a more profound issue at work. How far could one go in adopting the findings of modern intellectuals before compromising historic Mormonism out of existence? This was the real dilemma for these men. For Roberts, unless there was some accommodation, some reconciliation, many educated church members would drift away, unable to see how God could provide one record of his creation in nature and another in scripture. For Smith the issue was just as vital. Where do you stop once you have given up scriptural literalism? The faith of the Saints could easily be wrecked on the shoals of modernism.

The intense debate between Smith and Roberts ended inconclusively with the First Presidency declaring that neither side represented an official church position. However, the profound debate between these leaders is symbolic of a much wider spectrum of discussion over evolution that has gone on in Mormon society since the turn of the century.

Joseph Fielding Smith offered the most consistent opposition to evolutionary theory from Mormon sources. From his earliest published speeches to the publication of *Man: His Origin and Destiny* forty years later, the central theme of his position does not vary. Evolution is both untrue and destructive of faith. It is a Satan-inspired idea with which there can be no compromise. He was a Protestant fundamentalist in a Mormon setting.

Smith was not a scientist, and he would not have been prepared to argue against the theory on scientific grounds. Nor would he have wanted to. For him the word of God as revealed in the literal text of the scriptures was the only certain standard. Everything else would be tested against it. If it conflicted with the scriptures, it was wrong. His earliest published attack on evolution is entitled "The Word of the Lord Superior to the Theories of Men." This was the central concern of his attack thereafter. In an April 1930 address he spoke of his conviction, "The word of the Lord means more to me than anything else. I place it before the teachings of men. The truth is the thing which will last. All the theory, philosophy and wisdom of the wise that is not in harmony with revealed truth from God will perish. It must change and pass away and it is changing and passing away constantly, but when the Lord speaks that is eternal truth on which we may rely."[3]

Smith's concern for the literal accuracy of the scriptures was deeply related to a fundamental conviction that evolution would destroy orthodox Christian belief. In this he resembled one of his favorite sources, fundamentalist geologist George McReady Price, who once wrote, "No Adam, no fall; no fall, no atonement; no atonement, no savior."[4]

Smith was also convinced that orthodoxy stood or fell with a literal Adam and a literal fall. For him evolution denied the story of Adam. According to Smith, "If you believe in the doctrine of the evolutionist, then you must accept the view that man has evolved through countless ages from the very lowest forms of life up through various stages of animal life, finally into human form. The first man, according to this hypothesis known as the cave man, was a creature absolutely ignorant and devoid of any marked intelligence over the beasts of the field. Then Adam, and by that I mean the first man, was not capable of sin. He could not transgress, and by doing so bring death into the world; for, according to this theory, death had always been in the world. If, therefore, there was no fall, there was no need of an atonement, hence the coming into the world of the Son of God as the Savior of the world is a contradiction, a thing impossible. Are you prepared to believe such a thing as that?"[5]

For Smith anyone who adopted evolutionary views would end up rejecting the "fundamental doctrines of Christianity." The two were irreconcilable: "What I believe to be the most pernicious doctrine ever entering the mind of man [is] the theory that man evolved from lower forms of life. For its source we must go beyond the activities of men to the author of evil." Within such a context the next step was obvious. He wrote, "I do not believe that the falsely so-called scientific theory of man's origin has any more right to a place in public schools than the principles of the gospel of our Lord and Savior Jesus Christ have—and not half as much." He urged his audiences to protest the teaching of evolution in the schools, which, he believed, led people away from God.[6]

Smith denied that one could be a theistic evolutionist. He believed that there was only one true religion, one true theism, and that evolution was a naturalistic interpretation of the world with no need for God as creator and father of the human race. Furthermore, he believed that evolutionists wanted a completely rational, progressing world in which miracles could not be allowed.[7]

In the course of his writings, he criticized every part of the evolutionary corpus. He denied that the earth was old. The scriptures implied that a day, according to God, was 1,000 years, so the computation of a 13,000-year-old-earth easily followed. He denied the specific thesis of organic mutability of species in uncompromising terms. There was an "eternal decree that animals of different families or species shall remain separate from other species and there are bounds they cannot cross." He took satisfaction in pointing out the hoax of the Piltdown man as an example of the willingness of science to be deceived.[8]

Smith often lumped several different views together and condemned them all. He attacked the idea of spontaneous generation, a naturalistic interpretation of the coming of life on earth, and said that the consistent evolutionist believed in this, which was not true. He also held that evolution demanded a belief in the inheritance of acquired characteristics, which was not the case. Finally he identified believers in evolution with students of "higher criticism" as "two groups of the same general class . . . each . . . bent on the destruction of the story of creation and the development of humanity as this story is told in the Bible."[9]

Though his lack of scientific learning led him into errors, he did see the difficulties of reconciliation between Mormon theology and evolutionary thought. The fundamental intuition of the evolutionist was gradual change from simple to complex, from primitive to sophisticated in nature and society. But the Mormon restorationist impulse made the present a copy of the past and had the effect of shortening the historical perspective. If present and past could be brought together in this way, the possibility of the kind of elaborate systems of social and cosmic evolution as that envisioned by Spencer would certainly be questioned. Furthermore Mormon anthropomorphism made God the prototype of man; Adam was literally his offspring. To think of a being made in the literal image of God as the result of descent from other forms of life was a difficult move indeed.[10]

Mormon thought, however, is a diverse complex of elements, and other thinkers found themes compatible with evolutionary speculations. One of the most fundamental of these was the conviction that truth was indivisible, and Mormonism encompasses all truth. There is not one set of truths in religion and another set of truths in science. All truths are part of one whole, one set of truths that do not conflict. This conviction led several important church authorities to attempt to account in some way for the mass of evidence that conflicted with the traditional views of the Creation and the coming of Adam.

The first church leader to attempt a reconciliation of sorts was Apostle James E. Talmage, a trained geologist, president of two universities, and a man who believed that modern scientific discoveries were important and could not be denied outright. But though he was sympathetic to science, his religious convictions prevented him from becoming an unqualified supporter of evolution. Ultimately he retreated into the world view of Bishop Ussher and the coming of Adam at 4004 B.C.E.

Talmage did not write or publish a great deal on evolution. His first discussion of the matter came in 1890 before he became an apostle. At the time he was president of LDS College in Salt Lake City and taught geology and natural science at the school. In an address to teachers in Utah County, he discussed evolution at some length. This speech set a pattern for Talmage's later discussions of evolutionary theory and the ideas surrounding it.[11]

In the speech Talmage distinguished between a general idea of evolution as a theory of development or change and the specific hypothesis of natural selection and organic mutability advanced by Darwin and his followers. Demonstrating a wide acquaintance with the history of evolutionary thought, he discussed the background of the Darwinian synthesis in Buffon, Lamarck, and Erasmus Darwin, Charles Darwin's grandfather.

Talmage criticized the evolutionary ideas of Darwin's most prominent supporter, Thomas Huxley. He dismissed the idea that life originated in some primordial protoplasm as the result of chance occurrence. Any such generation had not been demonstrated, he argued, and all attempts to find or create such matter had failed. Hence on this point the theistic conclusion was obvious: "Without spontaneous generation 'miracle' in the words of Strauss was and is still necessary to explain the advent even of the hypothetical primordial germ."[12]

Then he proceeded to argue against the central thesis of Darwinian synthesis, the organic mutability of species. The fixity of species was a hallmark of Talmage's thinking. Variations do occur, he admitted, but he called his audience's attention to the sterility of hybrids as a classic example of the "law" that species reproduce only "after their own kind." Each creation was a special work of the Creator adapted to its specific environment: "The insect is fitted for its abode on the leaf; the fish for the water; the bird for the air; each beast for its allotted life; and so man for his. No one form can be transmuted into another. The thought that it could be otherwise is far more wild than the alchemist's dream of transmuting base lead into royal gold. In the fable of old the frog burst when it tried to appear as an ox. Each after its kind—each to its sphere—this is the song of nature; and all praise to nature's God."[13]

This hostility to the idea of mutability of species did not prevent Talmage from adopting the language of evolution. There was, he said, a "true evolution" that was not subject to the attacks that he launched. This true evolution was signified by the idea of development and growth. "Is evolution true?" he asked. "Aye: true evolution is true. The evolution that means advancement, progress, growth to a full realization of the intended measure of all things, that is true."[14]

In line with many others, Talmage regarded Mormonism as the best expression of this true evolution. What more lavish evolutionary thought was there than that people could progressively develop into gods? The evolutionist who failed to see the cosmic evolution of the spirit in humankind was truly blind. Men were not the offspring of other animals, they were the offspring of God. They were evolving, developing, and progressing into divine beings themselves.[15]

Talmage recognized that certain hard facts from geological and paleontological studies could not be ignored. He seems to have been convinced of the necessity to account in some fashion for these well established facts. The most important statement from him in this regard was his 1931 address, "The Earth and Man," but during the same time period Talmage answered many letters on topics surrounding evolutionary theory. With these sources it is not difficult to reconstruct the main contours of his thinking.

Talmage began by admitting that the earth was considerably older than humanity. How old he did not know, but the church made no pronouncement on such matters and if geologists said that it was very old then that was probably true. Such a concession as this would not produce shock waves anywhere. American theologians had been saying it since the 1830s without great difficulty, and inside the LDS church many were prepared to accept it. His next move was more challenging. Plants and animals had existed for ages before the coming of man. Furthermore they had lived and died during these countless ages. This was the major concession in the 1931 address: "According to the conception of geologists the earth passed through ages of preparation during which countless generations of plants and animals existed in great variety and profusion and gave in part the very substance of their bodies to help form certain strata which are still in existence as such."

As it stands this statement could be interpreted as merely a report of what geologists believe about earth history. But in a letter a few months later he was explicit about his own belief: "I cannot agree with your conception that there was no death of plants and animals anywhere upon this earth prior to the transgression of Adam, unless we assume that the history of Adam and Eve dates back many hundreds of thousands of years. The trouble with some theologians—even including many of our own good people—is that they undertake to fix the date of Adam's transgression as being approximately 4000 years before Christ and therefore about 5932 years ago. If Adam was placed upon the earth only that comparatively short time ago the rocks clearly demonstrated that life and death have been in existence and operative in this earth for ages prior to that time."[16] Talmage admitted life and death of animals for those countless ages but still believed in the biblical chronology for the coming of Adam.[17]

If Adam only came 4,000 years before Jesus Christ, then Talmage was clearly headed for difficulty. In the 1931 speech he tentatively suggested that there might have been men on earth before Adam—"pre-Adamic men." He suggested that whatever came before the "Adamic race" (his term) was a completely different dispensation with which we are not to be concerned. Talmage realized that dogmatic assertions were not helpful. In his journal on the day the First Presidency gave its decision in the controversy between Smith and Roberts, he wrote, "This is one of the many things on which we cannot preach with assurance, and dogmatic assertions on either side are likely to do harm rather than good."[18]

In a letter written a few months before his death, Talmage articulated his fundamental scheme of reference which had varied little in forty years: "Undoubtedly true evolution is true, meaning progress from the lower to the higher, from the simple to the more complex. We cannot sweep aside all the accumulated knowledge in geology, archeology or any other branch of science simply because our interpretation of some isolated passage of scripture may seem to be opposed thereto. I do not believe that Adam derived his mortal body by evolutionary processes from the lower animals. The adamic race of men are of an entirely different order."[19] In the end Talmage's thinking on evolution is an amalgam of diverse impulses, the mark of a man with divided loyalties. As a scientist he knew that the evidence could not be denied. But the safe harbor of special creationism was appealing to him.

Talmage's attempt at some reconciliation between scientific facts and received faith was greatly amplified by B. H. Roberts. Late in his life Roberts attempted to understand evolution and paleontology in a monumental manuscript that has remained unpublished. Through this manuscript it is possible to look at some of the ways Roberts dealt with central questions of evolutionary theory.[20]

Roberts believed the evidence for the antiquity of the earth and its life forms could not be denied. There were millions and billions of years of earth history, stretching back to the beginning when God created the world. Roberts included in the manuscript citations claiming that the world was at least two billion years old. The clear implication of the text is that he was prepared to accept any such figure that science could demonstrate as accurate.[21]

More importantly Roberts was prepared to accept the established fossil records of life and death stretching back hundreds of millions of years. Of these records the most important were those relating to the antiquity of humankind. This was clearly an important question for Roberts. The manuscript is filled with pages of evidence concerning the discoveries of the fossil remains of prehistoric people. He quoted extensively from experts concerning the evidence of the antiquity of the human species all over the earth. The evidence, he said, was so extensive that he could not present nearly all of it.[22]

If the human race was this ancient, then Genesis was clearly in for difficulties. But Roberts did not tamper with the Genesis history in any fundamental way. Rather he turned to the Mormon idea of a physical and a spiritual creation. If this were true, then the first chapter of Genesis might be a record of the spiritual creation and the second might be the record of the material or physical creation. But the second chapter implies that man appeared on a barren world before anything else. Hence Roberts seemed to find some scriptural warrant for the idea of some great cataclysm that destroyed all life on earth before the coming of Adam.[23]

Like Talmage, Roberts addressed the dilemma of the antiquity of human beings by positing a race of pre-Adamite humans. The antiquity of the present human race stretched back about 4,000 years, but before this the earth existed for ages: plants and animals, men and women had lived and died for millions of years. Then some great cataclysm destroyed all other beings on the earth. "Why not recognize that truth and see that which is inevitable," Roberts wrote, "that in the advent of Adam the time had come for the achievement of some special purpose in relation to man—some spiritual relationship that brought about the introduction of the adamic dispensation? Otherwise the whole volume of facts as they are disclosed are thrown into confusion; and the revealed truths themselves for most men rendered doubtful, being out of harmony with the facts ascertained as to man's antiquity."[24]

Roberts relied not only on scientific sources but also Mormon ones for his theory of pre-Adamite people. Among other support was an 1854 address by Apostle Orson Hyde. Hyde had argued that if Adam had been commanded to "re-plenish the earth," how could this have been unless the earth had already been populated. To a scriptural literalist the argument seemed sensible. Furthermore Roberts said that Brigham Young had agreed with Hyde's speech, and thus the argument seemed to have prophetic approval. Whether this was actually the case is questionable. Hyde's talk was primarily on marriage. Brigham Young began his own talk by saying, "I do not wish to eradicate any items from the lecture Elder Hyde has given us this evening." It seems more plausible that Young was referring to the discourse as a whole rather than to any particular point.[25]

This elaborate dispensationalist argument was most clearly not a theory of evolution. It did not deal at all with the central thesis of evolution—the mutability of species and descent with modification. Roberts's discussion of this issue in the manuscript is ambiguous. He was greatly influenced by the biblical argument that species reproduce only "after their own kind." He refers to this several times as the "great law of life." But he also was greatly impressed with the variation among offspring in nature. He wanted some way to balance these two perspectives of stability and change in nature.[26]

Roberts called his answer to this problem "the development theory." He thought this theory would preserve the "great law" of reproduction and yet leave room for wide variation within certain bounds. It recognized "the eternity of some life forms, and the possibilities of these forms—perhaps in embryonic status, or in their simplest forms (same as to man) are transplanted to newly created worlds there to be developed each to its highest possibilities, . . . "[27]

This view evades the central issue. What are these primeval life forms out of which other forms develop? There is no logical reason why all species could not have developed from one primeval life form if the immutability of species is broached. In a later passage he was even more unclear but intriguing: "And from a few other forms of life transported to earth there could be development of varied kinds of life yet adhering closely to the great law of life so constantly repeated—'each after its own kind.' Not necessarily limited to stereotyped individual forms, but developing the kinds from the subdivisions of vegetable and animal kingdoms into various species through development from primeval forms."[28] Clearly Roberts's "development view" led him to the edge of evolutionary descent.

To handle the problem of human antiquity, Roberts has adopted a dispensationalist framework and the idea of a cataclysm destroying all life on the earth prior to the coming of Adam. Here he clearly argued for an orderly unfolding of life forms. Humankind in this scheme comes not on a barren world but a world already populated with an infinite variety of plants and animals.[29] It is doubtful that any workable reconciliation between these two perspectives could be maintained. Roberts saw clearly that there was a great deal of evidence that could not be squared with the traditional interpretation of Genesis. But he was unwilling to attempt a reconciliation grounded in a firm commitment to evolution. Later, others would make the attempt.

Few Latter-day Saints have been more open about their acceptance of organic mutability than Fredrick Pack. Pack was James Talmage's assistant at the University of Utah, and when Talmage resigned to become an apostle, Pack was appointed his successor as Deseret Professor of Geology. Pack had impressive credentials both for a churchman and a scientist. He was a member of the church Sunday school board and wrote many books for the church. He was a prominent foe to tobacco and a leader in the 1920s church-organized campaign to prohibit smoking in public. He was also a 1904 graduate of the University of Utah and a Ph.D. graduate from Columbia University in 1906 with a string of scientific treatises on the geologic structures of Utah and the Wasatch Fault.[30]

In 1924 Pack published his major discussion of evolution in *Science and Belief in God*. Here he was forthright and uncompromising in his defense of organic evolution. Evolution was as true as Mormonism for him, and two truths could not conflict. Pack began by arguing that nothing in nature was immutable, including species. Change, not stability, was the hallmark of the natural world: "The essence of evolution is the essence of continuous change. . . . evolution is essentially a series of changes brought about by the laws of nature." Pack claimed that the notion of the change in species is supported by an "almost unlimited array of evidence in favor of the doctrine of organic evolution." Pack dismissed the characteristic line of reasoning about horses only birthing horses. "Such a statement scarcely merits serious consideration," he wrote, "since no form of the doctrine contemplates the likelihood of a change of that character." The time span envisioned for the development of new species made this argument ridiculous as an attempted disproof of evolution.[31]

Although the fact that evolution had occurred was irrefutable, Pack admitted the mechanism that had produced this change was open to question. "The fact that scientists do not agree as to the manner in which evolution operates is often interpreted to mean that they disagree in the matter of the validity of the principle itself. This is of course all wrong." Pack emphasized that the "doctrine of organic evolution is at present more widely accepted than ever before."[32]

Pack himself saw natural selection as an insufficient explanation of the process and recognized that Darwinism with its ultimate reliance on chance had no place for the operation of an overarching purpose in nature. The idea of organic evolution, including the mutability of species, posed no threat to Pack's faith. Darwinism as an explication of the evolutionary process did.[33]

Contrary to orthodox Darwinists, Pack argued that the record does not indicate a random development devoid of plan or purpose but rather shows that life developed along "well directed lines." By adding a concept of plan and purpose, Pack thought the requirements of theism could be satisfied. Further this purposeful law of evolution did not require "the immediate interposition of Deity." For him it was a nobler view of God to think that he could set up a process requiring little supervision. A builder whose machine requires constant repair is not a great craftsman.[34]

Pack was more cautious in discussing the place of humans in this scheme, but he remained an evolutionist. He suggested that the evidence was not conclusive in proving that present people had descended from more primitive people and thence from lower primate forms. But it was very persuasive. "To assert as some theologians do that science has failed utterly in its search for evidence connecting man with lower forms of life could only be done by ignoring very pertinent discoveries." Do all animal forms represent one continuous line of descent down to and including humanity? he asked. "Speaking for the great mass of scientists the reply would be an emphatic 'yes.'"[35]

Pack thought that none of this upset belief in God or faith in the Genesis account. "The search for the origin of man is not a question as to whether or not Deity is the author of his existence. On the other hand the question is merely one of how man reached his present state of development. . . . the doctrine of anthropoid origin of man is not opposed to belief in the Fatherhood of God; it simply attempts to explain the way in which nature operates." If God was "the greatest teacher in the universe," then it seemed reasonable that he would teach his children in accord with their ability to understand. "It should not be a source of surprise therefore that many of the scriptural narratives intended for ancient Israel appear to us at least in places to be primitive and even crude."

Pack suggested that scientific research might be God's way of giving us new information on the creative process: "If God were to repeat the story of man's origin He would probably clear away many of the obscurities surrounding the account contained in the Jewish scriptures. Doubtless, however, as people become more and more anxious to know the truth, He will supply means for their enlightenment, but no one would care to say whether this enlightenment will come as a direct revelation from God or through the searchers of science."[36]

Pack attempted to turn the tables on critics by using evolutionary progression to prove the inspired character of Genesis. He thought that Genesis represented the successive stages of the creation process and that the geological record told exactly the same story. Moses must have received his information from elsewhere since no one except God could have told him such truths. Pack's biblical defenses of evolution were published in no other than the official church periodical, *The Improvement Era*.[37]

As Thomas Kuhn has argued, scientific departures from orthodoxy can be tolerated so long as the exponent of the new is viewed as a defender of orthodoxy. On the important question for Mormon society during the period, the moral purity of its members as distinct from the Babylon around them, Pack was a staunch defender of the faith. He published tracts against smoking, he exposed the evils of caffeine in talks and forums. As a defender of orthodoxy in areas of great concern, he could be permitted his own ideas in other areas without harm to his standing in the community.[38]

Though Pack published the most rigorous defense of evolution, others engaged in elaborate speculations. One of the boldest attempts to expound an elaborate system of cosmic evolution was that of Nels Nelson. Nelson taught English at Brigham Young University from 1883 until 1920 with some time out for a mission and study in the East. He also taught philosophy, religion, and public speaking during his varied career at the university.[39]

The most important of Nelson's discussions is contained in his *Scientific Aspects of Mormonism*. This book was first published in 1904 with the financial and moral support of the LDS church. In a circular sent around to advertise the book, Nelson quoted from Anthon Lund of the First Presidency praising the book. The First Presidency was so interested in having the book published that they loaned Nelson $800 to pay the publisher. Church president Joseph F. Smith thought so highly of Nelson that he sent him manuscripts to review before deciding whether they should be published by the church. From the mass of letters between Nelson and church leaders it is clear that he was on close terms with Smith and others.[40]

The intention of Nelson's work was to demonstrate that Mormonism was compatible with the best scientific thought of the era. He claimed that Mormonism would be shown to be a scientific religion. Moreover, he thought that any religion that "is not scientific is scarcely worthy of the credence of our enlightened age." Unless religion agreed with "the Book of Nature" it would fail the test of believability.[41] With this belief Nelson set out to demonstrate that Mormonism is uniquely in agreement with the best "scientific" thought of the age.

In the course of this demonstration, Nelson developed a vast system of biological, spiritual, and intellectual evolution, including an unfortunate theory of racial evolution.[42] In fact evolution and progress are the key words of his work. What he did was to link the notions of evolution and progress that were popular at the time with Mormon ideas of eternal progression. Like his mentors Fiske and Spencer, Nelson saw the whole universe moving toward increasing vistas of intellectual, moral, and spiritual growth. In the end he interpreted the most miraculous of Christian events, the resurrection of the dead, in terms of gradual evolution.[43]

For Nelson the world was neither the product of chance nor was it the outcome of some instantaneous event. It was the product of gradual growth and development overseen by God. "If to the idea of evolution there be added the idea of constant oversight, that things happen not by drifting but by direction, then we have fairly the Mormon idea of evolution." This evolution was taking place in all spheres of human life. In the intellectual sphere Nelson argued that humankind's ideas of God were developing as their environment and their ideals were changing: "The honest man's conception of God is a progressively growing ideal." People project onto God their ideals. Any attempt to prevent men and women from developing even more noble ideas of God should be rejected: "Let no council of ecclesiastics presume to lay an embargo on his soul by pronouncing once and for all what God is or is not." This would only be another form of "priestcraft."[44]

Nelson carried his system of spiritual evolution to the conclusion that heaven was evolving with the race. Heaven is described as "that state which is the sum total at any moment of what God has achieved." Heaven is thus not so much a place as a state of the soul, and of course states of the soul are always changing: "That is to say heaven is always a present, not a future state of the soul; and if any being would know the extent, the heighth, the depth and the breadth, of bliss which the universe has in store for him at any time, let him take stock of how much heavenly beauty he sees and feels and [that] lives in the creations immediately around him. . . . He is in the highest heaven who sees most beauty, feels most harmony in the creations immediately around him." The evolution of the whole universe was Nelson's theme, and in this vista even the most central themes of Christianity were changing as they were given new meaning by developing beings.[45]

Nelson had a place for almost everything, including Darwin: "It must by this time have dawned on the reader that Mormonism is a transcendent system of evolution—a system so vast and far reaching that by comparison the researches of Darwin and his collaborators important though they have been are but links in an endless chain." Darwinism was true, but it was an insignificant part of the vast evolutionary system under the control of God. Nelson was prepared to adopt anything that science might discover about the process of creation: "Science has traced better than theology can the history of creation since the beginning of the operation of this law; and with the facts of science Mormonism has no controversy. Ask me how God created the world and I shall answer: 'In the way it could be created and not in the way it couldn't.' Ask me how long it took Him and I shall say: 'As long as it needed to take.' That is the only commentary of Mormonism on the first chapter of Genesis." The only thing that Mormonism would add to science was the provision that all processes were under the control of God not chance.[46]

Nelson's system could thus accommodate the mutability of species. On this he is open and direct: "Surely it is a sensible, an economical, a beautiful way of introducing variety into the flora and fauna of the earth; and if it is God's way—and it surely is if it is the way at all—let us accept it as a truth with all reverence and humility." Nelson extended his acceptance of the mutability of species into the spiritual realm. He believed in Mormonism's dual creation, the spiritual and the temporal. For him this becomes a "dual evolution." Even "spirit species" evolved: "Now whether God created but one such spiritual germ and produced all the other forms by modification afterwards or whether He created, let us say, many such original organisms, who shall tell: In any event why should there be bitterness about it? Whichever plan we assume one thing is fixed: it is God's way of transmitting the formless and limitless into the formed and the limited."[47]

An equally important part of Nelson's system was an all encompassing theory of racial and social evolution. Nelson believed that the world's population could be divided into races and each race would have a role to play in the progressive evolution of humankind. As human society progressed each race came to the fore as leaders for a season, soon to be followed by the next race in the developmental scheme, until the Mormons would appear: "Tall and straight and comely, gifted with intellectual vigor and spiritual insight they are among the flower of Shem reserved for this conflict with falsehood and artificiality." At Nelson's hand, Mormonism became a sub-race destined to rule the world at the final stage of social progress and racial development.[48]

In a letter written to President Joseph F. Smith after publication of his book, Nelson proclaimed that his only purpose in writing was "to make men and women think not of what the principles of Mormonism are merely but of what they mean in our lives."[49] These were the words of a modernist intellectual. The separation of eternal truth from changing and growing meaning was central to reinterpreting the theological framework in light of late nineteenth-century evolutionary understanding.

Though his system was vast, Nelson did not deal with the story of Adam. He seemed to claim at one point that Adam came as a divinely directed being and that his physical body was the product of descent. But he hedged by saying that however it was, it was God's way. After Nelson's death, his son brought out a collection of his writings that discuss the Eden story in some detail. There Nelson argued that the garden story was "manifestly divine camouflage to satisfy the questioning spirit of man till his intellect should be ripe enough for the real story," which was being discovered by science. He argued at some length that the garden could not have been real but that the essential element, the idea of a fall, really did happen to a real Adam in a spiritual domain prior to his coming to earth.[50]

One may not think a great deal of Nelson's system of evolutionary theism—in some cases it was only a mass of bizarre, racist, apologetic speculations—but the attempt to deal with evolutionary thought in an all-encompassing framework is important. Nelson's relationship to President Smith suggests some support for the speculative intellectual option he represented.

A more impressive example of Nelson's open and speculative approach is represented by the writings of William H. Chamberlin. He was one of the guiding spirits for a whole generation of young Mormon intellectuals who came of age after the turn of the century.

Chamberlin had an impressive background. In 1891 he obtained his B.S. from the University of Utah and began teaching science and math at LDS College in Salt Lake City. Following a three-year proselyting mission to Tahiti, he returned to a temporary teaching position at Brigham Young College (BYC) in Logan, teaching geology and then math. He spent two summer terms studying ancient languages and biblical studies at the University of Chicago, and was made a professor of theology at BYC. In 1906 he obtained an M.A. in philosophy from the University of California under George Howison, and in the school year 1907-1908 he studied at Harvard with Josiah Royce, spending a summer studying psychology back at the University of Chicago. From 1910 to 1916 he was professor of philosophy and ancient languages at Brigham Young University in Provo. He also taught psychology. In 1916 he resigned from BYU and spent the next year studying at Harvard. He returned to Utah and first taught at the University of Utah and then finally spent his last year, 1920-21, as director of theology at BYC. He died in 1921 at the age of 50.[51]

Chamberlin's system was clearly modeled after that of his teachers Howison and Royce. He was fond of Howison, Royce, Bowne, and A. K. Rogers and quoted from them in his work. At a later time he studied writings of Henri Bergson, the French vitalist. In the spring term of 1916 he gave a seminar at BYU on Bergson.[52] Chamberlin was an evolutionist who thought he could work out a systematic reconciliation of evolutionary thought and revealed religion on the foundation of personalistic idealism and its related cousin, the vitalism of Bergson.

The heart of his position was in the emphasis he placed on divine immanence. For Chamberlin a basic belief was that nature is a living whole. For example, he began an important defense of evolution by exclaiming, "The world not only moves but it lives! It is involved in and is a part of a vast dynamic purposive process." The natural world around humanity was for Chamberlin a living whole, almost a living being itself, permeated with the spirit of God. He was fond of Doctrine and Covenants 88, which speaks of "the light which is in all things, which giveth life to all things which is the law by which all things are governed, even the power of God who sitteth upon his throne who is in the bosom of eternity, *who is in the midst of all things.*"[53]

This passage is almost a summary of Chamberlin's thought. For Chamberlin the living whole of nature was in a real sense the body of God. God is not nature itself as a strict pantheist would hold. God is rather "in the midst of all things." God is at work in and through nature, but God is not nature. This distinction is important for understanding Chamberlin. It allows for organic change in nature but not change in the purposes of God. The natural world evolved under the control of the Divine Immanence who was working out his purposes in and through nature.[54]

Chamberlin thought that nature manifested personality, with distinctive "attitudes" far beyond such routines as photosynthesis.[55] "Whenever or wherever physical changes of note have taken place in the history of the world," he wrote, "then and there, there has been as it were a struggle on the part of the Life of extra human nature to modify its adjustments so that externally viewed, new forms or species such as could live on in the changed and new stable environment have been produced."[56] Nature is constantly creating new physical forms in response to new and more complex situations.

Chamberlin argued nature manifested all of the personal qualities which have traditionally been attributed to Deity, and it is the source of individual human lives in much the same manner in which God is said to be the creator of humankind. Chamberlin said it was upon this God that we depend for our physical bodies created by him through millions of years of activity. God furthermore was constantly at work calling forth more noble qualities from us. God had engaged in numberless activities on our behalf such that "without much apparent effort on our part a large number of powerful and valuable habits have been formed in us." This activity was the measure of God's love for us: "Through the development of such attitudes, God has shown his love for man, an eagerness to have him develop in more of his unique life, and reverence for his individuality, a desire to cultivate it."[57]

Chamberlin thought that evolution would provide a firmer support for belief in the resurrection and for theism in general. First, evolution supported belief in the immanence of God in nature. Second, the millions of years required to create the human body imply "a measureless interest in our welfare." Hence there is a strong prima-facie reason to expect a resurrection: "In conclusion then let us repeat that if a Divine purpose is immanent in nature, nature's forms must be thought of as evolving in a way parallel to the unfolding of the Divine purpose. The use of the theory is a most important means of advancing to a realization of God's immanence in nature and life and a great remover of intellectual difficulties that hamper faith in so many. And finally the theory awakens within us from the above point of view an expectation of the resurrection, or a renewal of God's reactions to our lives, the restoration of the spirit to the body without which there can be little or no life or happiness. That God can do this seems certain and that he will do it is at least as certain as that the uniformity of nature that all science presupposes shall continue. Both the uniformities in nature and the resurrection depend upon the Father's love."[58]

Nature is the tabernacle of God through which he works to bring to pass his ends. The year before his death Chamberlin wrote: "The material elements, as they seem to hide their cause from our view, can be said to be the covering or tabernacle of God and vanishing human forms are elements of that tabernacle. . . . God is the fixed or eternal cause of most things visible or changing in material nature. And so anyone who has seen nature has in a sense seen God."[59]

To some the immanent personalism of Chamberlin may not sound like Mormon orthodoxy. But the latter is notoriously difficult to define. If anything the preceding discussion should have suggested the impossibility of defining a consistent standard of orthodoxy on the issues discussed. Chamberlin himself drew on Mormon scripture and the writings of church leaders for support. He was particularly fond of Doctrine and Covenants 93 and 88. He was conversant with Apostle Parley P. Pratt's *Key to the Science of Theology*, which contains a discussion of the Holy Spirit not unlike his own theological system. Though Chamberlin never seemed to have quoted him, Parley's brother Apostle Orson Pratt discussed the idea of God in terms that could have been easily adopted by Chamberlin.[60]

Chamberlin's Mormon commitment was deep and genuine. No one who reads his mission journals, his early article in praise of Joseph F. Smith, or some of the letters he wrote in 1917 after his last year at Harvard could say otherwise. But his work was threatening on several fronts. The philosophical acumen was threatening to a religious leadership that wanted practical men, not speculative theologians. Mormonism was a religious system that had a unique impact on the lives of many common people. Mormon theological simplicity and scriptural literalism brought the central theological symbols and beliefs into the world of common people.

But Chamberlin was thinking of another audience, the sons and daughters of the church who were studying secular ideas and naturalistic sciences. Unless the great features of the Mormon theological system could be expressed in ways at least compatible with modern knowledge, would they be any match in the marketplace of ideas? This was a threat to the community of faith, which Chamberlin could address.

LDS church historian Leonard Arrington once argued that a bias in writing Mormon history has been a perception of unity.[61] Frequently the desire to see unity on important intellectual or theological issues has led to ignoring or distorting the evidence. The response of Mormons to the challenge of evolutionary thought has been as diverse as anything found outside of Mormondom. The spectrum of opinion in Zion has been a microcosm of the spectrum of opinion in other religious communities. To a large measure diversity is healthy, for it prevents people from absolutizing their own private perspectives. But groups also require some set of beliefs, values, or loyalties common to all members. The profound diversity of Mormon reactions to evolutionary thought suggests an even deeper struggle with the increasing pluralism of the twentieth century. The conservatives want a firm standard, the literal word of scripture, as a guide and test of loyalty and orthodoxy. Their critics see too much truth in modern thought to accept simple denial. The struggle of these two outlooks has been the agony of every major religious system in the modern west. In Mormonism the discussion is currently muted but no less real.

NOTES

1. B. H. Roberts to Rudger Clawson, 31 Dec. 1930, Clawson Papers, Archives, Historical Department, Church of Jesus Christ of Latter-day Saints, Salt Lake City, Utah (hereafter LDS archives).

2. Joseph Fielding Smith to Rudger Clawson, 14 Dec. 1931, Clawson Papers.

3. Joseph Fielding Smith, "The Word of the Lord Superior to the Theories of Men," *Liahona* 15 (Apr. 1918): 641-44. The quotation is from Smith's "Faith Leads to a Fullness of Truth and Righteousness," *Utah Genealogical and Historical Magazine* 21 (Oct. 1930): 148.

4. On Price, see Norman Furness, *The Fundamentalist Controversy* (New Haven: Yale University Press, 1954), 16. For other examples of this general argument, see Willard Gatewood, ed., *Controversy in the Twenties:*

Fundamentalism, Modernism, and Evolution (Nashville: Vanderbilt University Press, 1969).

5. Joseph Fielding Smith, *Man: His Origin and Destiny* (Salt Lake City: Deseret Book, 1954), 50-51; Joseph Fielding Smith, "The Origin and Destiny of Man," *Improvement Era* 23 (Mar. 1920): 387.

6. Smith, *Origin and Destiny*, 133; Smith, "The Word of Lord Superior," 641-44; Joseph Fielding Smith, "Entangle Not Yourselves in Sin," *Improvement Era* 56 (Sept. 1953): 646-47, 671-78.

7. See Smith, *Origin and Destiny*, 16, 79; also "Church News Section" of *Deseret News*, 15 Apr. 1939: "The theistic evolutionist is a weak-kneed unbelieving religionist who is always constantly apologizing for the miracles of the Scriptures and who does not believe in the Divine mission of Jesus Christ"; Smith, "The Origin and Destiny of Man," 386; and *Origin and Destiny*, 213.

8. Joseph Fielding Smith, *Doctrines of Salvation*, 3 vols. (Salt Lake City: Bookcraft, 1954-56), 1:79-31; Smith, *Origin and Destiny*, 167, 266, 157, 154.

9. Ibid., 137-38; Smith, "The Origin and Destiny of Man," 374-82; Smith, *Origin and Destiny*, 179; Loren Eisely, *Darwin's Century* (Garden City, NJ: Doubleday and Co., 1958), 205-31; Smith, *Origin and Destiny*, 33.

10. Ibid., 248.

11. James E. Talmage, *The Theory of Evolution* (Provo, UT: Utah County Teachers Association, 1890).

12. Ibid., 9.

13. Ibid., 17.

14. Ibid., 16.

15. James E. Talmage, "What Mormonism Stands For," *Liahona* 6 (Feb. 1909): 829-32; and Talmage, "Fallen But He Shall Rise Again," *Improvement Era* 22 (Oct. 1919): 1067-68.

16. James E. Talmage, "The Earth and Man," *Deseret News*, 21 Nov. 1931; also Talmage to Bee Gaddie, 28 Mar. 1930, Talmage Papers, LDS archives; Conrad Wright, "The Religion of Geology," *New England Quarterly* 14 (Fall 1941): 335-58; Talmage, "The Earth and Man"; Talmage to Heber Timothy, 28 Jan. 1932, Talmage Papers.

17. Talmage to Daryl Shoup, 10 Dec. 1930, and Talmage to Heber Timothy, 19 Mar. 1932, Talmage Papers.

18. Talmage, "The Earth and Man," 5; Talmage Journal, 7 Apr. 1931, Archives and Manuscripts, Harold B. Lee Library, Brigham Young University, Provo, Utah.

19. Talmage to F. C. Williamson, 22 Apr. 1933, Talmage Papers.

20. B. H. Roberts, "The Truth, The Way, The Life," manuscript, LDS archives. Truman G. Madsen has argued that Roberts's discussion of evolutionary thought and his speculations about a pre-Adamite race are not

integral to the manuscript and could easily have been left out. I believe that this interpretation ignores two very crucial points that suggest the importance of this section in the manuscript. First, Roberts himself obviously felt that it was so important that he would not cut it out even when that was the only way to get the book published. In fact he added material on discoveries of prehistoric men after the reading committee of church authorities told him to remove the section. Second, it is clear from the discussion surrounding the manuscript that he felt keenly the need to effect a reconciliation between the indisputable facts of science and the received Mormon tradition. Without this he was concerned that many educated individuals would desert the church. Given the times the single most explosive area of confrontation was clearly the theory of evolution and the record of prehistoric humans discovered by paleontology. It thus seems that to be consistent with one of Roberts's great concerns, the manuscript would have to attempt some such reconciliation. See Truman Madsen, "The Meaning of Christ—The Truth, The Way, The Life: An Analysis of B. H. Roberts's Masterwork," *Brigham Young University Studies* 15 (Spring 1975): 259-92.

21. Roberts, "The Truth, The Way, the Life," chap. 24; chap. 31, pp. 3-4.

22. Ibid., chap. 31.

23. His discussion of the idea of two creations is in chap. 30, while references to the great cataclysm are in chap. 32, pp. 1-3.

24. Ibid., chap. 31, pp. 29.

25. *Journal of Discourses*, 26 vols. (Liverpool and London, 1854-86), 2:79-88.

26. Roberts, "The Truth, The Way, The Life," chap. 25, pp. 3-4, 8.

27. Ibid., 5-6.

28. Ibid., 10-11.

29. Ibid., 8.

30. Basic biographical information from Andrew Jenson, *Latter-day Saints Biographical Encyclopedia*, 4 vols. (Rpt.; Salt Lake City: Western Epics, 1971), 4:218-19.

31. Fredrick Pack, *Science and Belief in God* (Salt Lake City: Deseret News Press, 1924), 79, 85, 91.

32. Ibid., 96.

33. Ibid., 108-18.

34. Ibid., 120, 124.

35. Ibid., 193, 173.

36. Ibid., 296, 206, 179.

37. Fredrick Pack, "The Creation of the Earth," *Improvement Era* 13 (Sept. 1910): 1023-27; 13 (Oct. 1910): 1121-27; 14 (Jan. 1911): 220-30; much of this same argument is found in the book, 248-60.

38. Fredrick Pack, *Tobacco and Human Efficiency* (Salt Lake City:

Deseret News Press, 1918); Pack, "How the Impending Tobacco Crusade Can be Avoided," *Improvement Era* 24 (Jan. 1921): 218-28; Pack, "Should Latter-day Saints Drink Coca-Cola?" *Improvement Era* 21 (Mar. 1918): 431-35.

39. The basic biographical information is contained in T. Earl Pardoe, *The Sons of Brigham* (Provo, UT: Brigham Young University Alumni Association, 1969). Also important on another phase of Nelson's work is Davis Bitton, "N. L. Nelson and 'The Mormon Point of View,'" *Brigham Young University Studies* 13 (Winter 1973): 157-71.

40. A copy of this notice is in the LDS archives. See letters of Joseph F. Smith to N. L. Nelson, 11 May and 9 July 1904, and N. L. Nelson to Joseph F. Smith, 9 May, 12 May, and 8 June 1904, Smith Papers, LDS archives; a letter from Joseph F. Smith transmitting a manuscript for Nelson to review: the date cannot be made out clearly but it is probably October 1904. Nelson's reply, obviously on the same manuscript, is dated 8 November 1904.

41. Nels Nelson, *Scientific Aspects of Mormonism* (New York: E. P. Dutton, 1904), 9.

42. Ibid., 91, 94-96, 101-93.

43. Ibid., 229.

44. Ibid., 62, 18-20.

45. Ibid., 38, 56, 60.

46. Ibid., 61, 65.

47. Ibid., 66, 71.

48. Ibid., 97-98.

49. N. L. Nelson to Joseph F. Smith, 5 Jan. 1905, Smith Papers.

50. Nels Nelson, *What Truth Is* (Salt Lake City: Stevens and Wallis, 1947), 54-60.

51. The basic biographical information is contained in Ralph Chamberlin, *Life and Philosophy of W. H. Chamberlin* (Salt Lake City: Deseret News Press, 1925).

52. Ibid., 209.

53. W. H. Chamberlin, "The Theory of Evolution as an Aid to Faith in God and Belief in the Resurrection," *White and Blue* 14 (14 Feb. 1911); D&C 18:13. *White and Blue* was the BYU student publication at the time.

54. See his *Essay on Nature* (Provo, UT: Privately Printed, 1915).

55. Ibid., 15.

56. Ibid., 19.

57. Ibid., 24, 27.

58. W. H. Chamberlin, "The Significance of the Resurrection," *White and Blue* 16 (11 Mar. 1913): 295. Also see *The Parables of Jesus*, Brigham Young College Bulletin, no. 2 (Jan. 1904): 3; "A Christmas Message," *White and Blue* 16 (10 Dec. 1912): 7; and *An Essay on Nature*, 41-44; "The Theory of Evolution," 4.

59. W. H. Chamberlin, *The Life of Man: An Introduction to Philosophy*

(Logan, UT: Privately Printed, 1920), 12.

60. His fondness for Pratt appears in an unpublished essay sent to President Joseph F. Smith entitled "The Origin and Destiny of Man," in Smith Papers.

61. Leonard J. Arrington, "The Search for Truth and Meaning in Mormon History," *Dialogue: A Journal of Mormon Thought* 3 (Summer 1968): 64.

6.
The B. H. Roberts/ Joseph Fielding Smith/ James E. Talmage Affair

Richard Sherlock and *Jeffrey E. Keller*

FEW CHAPTERS IN TWENTIETH-CENTURY MORMON THOUGHT ARE MORE thought-provoking than the events following B. H. Roberts's efforts to publish *The Truth, The Way, The Life.* The hottest issue addressed by Roberts's manuscript was organic evolution.[1] His assertion that the earth was much older than a few thousand years was hardly remarkable.[2] But his assertion that countless plants and animals lived long before the biblical chronology was controversial. The problem was to account for this in terms of a scriptural framework. Roberts was never prepared to do away with a literal Adam, who he believed was a real person with a special divine mission. He was not, however, the earliest man on this planet. Before him a whole race of human beings lived and died on earth. These "pre-Adamites" were destroyed in a great cataclysm that "cleansed" the earth, leaving only fossilized remains as the meager evidence of their presence.[3] Roberts also undertook a vaguely worded and somewhat contradictory account of the evolutionary development of life forms on earth—a "transmutation" of species.

With so many concessions to science it is not surprising that Roberts's manuscript received unfavorable criticism. What is surprising is how narrowly focused this criticism was at first. The manuscript was first reviewed by a reading committee of the Council of the Twelve who drew up a "list of points of doctrine in question." There were thirty-seven items on the list, almost all minor. The committee felt, for example, that Roberts overstated the evidence in saying that the tree from which Adam and Eve ate contained the seeds of life and death. The scriptures referred only to the seeds of death. Other similarly minor issues were raised.[4]

The real sticking point was the theory of pre-Adamites. In a cover letter to the council, the reading committee noted that there were "objectionable doctrines advanced which are of a speculative nature and appear to be out of harmony with the revelations of the Lord and the fundamental teachings of the Church. Among the outstanding doctrines to which objection is made are: The doctrine that Adam was a translated being who came to this earth subject to death, and therefore did not bring death upon himself and his posterity through the fall."[5] The committee further reported that they had met several times with Roberts to get him to delete offending chapters. He had refused and even added material referring to recent finds of pre-historic humans in China. At one point he threatened to publish the book on his own if he could not get church approval.

After the report of the reading committee, the full council reviewed the matter and reached virtually these same conclusions in its own report to the First Presidency. The council report, however, also stressed a more basic theme: "It is the duty of the General Authorities of the Church to safeguard and protect the membership of the Church from the introduction of controversial subjects and false doctrines which tend to create factions and otherwise disturb the faith of the Latter-Day Saints. There is so much of vital importance revealed and which we can present with clear and convincing presentation and which the world does not possess that we, the committee, see no reason for the introduction of questions which are speculative to say the least: more especially so when such teachings appear to be in conflict with the revelations of the Lord."[6]

Even as this letter was being sent, Roberts's position was attacked publicly by a member of the council (and of the reading committee). In an address to the April 1930 genealogical conference, Joseph Fielding Smith went beyond the questioning of the council. In his mind the issue was clear: Roberts was teaching false doctrine. While this is debatable, Roberts certainly was repudiating positions staked out earlier by Smith himself.[7] In his speech Smith was characteristically blunt: "Even in the Church there are a scattered few who are now advocating and contending that the earth was peopled with a race—perhaps many races—long before the days of Adam. These men desire, of course, to square the teachings in the Bible with the teachings of modern science and philosophy with regard to the age of the earth and life on it. If you hear anyone talking this way you may answer them by saying that the doctrine of pre-adamites is not a doctrine of the Church and is not advocated or countenanced in the Church. There is no warrant for it in scripture, not an authentic word to sustain it."[8]

When this address was printed in the October issue of the *Utah Genealogical and Historical Magazine*, Roberts could not remain silent. In December he appealed directly to President Heber J. Grant. In a strongly worded letter, he objected to the "strictly dogmatical and pronounced finality of the discussion." If Smith had been speaking for the church, this fact should have been stated clearly. In the likely event he was speaking only for himself, Roberts wrote: "If Elder Smith is merely putting forth his own position I call in question his competency to utter such dogmatism either as a scholar or as an apostle. I am sure he is not competent to speak in such a manner from general learning or special research work on the subject; nor as an Apostle as in that case he would be in conflict with the plain implication of the scriptures, both ancient and modern, and with the teaching of a more experienced and learned and earlier apostle, and a contemporary of the prophet Joseph Smith—whose public discourse on the subject appears in the Journal of Discourses and was publicly endorsed by president Brigham Young, all of which would have more weight in setting forth doctrine than this last dictum of Elder Smith. My question is important as affecting finally the faith and status of a very large portion of the priesthood and educated membership of the Church. I am sure and I trust this matter will receive early attention."[9]

After receiving this letter, Grant referred the matter to the council for a discussion of the issues. The council resolved to hear both men in separate sessions. On 7 January 1931 Roberts made his presentation to the assembled apostles.[10] While a copy of the lengthy paper has not been located, from his letters and manuscript he apparently repeated the arguments from science, scriptural authority, and apostolic teaching (primarily Elder Orson Hyde). Two weeks later Smith appeared with his own lengthy paper. His was a defense of a scriptural literalism: "The Latter-day Saints are not bound to receive the theories of men when they do not accord with the word of the Lord to them." What Roberts was preaching was not just erroneous, he was compromising with satanic forces: "The doctrine of organic evolution which pervades the modern day sciences proclaiming the edict that man has evolved from the lower forms of life through the Java skull, the Heidelberg jaw, the Piltdown man, the Neanderthal skull and last but not least the Peking man who lived millions of years ago is as false as their author who lives in hell."[11] To Smith, Roberts's view was dangerous because he was willing to depart from the most literal reading of the first chapter of Genesis. Once started on this process, Smith argued, you cannot stop. Those who followed this course were bound to wander in a desert of their own creation, ultimately forsaking the historic faith of the church for their own theories.[12]

After hearing both men the council noncommittally referred the matter back to the First Presidency, noting only that they regarded Roberts's language as "very offensive" and as "failing to show the deference due from one brother to another brother of higher rank in the priesthood."[13]

Roberts continued to press his case. In early February he again wrote directly to Grant saying he would like an opportunity to point out the "weaknesses and inconsistencies" in Smith's paper, which he characterized as "sleighter than a house of cards." He also made pointed reference to his now overshadowed manuscript: "It was . . . such pablum as this that suspended the publication of my book—now in manuscript—*The Truth, The Way, The Life*. This book from my judgment of it is the most important work that I have yet contributed to the Church, the six volume comprehensive history of the Church not omitted. Life at my years and with an incurable ailment is very precarious and I should dislike very much to pass on without completing and publishing this work. . . . If the position he has taken can be met successfully, then I think that the principle cause suspending the publication of my work will be removed."[14]

Roberts did not get his chance. Two months later the First Presidency replied in a memorandum circulated to the hierarchy. An entry from Grant's journal makes the attitude of the presidency clear:

"After reading the articles by Brothers Roberts and Smith, I feel that sermons such as Brother Joseph preached and criticisms such as Brother Roberts makes of the sermon are the finest kind of things to be left alone entirely. I think no good can be accomplished by dealing in mysteries, and that is what I feel in my heart of hearts these brethren are both doing."[15]

The memorandum from the First Presidency made several specific points. First, it called attention to the care which must be exercised by any of the authorities when they speak publicly on controversial topics: "We call attention to the fact that when one of the General Authorities of the Church makes a definite statement in regard to any doctrine, particularly when the statement is made in a dogmatic declaration of finality, whether he expresses it as his opinion or not he is regarded as voicing the Church [position] and his statements are accepted as the approved doctrines of the Church, which they should be."[16]

Second, it noted that both Smith and Roberts had produced scientific evidence, scriptural texts, and quotations from previous church authorities to bolster their respective arguments. So far as the First Presidency was concerned, however, neither side was able to carry the day. In this crucial section they wrote: "The statement made by Elder Smith that the existence of pre-adamites is not a doctrine of the Church is true. It is just as true that the statement 'there were not pre-adamites upon the earth' is not a doctrine of the church. Neither side of the controversy has been accepted as a doctrine at all."[17]

Given this conclusion on the doctrinal issues, the instruction to church authorities was obvious: cease public discussion of the controversial topics. Concern yourselves instead with the simple truths of the gospel: "Upon the fundamental doctrines of the Church we are all agreed. Our mission is to bear the message of the restored Gospel to the people of the world. Leave geology, biology, archaeology and anthropology, no one of which has to do with the salvation of the souls of mankind, to scientific research, while we magnify our calling in the realm of the Church.

"We can see no advantage to be gained by a continuation of the discussion to which reference is here made, but on the contrary are certain that it would lead to confusion, division and misunderstanding if carried further. Upon one thing we should be able to agree, namely, that Presidents Joseph F. Smith, John Winder and Anthon Lund, were right when they said: 'Adam is the primal parent of our race.'"[18]

When the Roberts-Smith controversy first arose, Apostle James Talmage was not appreciably involved. Although he was a trained geologist and regular speaker on the science/religion theme, he had not been part of the reading committee that reviewed Roberts's book and so had little contact with the discussion. This changed in 1931 when the entire Quorum of the Twelve was required to hear the protest that Roberts made against Smith.

Talmage's views were already well known, both within the church hierarchy and among the membership at large. Much of his adult life had been devoted to harmonizing science and religion. As early as 1881, as a twenty-year-old teacher at Brigham Young Academy, he had resolved "to do good among the young—probably lecture . . . on the subject of harmony between Geology and the Bible—a subject upon which so many of our people have mistaken ideas."[19] Talmage unquestionably accepted as established fact the great age of the earth as well as the existence and death of life forms before the time of Adam. Although these views were not always presented conspicuously in his talks, he was consistent in affirming these ideas whenever he addressed them publicly. On the question of pre-Adamic people, however, he created uncertainty as to his personal views by avoiding public comment. Partly because of this ambiguity in the public record, some have concluded that Talmage may have rejected both the theory of evolution *and* the existence of pre-Adamites. But to the contrary Talmage was described by his geologist son, Sterling, as having expressed in 1920 a concept of pre-Adamites which "went beyond anything that I had dared to think."[20] Talmage thus appears to have been confident of the validity of notions demonstrated by his field of study, geology, but less so of ideas derived from related fields such as biology, with which he was less familiar.

Talmage's views during the 1931 discussions in the quorum were presumably sympathetic to much of the spirit of Roberts's efforts. Unfortunately, not a great deal is known about the views he expressed during these discussions. What is known, however, is revealing. Talmage was particularly upset by Smith's use of George

McCready Price as an authority in geology. Price was professor of geology at a small parochial college in the midwest and author of many books purporting to vindicate orthodox Christian belief by exposing the weaknesses of scientific theory.[21] After a quorum meeting in which Smith quoted extensively from Price's *The New Geology*, Talmage decided to prepare himself more fully for a debate on the merits of this type of evidence. He wrote to his eldest son, Sterling, for an opinion of the book. Sterling was a professor of geology at the New Mexico School of Mines.

The younger Talmage responded by pointing out a number of technical errors in the specific passages quoted by Smith and then added: "You ask 'how Price is held in the opinion of geologists in general.' As far as I can tell (and it seems to be the unanimous opinion of those who know his book, at least so far as I have talked with them), he is considered as a theological fanatic, who has gone off on a tangent that most geologists seem to find funny. I never heard his book discussed . . . without the element of comedy being dragged in. All of Price's arguments, in principle at least, were advanced and refuted from fifty to a hundred years ago. They are not 'new.' His ideas certainly are not 'Geology.' *With these two corrections*, the title remains the best part of the book."[22]

Armed with this response Elder Talmage brought up the subject of Smith's paper in the April 1931 meeting called to bring the issue to a final solution. In this heated meeting, as he later wrote to his son, Talmage used Sterling's evidence to "show up James McCready Price in all his unenviable colors." Moreover, he "was bold enough to point out that according to a tradition in the Church based on good authority as having risen from a declaration made by the Prophet Joseph Smith, a certain pile of stones at Adam-ondi-Ahman, Spring Hill, Mo., is really part of the altar on which Adam offered sacrifices, and that I had personally examined those stones and found them to be fossiliferous, so that if those stones be part of the first altar, Adam built it of stones containing corpses, and therefore death must have prevailed in the earth before Adam's times."[23] Finally, Talmage made it clear to his assembled brethren that all reputable geologists recognized the existence both of death and "pre-Adamites" prior to 6,000 years ago, the presumed date of the fall of Adam.

This view, of course, was vigorously denied by Smith, and "a serious disruption between and among certain brethren" was in the offing.[24] It was at least partly to avoid such disruption that the First Presidency sought to settle the dispute quickly without committing themselves to one side or the other with their memo of 7 April. That same day Talmage wrote in his journal: "As to whether pre-Adamite races existed upon the earth there has been much discussion among some of our people of late. The decision reached by the First Presidency and announced to this morning's assembly . . . is a wise one on the premises. This is one of the many things upon which we cannot speak with assurance and dogmatic assertions on either side are likely to do harm rather than good."

Three days after the decision was issued, council president Rudger Clawson wrote to George Albert Smith, chair of the first reading committee, asking him to "make an earnest effort to compose matters" with Roberts and get him to drop the affected material from his manuscript so that "an excellent work may not go unpublished and be lost to the Church." If Roberts refused he was to be told that the book definitely would not be published without the needed changes.[25] The committee did not succeed in this mission; for better than a year later Roberts was still trying to have the book published "as is." His last letter on the subject reveals a sadness and bitterness over the fate of what to him was the culmination of his ministry on behalf of the church: "It had been my hope that the volume still in manuscript, unpublished, which would make a work of about 700 pages—*The Truth, The Way, The Life*—would be the climax in the doctrinal department of my work. . . . [T]he matter of this book grew up during more than fifty years of my ministry crystallizing practically all my thought, research and studies in the doctrinal line of the Church. It was not the hasty product of the paltry six months at the close of my eastern states mission administration—as some have supposed. . . . [T]hat manuscript may not likely be printed in my lifetime, comment of course will not be necessary."[26]

The First Presidency's council in April 1831 to discontinue discussion was designed to maintain a neutral position. But in practice, their injunction did not have this effect. Only one side of the argument had been given any publicity—Joseph Fielding Smith's "Faith Leads to a Fullness of Truth and Righteousness." Many students, Talmage later recounted, "inferred from Elder Smith's address that the Church refuses to recognize the findings of science if there be a word in scriptural record in . . . seeming conflict with scientific discoveries or deduction, and that therefore the 'policy' of the Church is in effect opposed to scientific research."[27] Nor was Talmage alone in this concern, for he recalled on observation by an unnamed member of the First Presidency early in the discussions that "sometime, somewhere, something should be said by one or more of us to make plain that the Church does not refuse to recognize the discoveries and demonstrations of science, especially in relation to the subject at issue."[28]

Sterling Talmage in particular had been upset by arguments set forth in Smith's genealogy society talk, a copy of which had been forwarded to him by his father. Writing to Apostle Talmage in June, just a few weeks after the apparent resolution of the Roberts-Smith confrontation, Sterling recounted how "For several years I have been annoyed and irritated,—those terms are too mild, 'affronted' and 'challenged' would be better—by the type of thing you mention regarding no death on the earth, etc." While he had refrained in the past from branding such doctrine as "ignorant dogmatism," he felt motivated to protest now.[29]

Rather than involve himself in the already sensitive pre-Adamite debate, Sterling felt he could make his point just as well by dealing with another aspect of Smith's remarks. In the genealogy society address under the sub-heading "Miracles Not Inconsistent with Reasons," Smith had discussed Joshua's command to the sun to stand still (Joshua 10:12-14). He explained this miracle by asserting that the Lord had stopped the earth's rotation. The chaotic centrifugal effects science would expect from such a phenomenon, Smith asserted, were avoided by slowing the earth down gradually. To Sterling this was "so absurd that it will not stand the test of fifth grade arithmetic."[30] He prepared what was to become an "Open Letter to Elder Joseph Fielding Smith." He forwarded the letter to his father for critique.

Sterling affirmed that there were two basic reasons why Smith's hypothesis was unreasonable. First, he observed, a point on the surface of the earth in Palestine is moving at the rate of almost a thousand miles per hour. To bring that spot to a halt without causing inertial effects would take days or weeks instead of hours. Second, even were the earth to slow down gradually, winds would be generated "fully six times as great as in the most violent recorded hurricane." Of course, Sterling conceded, the Lord could have accomplished all of this by fiat, but he felt that neither he nor Smith was willing to accept that explanation because both conceived of a God who operated within a framework of natural law. To the younger Talmage, it seemed reasonable that the stopping of the sun was in reality an optical illusion caused by unusual atmospheric conditions which could bend the rays of sunlight over the horizon. He cited recorded examples of similar phenomena.

The implications of all this and the real reason for writing the letter were made quite explicit: "*some of the authorities have made statements that are not worthy of belief.*" Smith's hypothesis for Joshua's miracle was one example. The danger in this was that if a young person correctly disbelieves such a statement, "it is only a short step to doubting" all the authorities of the church. In sum Smith was out of place in referring to scientists as "Miserable Fools" as he had once in the past and should not discourse in areas in which he was "not informed."[31]

Apostle Talmage received his son's proposed letter enthusiastically. He strongly recommended sending the letter with a few revisions and suggested that Sterling give it wider distribution than originally planned: "I think it should be put into final shape and sent to its intended addressee without delay. . . . The conditions are peculiar but in my judgment and *in that of certain others* it is well to follow the course intended. I wish I could write in fuller measure of the conditions that have called forth your letter. But you have done . . . a good work. Finish it up."[32] After incorporating the changes suggested by his father, Sterling sent a copy in late June both to Smith and the First Presidency.

Apostle Talmage seems to have felt that he should play a more active role himself in correcting some lingering misconceptions among the membership. In July, just four months after the 7 April decision, Talmage chose to make a passing reference to the subject of pre-Adamites in one of his weekly radio addresses—in order, as he wrote Sterling, to "test the sensitiveness of at least some of our people on the subject." The response he received led him to conclude that the time was right to make clear at least by inference what was and was not the official position of the church.[33]

Elder Talmage undertook this task in a speech in the tabernacle on 9 August 1931 entitled "The Earth and Man." In this he affirmed that plants and animals "lived and died, age after age, while the earth was yet unfit for human habitation." Perhaps because of the injunction against further discussion of the issue, he did not explicitly include pre-Adamites in his discourse. However, in comments on evolution reminiscent of his earlier talks, he stated that he did not regard "Adam as related to—certainly not as descended from—the Neanderthal, the Cro-Magnon, the Peking or the Piltdown man."[34]

Not surprisingly the controversy that apparently had ended four months earlier was reopened. Should "The Earth and Man" be published? Several meetings of the quorum were devoted to the talk. The deliberations, Talmage later wrote to Apostle John Widtsoe, who was in Europe, "revealed a very strong feeling on the part of a minority of the Brethren against giving public sanction to the views of geologists as set forth in the address." In particular, "The insistence on the part of three of our brethren—really to the effect that all geologists and all geology are wrong in matters relating to the sequence of life on earth—has been surprising. The author of the genealogical society address holds tenaciously to his view that prior to the fall of Adam there was no death of plants and animals upon the earth."[35]

Smith, according to his own account to Susa Young Gates, was supported within the quorum by Rudger Clawson, David O. McKay, and George Albert Smith.[36] The official report by Clawson to the First Presidency noted that "again the scientific theory, or claim, is set forth in the sermon to the effect that man finally emerged, or was developed from and through a line of animal life reaching back, into numberless ages of the past, to the protoplasm."[37]

Those members of the quorum who supported publication included in addition to Talmage himself Reed Smoot,[38] Joseph F. Merrill,[39] John A. Widtsoe (whose opinion was solicited by mail),[40] and Richard R. Lyman and George F. Richards, who were present when Talmage delivered his address and expressed their "tentative approval" to him at the time, as well as Anthony W. Ivins who was similarly supportive.[41] There apparently was additional support within the quorum, for both Talmage and Smoot speak in their journals of a "majority" favoring publication.[42]

Despite this reported distribution of opinion, Clawson's official report states that "A motion was made and seconded to the effect that in the opinion of the Twelve, the sermon should not be published. This motion, after some further discussion, was followed by a substitute motion to the effect that the sermon be returned to Brother Talmage and that he be requested to remodel it if possible by cutting out the objectionable features. Brother Talmage consented to do this. The substitute motion was adopted."[43]

The quorum ultimately was unable to come to the requisite unanimity concerning publication despite Talmage's willingness to state explicitly that opinions expressed were those held by himself or by contemporary geologists. (This of course would still accomplish the desired goal of showing the acceptability of the views cited; it was not Talmage's intent to assert them as *the* church position on the subject.)

As with the Roberts-Smith case, the First Presidency again was called on to settle the controversy. This time they ruled in Talmage's favor. President Heber J. Grant made note of the decision in his journal, 17 November 1931: "At 11:30 Brother James E. Talmage called, and we went over his address delivered in the Tabernacle a number of weeks ago, and authorized its publication and also gave authorization for it to be printed in the same form as the radio addresses, for distribution."[44] Four days later the *Deseret News* "Church Section" carried the text of Talmage's remarks. It also was issued in pamphlet form.

Publication of "The Earth and Man" marked the final chapter of James Talmage's involvement with questions of science and reli-gion. He died less than two years later, just before his seventy-first birthday. Coincidentally, the seventy-seven-year-old B. H. Roberts died exactly two months later. The third principal, Joseph Fielding Smith, only fifty-seven at the time, continued as an influential presence for four more decades.

In 1934, just a year after Talmage's death, battle was again joined, but this time between Joseph Fielding Smith and Sterling Talmage. This episode began when Smith approved for publication in the *Deseret News* "Church Section" an article by Major Howard O. Bennion entitled "Is the Earth Millions of Years Old?" Bennion, at the time a retired civil engineer, had served in several army and government engineering posts and had studied geology as a hobby. He answered the earth question negatively, stating that scriptural and scientific accounts of the earth's creation were mutually exclusive, that the theory of evolution (including theistic evolution) was scripturally absurd, and that the principle of uniformitarianism upon which much of science depended was demonstrably false.[45]

Sterling Talmage immediately responded with a lengthy rebuttal to Bennion's article, which he sent to Apostle John A. Widtsoe (a close friend to both Sterling and his father) and to the *Deseret News*. Widtsoe, now back from Europe, responded favorably to Sterling's article. He wrote Sterling that he had "expressed myself as forcefully as I knew how to the brethren when the [Bennion] article was being discussed" but felt he could not formulate a direct reply himself because of the guidance against further discussion by ranking church authorities. He could, however, make sure that Talmage's article was published. The matter was discussed with Elder Smith, who, according to Widtsoe, agreed that both sides of the argument should be aired.[46] Talmage's "Can We Dictate God's Times and Methods?" was printed one month later.[47]

Sterling thus began to function for Widtsoe much as he had once served his father, as surrogate spokesperson for the ideas these brethren were constrained from discussing in print. (Howard Bennion served the same function for Smith.) Widtsoe went so far as to offer to act as Talmage's "unofficial agent in bringing matters before the public at home."[48] This was clearly set forth in his published essay: "As a geologist, I object to erroneous explanations of geological theories offered by one, who according to his own admission, had only a smattering acquaintance with geology. . . . As an upholder of the authority of the Church, I object to any statements from a non-authoritative source, of what constitutes 'the doctrines of the Church,' especially when some of these statements are in direct contradiction of the latest authoritative statements that have come to my attention."[49]

The "latest authoritative statement" referred to was of course "The Earth and Man" address by his father. As to the "authority" of the address, Anthony W. Ivins, first counselor to the president at the time of the speech, had reportedly informed Sterling that the talk did have approval of the presiding quorums.[50] Significantly, however, Widtsoe counseled Sterling immediately before publication of the rebuttal that "there appears to be no evidence on file that your father's splendid article, 'The Earth and Man,' went out with what is held to be full authoritative approval, that is, the vote of approval of the Presidency and the Twelve."[51]

Both Bennion and Talmage wrote follow-up articles. Bennion's, entitled "Further Observations on the Age of the Earth," did not address the issues raised by Talmage but simply reiterated much of the same material from his first article.[52] In the "Church News" that contained Talmage's second article, Sidney Sperry, a well-known Mormon Bible scholar, published an article supporting Bennion's position on scriptural grounds and attempting a specific reply to Talmage's charges. In this Sperry maintained that "The Earth and Man" address, so heavily relied upon by Sterling Talmage, was an inappropriate airing of James Talmage's own views "for which the Church should not be held responsible."[53]

Agitated by Sperry's criticism of his father, Sterling drafted a scathing rebuttal, but there is no evidence in his correspondence that it was ever sent to the *Deseret News*. A partial explanation may be found in the fact that he also addressed a letter to President Anthony W. Ivins: "I do not like to come out in print, and brand another member of the Church as a plain liar, even though under the circumstances the designation seems strictly accurate. Dr. Sperry's accusation that my father assumed personal responsibility for portions of 'The Earth and Man' that were not in accordance with the doctrines of the Church is utterly and unqualifiedly false." Talmage requested the First Presidency to officially correct this "misstatement . . . with reference to my father's sermon."[54] Although a copy of the First Presidency's reply to Talmage is unavailable, it is apparent that they declined to comply with his request.

In the summer following, Joseph Fielding Smith discovered an article by Dudley J. Whitney, introduced as "Esq., B.S. of Exeter, California," in the *Journal of the Transactions of the Victorian Institute*, purporting to prove that the earth was 6,000 years old.[55] Smith, impressed by the article, wrote to Whitney asking him to respond to the Bennion-Talmage debate.[56] Whitney subsequently drafted a series of articles, the first of which, "The Fiat Creation of the Earth," was published in the *Deseret News* but not in the "Church Section."[57]

Since the Whitney article was neither written by a Mormon nor published in a church periodical, Talmage paid little attention to it. W. W. Henderson, professor of zoology at Utah State University, wrote to the *News* stating that since "people generally take seriously whatever articles of this kind they find published in the *News*, it is unfortunate to publish such a paper."[58] As a result of this and other protests, the *Deseret News* decided against printing the last three or four articles in the Whitney series. In writing to Whitney of their decision, they suggested he take up the matter personally with Talmage or Henderson if he wished. Talmage subsequently received an angry letter from Whitney offering Sterling $100 to participate in a debate on the merits of the case for the fiat creation.[59]

Talmage was astonished by Whitney's letter, especially since he had had nothing to do with discontinuing the series. In his letter Whitney mentioned that "our mutual friend, Mr. Joseph Fielding Smith, the Church Historian," had been responsible for publication of Whitney's articles at the *Deseret News*. Talmage therefore wrote to Smith for an explanation.[60]

Smith replied that he had indeed favored publication of the Whitney articles: "As you know I am not in accord with many of the theories of the present day, including organic evolution and other theories taught by geologists, biologists, and others. For this reason I thought articles might be of interest showing there is another side to the questions. . . . While scientists are not atheists and are led to believe in some kind of a God, yet the tendency of the times is to destroy the Son of God and the plan of redemption."[61] Talmage expressed appreciation of Smith's reply in a return letter, although noting that Smith had merely re-emphasized the points of basic disagreement between them.[62]

Although Talmage declined Whitney's offer to debate publicly, he did attempt to spell out his objections to Whitney's articles in private correspondence. To this Whitney replied, "I confess with deepest penitence that in discussing the essentials of my case I hurried over one part of the subject with some generalizations that were not strictly correct." He still felt, however, that his basic thesis was "unanswerable." As a matter of fact, "I figure that if about seven or eight of [my] series had been published, the teachings of evolution would have been pretty badly demoralized in the Inter Mountain States."[63] With this the Whitney-Talmage exchange seems to have ended.[64]

Scarcely one year later Elder Smith approved an article similar to those of Whitney and Bennion for publication in the "Church News." This one was by Floyd Day, unintroduced in the article, and was entitled "Can the Scriptures Be Relied On?" If so, according to Day, the earth was only 13,000 years old, there was no death before the fall of Adam 6,000 years ago, and the principles of organic evolution were blasphemous.[65] Talmage once again protested strongly to the First Presidency that "the scriptural quotations are strained and misapplied." He pointed out again that the article was in direct contradiction to his father's "Earth and Man" address, which "is to be considered an apostolic utterance." Perhaps wearied by the persistent appearance of such articles, he also informed the presidency that he did not intend to draft a direct rebuttal, commenting only that "the present article . . . is so puerile that it carries its own refutation."[66]

Smith, shown a copy of Talmage's letter, was upset that "The Earth and Man" should be considered "an apostolic utterance delivered by appointment." He wrote Sterling that he knew personally that the talk had been issued "arbitrarily, in the absence of the President of the Church, and over the protest of the majority of the Council of the Apostles."[67] To Sterling, Smith's statement was tantamount to a charge that James Talmage in publishing his talk was guilty of unethical, clandestine behavior. He responded to Smith that "I knew my father better than that; and so did you. I must admit that the paragraph carries a note of personal resentment against what appears to me to be an utterly unfair aspersion relative to my father's methods and motives."[68]

At this point Talmage again sought confirmation of the status of his father's talk in a letter to "President Heber J. Grant and Counselors." The First Presidency replied with a letter outlining a history of publication of "The Earth and Man." Contrary to Sterling's belief that the sermon was authoritative, they asserted that it was twice "the unanimous view of the Twelve minus one, that the sermon not be published." It was their memory that "President Ivins withdrew the sermon from the consideration of the Council and himself decided that it should be published. It was printed within two or three days thereafter." According to the letter, President Grant had been away at the time and was apparently not consulted. The presidency continued, "You can see from the foregoing that the sermon 'The Earth and Man' cannot be regarded as an official expression of the Church." However, "we make this foregoing statement without making any comment at all upon the matters discussed in the sermon." Whether the sermon was prepared "by appointment," the presidency stressed that "These 'appointments' are made merely in order that certain work shall be done . . . but that does not mean that the Church must approve everything" that is said or done "by appointment."[69]

This account of events surrounding publication of "The Earth and Man" is remarkable in that it disagrees with almost every other account available, including Heber J. Grant's journal and Rudger Clawson's official report. One wonders what sources the 1935 presidency consulted. A satisfactory explanation for this discrepancy is unavailable, because of the inaccessibility of critical historical records. It is probably relevant to note that when this explanation was sent to Sterling Talmage, only President Grant remained of those who were in the First Presidency in 1931. Second counselor Charles W. Nibley had died in December 1931 and first counselor Ivins in 1934. J. Reuben Clark, the new first counselor and a frequent official respondent to inquiries to the First Presidency during the later Grant years, had not been a church authority in 1931 and was not party to the earlier discussions. The new second counselor, David O. McKay, was formerly of the Quorum of the Twelve.

Whatever the explanation for the letter, its effect on Sterling was profound. He replied to the presidency and to Smith in a highly conciliatory manner: "I am very grateful to you for clarifying my mind in this respect. I shall not again, either in publication or in private correspondence, place undue stress on the authoritativeness of this document, or any statements contained in it."[70] Thereafter he was never again so willing to commit himself publicly in disagreement with the conservative elements of the church, although he had several opportunities to do so.[71] Three years later when Apostle Widtsoe decided to involve himself in the public defense of science against scriptural traditionalism, Talmage published one last article on the age of the earth in the *Improvement Era* in support of Widtsoe.[72] He did not, however, follow through with plans to publish a series of articles written with Widtsoe's approval defending the theory of evolution.[73] Although he completed a book-length manuscript called *Can Science Be Faith Promoting?* he was unable to publish this work before his death in 1956.[74]

The extended debate generated by Roberts's manuscript ended inconclusively. Church leaders did not want to encourage the theological speculation which it would have engendered. But if they discouraged speculative discussion, they at the same time refused authoritative pronouncement. John Widtsoe amidst the controversies of the early thirties expressed his frustration at having been "afflicted with these questions [of science] for a generation of time." It seemed to him that it was "high time that the Church answer them definitely or declare that it does not know, so that more important questions may engage the minds of young and old."[75] But despite decades-old infighting for authority to speak in the name of the church about science, neither the issues of science nor those associated with doctrinal authority have yet been resolved.

NOTES

1. Roberts's views are also discussed in Richard Sherlock, "A Turbulent Spectrum: Mormon Reactions to the Darwinist Legacy," *Journal of Mormon History* 5 (1978): 33-59.

2. Many church leaders otherwise hostile to evolution, such as Charles Penrose, were prepared to admit that the earth was very old. American religious leaders in general had been doing it since the 1830s. See Charles Penrose, "The Age and Destiny of the Earth," *Improvement Era* 12 (May 1909): 506-9; Conrad Wright, "The Religion of Geology," *New England Quarterly* 14 (1941): 335-58.

3. The idea of pre-Adamite races goes back to the seventeenth century. It had its most complete statement in Isaac de la Peyrere's two works, *Men before Adam* (1656) and *Prae-Adamitae* (1655); on this, see especially Richard Popkin, "The Pre-Adamite Theory in the Renaissance," in *Philosophy and Humanism*, ed. E. P. Mahoney (Leiden: Brill, 1976), 50-69; and his more encyclopedic treatment in *The History of Skepticism from Erasmus to Spinoza* (Berkeley: University of California Press, 1979). While the theory was not new, Roberts seems to have been the first to place it in a dispensationalist framework.

4. George Albert Smith, chair of the reading committee, to Rudger Clawson, council president, 10 Oct. 1929, Clawson Papers, archives, Historical Department, Church of Jesus Christ of Latter-day Saints, Salt Lake City, Utah (hereafter LDS archives). The other members of the committee were Joseph Fielding Smith, Melvin Ballard, Stephen L Richards, and David O. McKay.

5. Ibid.

6. Council of the Twelve to Heber J. Grant, 15 May 1930, Clawson Papers.

7. Joseph Fielding Smith, "The Word of the Lord Superior to Theories of Men," *Liahona* 15 (Apr. 1918): 641-44; "The Origin and Destiny of Man," *Improvement Era* 23 (Mar. 1920): 376-93.

8. Joseph Fielding Smith, "Faith Leads to a Fullness of Truth and Righteousness," *Utah Genealogical and Historical Magazine* 21 (Oct. 1930): 145-58.

9. Roberts to Heber J. Grant, 15 Dec. 1930, B. H. Roberts Papers, LDS archives; Roberts to Rudger Clawson, 31 Dec. 1930, Roberts Papers.

10. Roberts met with the council on 2 January at which time he outlined orally the charges he was making. James E. Talmage journal, 2 Jan. 1931, James E. Talmage Collection, Archives and Manuscripts, Harold B. Lee Library, Brigham Young University, Provo, Utah.

11. Manuscript on file at LDS archives, 2-3.

12. This outlook pervades the manuscript presented to the council. Richard Sherlock has discussed another example of it in "Faith and History: The Snell Controversy," *Dialogue: A Journal of Mormon Thought* 12 (Spring 1979): 27-41.

13. Council of the Twelve to the First Presidency, 21 Jan. 1931, Clawson Papers.

14. Roberts to Heber J. Grant, 9 Feb. 1931, Roberts Papers. Talmage indicates in his journal that he was called in for a private conference with the First Presidency on these matters on 14 January. This was after Roberts had made his presentation but before Smith had made his, indicating that even then they were preparing to make a final decision by getting some geological advice from a knowledgeable source.

15. Heber J. Grant diary, 25 Jan. 1931, Heber J. Grant collection, LDS archives.

16. Copy in our possession, 7.

17. Ibid., 6.

18. Ibid., 7.

19. Talmage journal, 12 Dec. 1881.

20. Sterling Talmage to John A. Widtsoe, 17 Apr. 1934, Sterling Talmage Papers, Special Collections, Marriott Library, University of Utah.

21. George McCready Price, *The New Geology* (Mt. View, CA: Pacific

Press, 1923). For example, Price writes of geology: "In geology, facts and theories are still *in-extricably comingled*, and in the ordinary college textbook of the science, the most absurd and fantastic speculations are still taught to the students with all the solemnity and pompous importance which might be allowable in speaking of the facts of chemistry or physics."

22. Sterling Talmage to James Talmage, 9 Feb. 1931, S. Talmage Papers; italics Talmage's.

23. James Talmage to Sterling Talmage, 21 May 1931, S. Talmage Papers.

24. Ibid.

25. Rudger Clawson to George Albert Smith, 10 Apr. 1931, Clawson Papers.

26. Roberts to Heber J. Grant, 30 Aug. 1932; see also Roberts to E. H. Lund, Roberts Papers.

27. Talmage Journal, 21 Nov. 1931.

28. Ibid.

29. Sterling Talmage to James Talmage, 15 June 1931, S. Talmage Papers.

30. Ibid.

31. Sterling Talmage, "Open Letter to Elder Joseph Fielding Smith," 28 June 1931, S. Talmage Papers. The reference to geologists as "miserable fools" had evidently been made by Smith at a stake conference attended by Sterling Talmage.

32. James Talmage to Sterling Talmage, 23 June 1931, S. Talmage Papers; italics Talmage's.

33. Ibid.

34. James E. Talmage, "The Earth and Man," *Deseret News*, 21 Nov. 1931.

35. James Talmage to John Widtsoe, 18 Nov. 1931, Talmage Papers.

36. Susa Y. Gates to John A. Widtsoe, undated, Widtsoe Collection, Utah State Historical Society, Salt Lake City.

37. When Clawson's report was read to the Council of the Twelve, the only objection voiced was that "some of the brethren took exception to the expression, *'reaching back, into numberless ages of the past, to the protoplasm.'* I presume I should have said, *'reaching back, into numberless ages of the past, to the single-celled protozoan'*" (see Report of Rudger Clawson to the First Presidency, Clawson Papers).

38. Smoot wrote Talmage that he hadn't "a word of complaint to offer against" the address (24 Nov. 1931, Talmage Collection).

39. Merrill was reported to have "upon hearing the sermon expressed a great pleasure and satisfaction and asked for a thousand copies of the sermon to distribute among his seminary teachers" (Report of Rudger Clawson).

40. Widtsoe wrote, "I am pleased, indeed, that the address was delivered publicly and hope it may soon be published" (Widtsoe to Rudger Clawson, 9 Sept. 1931, Widtsoe Collection).

41. Talmage wrote in his journal that "the other brethren named [Richards and Lyman], including President Ivins, expressed their tentative approval of what I had said" (21 Nov. 1931). Joseph Fielding Smith wrote in his small journals, "(attended) Tabernacle in the afternoon. Dr. J. E. T. spoke not edifying but questionable" (copy in Eugene Thompson Collection, Archives and Manuscripts, Harold B. Lee Library).

42. Smoot wrote, "I voted that the article with a few slight changes be published and a majority voted that way" (Reed Smoot journal, 29 Sept. 1931, Smoot Papers, Archives and Manuscripts, Harold B. Lee Library). Talmage wrote, "The majority of the Twelve have been in favor of the publication of the address from the time they first took it under consideration" (Talmage journal, 21 Nov. 1931).

43. Clawson Papers.

44. Grant Journal, 17 Nov. 1931.

45. Howard S. Bennion, "Is the Earth Millions of Years Old?" *Deseret News*, "Church Section," 17 Mar. 1934, 6, and 24 Mar., 4, 7.

46. John A. Widtsoe to Sterling Talmage, 11 Apr. 1934, S. Talmage Papers.

47. Sterling Talmage, "Can We Dictate God's Times and Methods?" *Deseret News*, "Church Section," 14 Apr. 1934, 3, 5, and 21 Apr., 3, 6.

48. John A. Widtsoe to Sterling Talmage, 11 Apr. 1934, S. Talmage Papers.

49. Sterling Talmage, "Can We Dictate?" 3, 6.

50. Sterling Talmage to President Heber J. Grant and Counselors, 30 Dec. 1935, S. Talmage Papers.

51. John A. Widtsoe to Sterling Talmage, 11 Apr. 1934, S. Talmage Papers.

52. Howard S. Bennion, "Further Observations on the Age of the Earth," *Deseret News*, "Church Section," 19 May 1934, 4; Sterling Talmage, "Some Lessons Involved in the Age of the Earth," *Deseret News*, "Church Section," 16 June 1934, 2.

53. Sidney Sperry, "What Shall We Then Believe?" *Deseret News*, "Church Section," 16 June 1934, 3.

54. Sterling Talmage to President Anthony W. Ivins, 1 July 1934, S. Talmage Papers. The health of the 81-year-old Ivins at this time is unclear. He died just two months later.

55. Dudley Joseph Whitney, "The Age of the Earth as Deduced from the Salinity of the Ocean," *Journal of the Transactions of the Victorian Institute* 65 (1933): 26-34. The Victorian Institute was a society established in 1867 in London, England, that had as its goal: "To investigate fully and impartially

the most important questions of Philosophy and Science, but more especially those that bear upon the great truths revealed in Holy Scriptures, with the view of defending these truths against the oppositions of Science, falsely so-called" (ibid., 1 [May 1867]: vi). While the society defended many scriptural "truths" such as creation *ex nihilo* that were not compatible with Mormon thought, Smith was impressed with their treatment of evolution. Most of the society's articles on this subject, which invariably denounced evolution as being incredibly unscientific as well as unscriptural, were written by recognized scientists. Almost all of the post-1930 references in Smith's *Man: His Origin and Destiny* are to the Victorian Institute's *Journal*.

56. Dudley J. Whitney to Sterling Talmage, 29 Sept. 1934, S. Talmage Papers.

57. Dudley J. Whitney, "The Fiat Creation of the Earth," *Deseret News*, 16 June 1934, 6.

58. W. W. Henderson to editor, *Deseret News*, 26 June 1934.

59. Dudley J. Whitney to Sterling Talmage, 22 Aug. 1934, S. Talmage Papers.

60. Sterling Talmage to Joseph Fielding Smith, 16 Sept. 1934, S. Talmage Papers.

61. Joseph Fielding Smith to Sterling Talmage, 29 Sept. 1934, S. Talmage Papers.

62. Sterling Talmage to Joseph Fielding Smith, 16 Sept. 1934.

63. Dudley J. Whitney to Sterling Talmage, 29 Sept. 1934, S. Talmage Papers.

64. John A. Widtsoe remarked concerning Whitney's articles. "Life within the Church does not hinge upon the age of the earth, nor does any vital principle within the Church body of doctrine" (John A. Widtsoe to Sterling Talmage, 27 Sept. 1934, S. Talmage Papers).

65. Floyd Day, "Can Scripture Be Relied On?" *Deseret News*, "Church Section," 16 Nov. 1935, 7.

66. Sterling Talmage to President Heber J. Grant and Counselors, 24 Nov. 1935, S. Talmage Papers.

67. Joseph Fielding Smith to Sterling Talmage, 4 Dec. 1935, S. Talmage Papers.

68. Sterling Talmage to Joseph Fielding Smith, 7 Dec. 1935, S. Talmage Papers. This letter contains a hint of the intense feelings that ran between the Talmage and Smith families after 1931. Sterling's sister Elsie referred to a "Smith-Talmage family feud" and quit her job with the *Improvement Era* to escape Elder Smith's influence (Elsie Talmage to Sterling Talmage, 11 Jan. 1935 and 12 Apr. 1935, George Albert Smith Collection, Marriott Library).

69. Heber J. Grant, J. Reuben Clark, and David O. McKay to Sterling Talmage, 19 Dec. 1935, S. Talmage Papers.

70. Sterling Talmage to President Heber J. Grant and Counselors, 30 Dec. 1935, S. Talmage Papers.

71. See, for example, Sidney Sperry, "Challenge to Scientists in the Church: Harmonize Learning, Faith," *Deseret News*, "Church Section," 4 Apr. 1936, 3; and Joseph Fielding Smith's eulogy to William Jennings Bryan, "Was the Hero's Death So Bad?" *Deseret News*, "Church Section," 31 Oct. 1936, 1.

72. Sterling B. Talmage, "Genesis and Geology," *Improvement Era* 42 (Mar. 1939): 143-44.

73. Widtsoe encouraged Talmage in this endeavor: "it is very likely that the time is ripe for someone to begin right now to prepare a wise, temperate, scientific statement of the doctrine of evolution. . . . Evolution, as a law, seems to me to have been demonstrated" (Widtsoe to Sterling Talmage, 20 Apr. 1934, S. Talmage Papers). It is not clear whether this series was not published because it could not receive the approval of the brethren or if Talmage voluntarily withdrew the manuscript.

74. The manuscript is currently being edited by Stan Larson for publication.

75. Widtsoe to Susa Y. Gates, 30 Oct. 1931, Widtsoe Collection.

7.
Harvey Fletcher and
Henry Eyring:
Men of Faith and Science

Edward L. Kimball

THE YEAR 1981 SAW THE DEATHS OF HARVEY FLETCHER AND HENRY
Eyring, men of great religious faith whose superb professional achievements placed them in the first ranks of the nation's scientists. Both
could be said to have had simple religious faith—not because they
were uncomplicated people incapable of subtlety, but because their
religious character was early and firmly grounded in a few fundamen-
tals. This freed them from a life of continuing doubt and struggle.

The two men, seventeen years apart in age, had a kind of
family relationship. Henry Eyring's uncle Carl Eyring (after whom
the Eyring Science Center at Brigham Young University was named)
married Fern Chipman. Harvey Fletcher married her sister Lorena.
After their spouses died Harvey Fletcher and Fern Chipman Eyring
married. As a result Henry Eyring called him Uncle Harvey. But that
was not unique. Nearly everyone else did too.

Harvey Fletcher was born in 1884 in a little frame house in
Provo, Utah. Among his memories are attending the dedication of
the Salt Lake temple and shaking LDS church president Wilford
Woodruff's hand. As a young boy he recited a short poem at a
program in the Provo tabernacle. After he finished, Karl G. Maeser,
principal of the Brigham Young Academy, stopped him before he
could resume his seat, put his hand on Harvey's head, and said, "I
want this congregation to know that this little boy will one day be a

great man." Instead of being pleased, Harvey was bothered. He perceived it as a prediction of political leadership, which he did not want.

Later when he was president of the deacon's quorum, his bishop called on him to speak extemporaneously to the other deacons. Unable to think of anything to say, he stood first on one leg, then the other, and rubbed his head. Finally he blurted out, "I'd rather be good than great," and sat down. He often said that this was his best sermon.

When he graduated from eighth grade and took a job as delivery boy for a grocery store, he considered his education ended, but friends who went to high school at BYU influenced him to follow. He failed physics because he did not complete his laboratory journal, but the next year he earned an A+ and was hired as a laboratory assistant.

He received a college degree from BYU in 1907, one of six graduates that year, taught at BYU in 1907-1908, married Lorena Chipman, took a leave of absence the same year, and went to the University of Chicago to obtain a Ph.D. He borrowed money for his first year of graduate work and then earned additional funds by teaching high school science and running the projector for lecture classes.

At the beginning of his second year Harvey Fletcher started work with Robert A. Millikan, then a young assistant professor. Fletcher tells what happened in this excerpt from his unpublished autobiography:

> I went to Professor Millikan to see if he could suggest a problem upon which I could work for a doctor's thesis in physics. He was a busy man and I had a hard time making an appointment with him. Finally, he told me to come down to one of the research laboratories where he and Professor Beggeman were working and he would talk to me. First he and Professor Beggeman showed me the research work that they were doing on the electronic charge, and reviewed the work that J. J. Thompson and Regener had been doing along this line in Cambridge, England.
>
> They had arranged a little box having a content of 2 or 3 cubic centimeters which was fastened to the end of a microscope. A tube was attached from an expansion chamber to the little box.

By opening suddenly a petcock, a sudden expansion of the air in the little box was made which caused a cloud of water vapor to form. When viewed through a microscope this cloud was seen to be composed of a large number of tiny water drops. The droplets would soon drop from the top to the bottom of the box under the influence of gravity. A conducting plate was arranged at the top and another one at the bottom of the box so that an electric field could be produced.

When this electric field was turned on it would retard the fall of some droplets. They were trying to make the field just right so that the droplet would be suspended in the air between the plates. From the speed of the droplet, that is the fall speed, and the intensity of the field to stop the droplet, one could calculate the electrical charge on the droplet. This was essentially repeating the experiment that Regener did in England. However, the water forming the droplet evaporated so fast that the little droplet would only stay in view for about 2 seconds. So it was difficult to get more than a rough estimate of the charge.

We discussed ways and means of getting around the difficulty, and I think we all agreed that we should have a droplet that did not evaporate if we could get it small enough and could control it. Mercury, oil, and two or three other substances were suggested. In a discussion of that kind, it is rather difficult to be sure who suggested what. I left with the impression that I had suggested oil for it was easy to get and to handle. However, in Professor Millikan's memoirs he said he had been thinking of this before this conference. Of course, I cannot say yes or no to that, but I do know what happened after this conference.

Professor Millikan said to me, "There is your thesis; go try one of these substances which will not evaporate." So out I went to do this and get started on my thesis. To build an apparatus like they were using would take considerable time. So I decided to make a crude setup in the laboratory and try it before designing an elaborate one. So I went out to the drug store that afternoon and bought an atomizer and some watch oil. Then I came back to the laboratory and set up the following apparatus:

First an arc light with two condensing lenses in front of it was set up. The combination made a bright beam of light. The experience which I had with projection lanterns for lectures made it possible to get this together very quickly. I then used the atomizer and squirted some oil spray so that it fell through the beam of light.

The light made these tiny drops of oil look like tiny stars. This indicated this part of the experiment would probably work. I then went down to the student shop and found some brass sheets about one-eighth of an inch thick. From them I cut two circular plates about 20 centimeters in diameter. Then I fastened (soldered) a stem onto each one so that they could be held by an ordinary laboratory stand with clamps. A small hole was then bored in the center of the top plate. These plates were then set up horizontally, being about 2 centimeters apart. In this first set-up the air between the plates was not enclosed. So I moved the stands holding the two plates over into the beam of light. I then put a large cardboard between the light and the plates and cut a hole just large enough to permit the light to go between the plates without touching them. I then found a cathetometer (an instrument commonly used around a physics laboratory) and placed it so the telescope on it was turned and raised and lowered until its line of sight went between the two plates and at about 120° from the direction of the light beam. The distance from the telescope to the plates was about one meter. I then tried out the apparatus. I turned on the light; then focused the telescope; then sprayed oil over the top of the plate; then came back to look through the telescope. I saw a most beautiful sight. The field was full of little starlets, having all colors of the rainbow. The larger drops soon fell to the bottom but the smaller ones seemed to hang in the air for nearly a minute. They executed the most fascinating dance. I had never seen Brownian Movements before; here was a spectacular view of them. The tiny droplets were being pushed first that way and then this way by the actual molecules in the air surrounding them. I could hardly wait until I could try an electric field upon them to see if they were charged. I knew there were two or three banks of small storage cells in the laboratory. A large number of these small storage cells had been connected in series and mounted in storage compartments on a small trunk. Each one of these units would produce 1,000 DC volts at its terminal. So I soon rolled these into place near my crude apparatus. Insulated wires were attached electrically to each of the plates. The other ends of these wires were attached through a switch to the two terminals of the 1,000 DC battery. I finished most of this that first afternoon. The next morning I spent some time adjusting it and installing a meter to read the volts applied by the big storage battery. I was then ready to try the battery on these tiny oil drops.

The atomizer was used to spray some of the oil across the

top plates. As I looked through the telescope I could see the tiny stream of oil droplets coming through the hole. Again I saw beautiful stars in constant agitation. As soon as I turned on the switch some of them went slowly up and some went faster down. I was about to scream as I knew then some were charged negatively and others positively. By switching the field off and on with the right timing one could keep a selected droplet in the field of view for a long time. I went immediately to find Professor Millikan, but could not find him so I spent the rest of the day playing with these oil droplets and got a fairly reasonable value of "e" [the charge on a single electron] before the day ended. The next day I found him. He was very much surprised to learn that I had a set-up that was working. He came down to the laboratory and looked through the telescope and saw the same beautiful sight of the starlets jumping around that I had already seen. He was very much excited, especially after turning on the field. After watching for some time he was sure he could get an accurate value . . . by this method. He stopped working with Beggeman and started to work with me. We were together nearly every afternoon for the next two years. He called the mechanic who worked in our physics shop and we outlined a new design for our apparatus and asked him to build it. The principal changes were to make the plates more accurate and enclose the air between the plates to prevent air drafts. Also we obtained a radium source or X-ray source which we could shoot at the chamber to produce a great ionization.

This took about a week after which we started in earnest on this research work which was later to become so famous. After working five or six weeks we had the press come into our laboratory and see and hear our results. We also made a popular presentation. The papers were then full of this wonderful discovery. It was the first real publicity that I had received. My name ran right along with Professor Millikan's in the newspaper. I spent considerable time showing these experiments to various VIPs from all over the country.

I remember one of them was the great hunchback from the General Electric Company [Charles Steinmetz]. He was one who did not believe in electrons. He could explain all the electrical phenomena in terms of a strain in the "Ether." After watching these little oil droplets most of one afternoon he came and shook my hand and said, shaking his head, "I never would have believed it; I never would have believed it," and then left.

This was all great publicity for Professor Millikan. At that time his rank was only assistant professor. He had never published a noteworthy research. But he and Gale—another faculty member—had published an excellent high school physics text. I began to wonder if this work was to be my thesis as Professor Millikan promised at that first conference. We had never spoken about it since that first conference in December 1909. However, during the spring, we started together writing a paper to be published about the new research.

I wrote more of it than he did, particularly about the modification of Stokes' law and the arrangements of the data. He went over it all and changed the phrasing somewhat to make it read better. All the time I thought we were to be joint authors.

Phyllis was born May 21, 1910, about the time we finished this paper. When she was about one month old, I was baby sitting with her. Answering a knock I went to the door and was surprised to see Professor Millikan. I wondered why he had come to our humble apartment. I soon found it was to decide who was to be the author of the paper referred to above. There were four other papers in the formative stage that were coming out of these oil drop experiments and I expected they would all be joint papers.

He said that if I used a published paper for my doctor's thesis that I must be its sole author. The five papers on which we did the experimental work together were:

1. The Isolation of an Ion, a Precision Measurement of its Charge and the Correction of Stokes' Law. *Science*, September 30, 1910—Millikan.

2. Causes of Apparent Discrepancies and Recent Work on the Elementary Electrical Charge. *Physik Zeitschrift*, January 1911—Millikan and Fletcher.

3. Some Contributions to the Theory of Brownian Movements, with Experimental Applications. *Physik Zeitschrift*, January 1911—Fletcher.

4. The Question of Valency in Gaseous Ionization. *Philosophical Magazine*, June 1911—Millikan and Fletcher.

5. A Verification of the Theory of Brownian Movement and a Direct Determination of the Value of Ne for Gaseous Ionization. *Physics Review*, August 1911, and *Le Radium*, July [19]11—Fletcher. This was my thesis.

It was obvious that he wanted to be the sole author on the first paper. I did not like this, but I could see no other out and I agreed to use the fifth paper listed above as my thesis and would be listed as the sole author on that paper.

People have frequently asked me if I had bad feelings toward Millikan for not letting me be a joint author with him on this first paper which really led to his getting the Nobel prize. My answer has always been no. It is obvious that I was disappointed on that first paper as I had done considerable work on it and had expected to be a joint author. But Professor Millikan was very good to me while I was at Chicago. It was through his influence that I got into the graduate school. He also found remunerative jobs for me to defray all my personal and school expenses for the last two years. Above this was the friendship created by working intimately together for more than two years. This lasted throughout our lifetime. Remember when we worked together he was not the famous Millikan that he later became. When he wrote his memoirs shortly before he died, he had probably forgotten some of these early experiences.

I graduated with a Ph.D. in Physics in 1911 with an honor "Summa Cum Laude." This was the first such high honor that was given to a physics student at Chicago.[1]

Fletcher had offers to teach at the University of Chicago and to work at Western Electric Laboratories upon graduation but chose to return to BYU which had granted him leave to pursue graduate studies. He served as head of the physics department but spent much of his time teaching elementary mathematics while continuing some further experiments growing out of those he started at Chicago.

Every spring I received a letter from Dr. Frank B. Jewett [of Western Electric] asking me this question, 'Which is more important in your mind this year, business or sentiment?' After five years of this I finally accepted his offer to have me join his organization in New York City.

When I told President [George H.] Brimhall of my intentions, he thought I was being disloyal to the church, and asked, Why don't you talk to President Joseph F. Smith and ask his advice? President Smith . . . was coming to Provo to attend a board meeting of the BYU and so I made a date to see him. I explained Dr. Jewett's proposition and then told him about the research department of the Western Electric Company. I said this department did most of the research and engineering for the entire American Telephone and Telegraph Company. So I just felt an urge to try my skill against the intellectual giants in this laboratory. After listening to my story he sat quietly in a thoughtful mood for a few minutes (it seemed forever) and then said, "Yes, I want you to go and take this position, but promise this, that you will keep your testimony strong and keep up your Church activities. If you do so you can do more good for the Church in New York City than you could do here at the BYU at the present time and you will be successful in your work. We need more Mormon boys to go out into the world of business and scientific research to represent our ideal of living."[2]

Fletcher spent the next thirty-three years with what later came to be known as Bell Telephone Laboratories. Because others were already engaged in working with electronics, he moved into acoustics, a field new to him. Out of these studies came a flood of wonderful acoustic devices, such as high fidelity recording, stereophonic sound, talking motion pictures, hearing aids, the artificial larynx, sonar, audiometers, and so on. An early hearing aid made especially for Thomas Edison weighed approximately one hundred pounds.

Fletcher was the first Latter-day Saint to be nominated to the National Academy of Sciences. He was nominated in three areas rather than one—in physiology for his study of the anatomy of speech (he had published *Sound and Hearing* in 1929), in engineering, and in physics.

Gradually he added administrative responsibilities, becoming director of acoustical research in 1925 and director of physical research in 1933. Under his administration three researchers at the Bell Laboratories developed the transistor and received the Nobel Prize for their work. Another researcher developed the semi-conductor.

His goal of reproducing sound with realism had its first public demonstration in 1933. The *New York Times* of 24 January 1934 said that the audience was "mystified" and "often terrified. . . . Had it not been for the knowledge that they were witnessing a practical scientific demonstration," the reporter stated, the audience "might have believed they were attending a spiritualist seance. Some women in the audience, admitting a feeling of 'spookiness,' left the auditorium in fright. Airplanes flew from the stage and circled over the heads of the audience with so much realism that all present craned their necks in fright." With the cooperation of Leopold Stokowski, Fletcher demonstrated stereophonic sound by transmitting to Constitution Hall in Washington, D.C., a live performance of the Philadelphia Orchestra from Philadelphia.[3]

He became the founding president of the Acoustical Society of America in 1928 and helped form the American Institute of Physics in 1932. He also served as president of the American Association for the Advancement of Science in 1937 and president of the American Physical Society in 1945. He belonged to other societies, honorary and professional, and six universities gave him honorary degrees.

When Fletcher retired from Bell in 1949 at age sixty-five, he taught at Columbia and then returned to BYU in 1952 as director of research and head of the Department of Engineering Sciences. He became first dean of the College of Physical and Engineering Sciences in 1954. The Engineering Sciences Laboratory Building was named in his honor. After a few years he returned to acoustical research and retired from teaching and administration. In his career he published more than fifty technical papers, held twenty patents, and received various medals and public recognitions.

Throughout Harvey Fletcher remained true to the commitment he made to President Joseph F. Smith. In New York City his house was the center of church life for the few members living there in the early days. He served ten years as president of the New York Branch and served beginning in 1936 as president of the New York Stake.

His coworkers knew what he stood for—at least in a general way. One day as Fletcher was riding the ferry to work in Manhattan, he overheard two other Bell Laboratory employees talking behind him. One said, "Did you know that Harvey Fletcher is a bishop in the Mormon church?" The other corrected, "Hell, he's not a bishop. He's an archbishop!"

A typical example of his kindly and realistic counsel was his wise approach to a member of the ward whose marriage was deteriorating. Fletcher pushed an apple under the man's chin and asked, "What do you see?" Baffled, the man replied, "Nothing." Fletcher then held the apple out where the man could see it clearly and said, "You're just too close to this tragedy now. You need to give it time.

Then you'll be able to see it in perspective." This homely illustration made the point.

Successfully rearing a faithful family far from the Mormon community could not have been done without Lorena Chipman Fletcher. In 1965 she was named Utah Mother of the Year and also national Mother of the Year. It pleased her husband Harvey to be able to take a supporting role for a change. He kept her scrapbook with care and showed it with pride.

The family's high standards are evident in the accomplishments of the five surviving sons, a son and daughter having died previously. Stephen was vice president and general counsel for Western Electric until his retirement; he then taught in the J. Reuben Clark Law School at BYU and was copyright lawyer for the LDS church. Harvey J. was professor of mathematics at BYU. James served as president of the University of Utah, then head of NASA twice, and later was engaged in energy research. Robert was executive director of the integrated circuit development division of Bell Laboratories. Paul was an administrator in the field of lasers in the government laboratory at San Diego.

Fletcher wrote a 1961 LDS Sunday school manual called *The Good Life*, a publication which deserves continued reading. He divided the good life into three aspects—love of God, love and use of knowledge, and love of fellow men and women. Few people have better exemplified "the good life" than he did, and the choice to be "good" was made early. When he was a boy in Primary, his teacher drew a chalk line on the floor of the classroom and said, "Here's the big difference in life—who's on the Lord's side and who isn't. I want you to make a decision whether you're going to be on the Lord's side or not." He remembered all his life the good feeling of rushing over to the right side of the line.[4]

Fletcher's colleague, Henry Eyring, was born in 1901 in Colonia Juarez, one of the Mormon colonies in northern Mexico. After initial hard times his father developed a 14,000-acre ranch with 600 cattle and nearly 100 horses. Henry remembered his childhood as an idyllic time, riding the range beside his father.

When he was four he suffered from typhoid fever. During the illness his Sunday school teacher, "Miss Allred . . . an attractive young lady," visited him. "I was proud and happy that she cared enough to visit me. She spoke to me cheerfully and, after a brief visit with my mother and me, went on her way. But something important had happened to me. . . . I learned that day how important it is to care about people even when they are small and may not seem very important."[5]

In 1912 the Eyring family became refugees from marauding bands of revolutionaries along with the approximately 5,000 other Mormon colonists. They spent a year in El Paso hoping to return to their homes. Henry illustrated early an unusual tenacity. He worked in an El Paso grocery store, rollerskating to work. At the bottom of his hill the sidewalk ended two feet above the road. Daily he tried to make the jump at full speed, nearly always falling and dropping his lunch pail. Only a few times during the year did he make a successful jump.

His father settled the family again in the Gila Valley of Arizona on a 98-acre farm only partly cleared of mesquite. The rigors of dirt farming in arid country gave him incentive to succeed at his studies as a way out and he received a county scholarship to attend college.

As he was about to leave for school, his father said to him, "Son, in this church you don't have to believe anything that isn't true. You go over to the University of Arizona and learn everything you can, and whatever is true is a part of the gospel. The Lord is actually running this universe. I'm convinced that he inspired the Prophet Joseph Smith. If you'll live in such a way that you'll feel comfortable in the company of good people and seek truth, then I don't worry about your getting away from the Lord." His mother advised him not just to be good but to be good for something.[6]

Young Henry waited on tables and graded papers at the university to support himself while he obtained a bachelor's degree in mining engineering, then went to work in the copper mines in Arizona. He says that having a rock smash his foot in the mine persuaded him to switch to metallurgy for a master's degree, and the noxious fumes of the blast furnaces then persuaded him to return to college for a career as a teacher. He obtained his Ph.D. in chemistry at Berkeley in 1927 under Professor George E. Gibson and was also greatly influenced by Gilbert N. Lewis.

With doctoral degree in hand he started teaching at the University of Wisconsin. At a Christmas party for Mormon students he met Mildred Bennion, then pursuing graduate study while on leave from her position as chair of the women's physical education program at the University of Utah. They married in 1928. At Wisconsin Eyring became interested in reaction kinetics and studied it for a year in Berlin and another year at Berkeley.

At Berkeley he used hydrogen and fluorine to test his theories. Conventional wisdom said that these chemicals united in pure form would explode, but Eyring's quantum mechanical calculations indicated no explosion at normal temperatures. He and a friend mixed the pure gases by remote control while they hid behind a barricade, and the mixture did not explode. To flush out the dangerous gases, they had arranged to use a tank of nitrogen but had forgotten to run the control to the place where they were sheltered. Eyring crawled across to turn the valve and the mixture promptly exploded, presumably catalyzed by material introduced from the nitrogen tank or the tubing. Fortunately, no one was injured by the flying glass.[7]

This vindication of his theoretical approach to chemistry drew an invitation from the American Chemical Society to participate in a special symposium on "Applications of Quantum Theory to Chemistry," and that exposure in turn brought him an invitation to join the faculty at Princeton University, which he accepted. His first public acclaim came in 1932 when he received a $1,000 prize from the American Association for the Advancement of Science for a paper that further illustrated how the principles of quantum mechanics applied to organic as well as inorganic chemical reactions.

In 1934 Eyring submitted a paper, "The Activated Complex in Chemical Reactions," to the *Journal of Chemical Physics*. The editor sent it out for review and the reviewer replied that "the method of treatment is unsound and the result incorrect." Eyring persisted, however, and obtained the endorsement of other scientists whose judgment carried more weight. They persuaded the editor to publish the paper, and it proved to be the single most influential paper he ever wrote. He later stated wryly, "Ego is no small thing in the success of a scientist." His absolute rate theory, as it is now called, is said to have been one of the most potent ideas to appear in chemistry in the last fifty years. It applies not only to chemical reactions but also to numerous physical and biological processes.

For this and other contributions to chemistry, he was repeatedly nominated for consideration by the Nobel prize committee. When asked about his not receiving the prize, he quipped, "I'm available!"[8] In all probability the fact that his most significant single contribution to science came so early in his career and was not immediately appreciated limited his chance to receive the highly publicized prize. At Henry Eyring's funeral Dr. Dan Urry, a colleague, called him "one of the principal architects of physical-chemical theory of this century" for his theory of rate processes, his structure theory of liquids, and his theory of optical rotation, among other things.

In awarding Eyring the Swedish Berzelius Gold Medal in 1979, King Karl Gustav of Sweden said, "You are the only true alchemist; you have turned the hydrogen atom into pure gold." Eyring had started the development of his theory of rate processes by treating the reactions of hydrogen atoms and had rapidly expanded it to the more complex reactions in polymers and textiles, chemiluminescence and enzyme mechanisms, biological connective tissue and membrane permeability, and the physical chemistry of nerve action.

In New Jersey Henry Eyring served his church well. He became branch president (1942-44) and then was called as president of the New Jersey District (1944-46), the spiritual head, as he said, of three million persons "though most of them were blissfully unaware of the fact."[9]

He flourished professionally, sometimes overly engrossed in his work. On one occasion he missed his train stop and went right on past Princeton. Getting off and boarding a return train, he missed Princeton a second time.

Albert Einstein was at the Institute for Advanced Study at Princeton during this period, and Eyring enjoyed that association. Of Einstein he said, "He was first rate, there is no question about it, . . . but the picture some people have of him as a lone intellectual giant is a wrong one. I prefer to think of him as a man with few peers. There are other people who are comparable. Neils Bohr was another physicist of comparable scientific influence."[10]

Of this period a former student of his recalled: "When I came into Henry's lecture room for my orals, only Henry was there. The other members of the committee had not yet arrived. He sensed my anxiety and in an attempt to relax me asked if I had ever seen him jump to the table from a standing position. I had never seen him do this, so he made a mighty jump which didn't suffice. He cracked both shins on the edge of the table. For a few moments I thought the oral would have to be canceled, but with pain and determination he backed off and tried it again, this time succeeding."[11]

In 1946 Eyring received an invitation from President A. Ray Olpin of the University of Utah (who by coincidence was Harvey Fletcher's former student, brother-in-law, and colleague at Bell Laboratories) to teach at the University of Utah and establish a graduate school. He considered the offer, then declined. When his wife Mildred learned of this decision, she wrote him a letter to read at the office expressing her feelings that it was time for them to "go home." He immediately wired President Olpin to disregard his earlier letter; he was coming.[12]

For twenty years he was dean of the graduate school, the catalyst and leader needed to establish the University of Utah as a respected research institution. In his career he published 622 scientific papers and a dozen books, with collaborators, edited thirty-eight volumes in several series, and served as the personal mentor for 118 doctoral students. He taught actively until his last illness at age eighty. Then university president David P. Gardner was quoted as saying, "Retirement? The university is not accustomed to retiring geniuses."[13] The university's chemistry building bears his name. Many other honors came to him, including fifteen honorary doctoral degrees, the National Medal of Science in 1967, the Priestly Medal in 1975, and the $100,000 Wolf Prize in Israel in 1980, as well as more than a dozen other major medals and prizes. He served as president both of the American Chemical Society and the American Association for the Advancement of Science. No Latter-day Saint scientist was as widely known as he.

Eyring prided himself on his fitness. He walked to and from his office, politely waving off offers to ride, did standing jumps from the floor to the top of his desk, and until 1978 challenged students to an annual foot race, putting up cash prizes for the first four places. He pursued his scientific work with the same vigor and irrepressible excitement.

An affable speaker, quick with a witty aside or self-deprecating remark, he was popular as a scientific lecturer and as a church speaker. As a teacher he made concepts vivid with images. Chemical reactions might involve bouncing ping pong balls, mountain passes, springs, or marching soldiers. "Dr. Eyring used to say that you must have a model before doing quantitative deductive thinking. A good model is best, but a bad model is better than none at all," recalled Dr. Milton Wadsworth, associate dean of the University of Utah College of Mines and Mineral Industries. "He said it's not a sin to be simple and wrong, but it is a sin to be complicated and wrong, and he had a marvelous way of simplifying complicated material."[14]

Something of Eyring's personality and style can be glimpsed in a report Donald Carr made to the head office of Phillips Petroleum Company during a visit in September 1961 to the company research facilities in Oklahoma:

> Henry Eyring took us over. I believe that this is the greatest "visitation" we have ever had (I use this much misemployed word deliberately, as one talks of visitations by kings, ghosts, and billionaires). . . .
>
> The spell of Eyring is magical. It is compounded of what? Enormous ability, curiosity, imagination, kindness, inexhaustible energy, the incredible combination of a poet's facility with the English language and an advanced physicist's gift for higher mathematics,—above all, *happiness*. I believe he is the happiest man I have ever met, and this spreads, as it must spread from all great geniuses. I wonder how many Eyrings there are in the world? If there were enough we would have nothing to fear, nothing at all to fear.
>
> A man of his accomplishments could afford complete egotism. But what was our toughest problem? To steer him with expedition through the laboratories, since he insisted on talking with everybody he met, asking him what he thought about this and that, fanning a little flame of genuine fellowship here, there, everywhere.
>
> Since the unexpected is what one expects of Henry, his last lecture on the superficially rather unappetizing subject of optical rotation was, to say the least, his best. Here he delved into the theory of origins of life and nature of things, even the true inwardness of light. With his beautiful surgeon's hands, he imitated a ghostly "dipoleness," a sort of Carrollian grin of the cat, being propagated

through space. He concluded that the most important thing in our history was that we were created as matter rather than anti-matter and close upon that was the biochemical triumph of the laevo rather than the dextro-alpha amino acids.

Even from the standpoint of time alone, he earned much more than his honorarium. His lectures were always at least two hours, and would have lasted longer, except for nervous monitors such as Don Smith and myself. His afternoon discussions were continuous eruptions of intellectual richness. At luncheon and in the evening, his charm dominated every table, every minute.

Even in the most complicated presentation in the Adams Building auditorium, he managed with his resonant actor's voice (without loudspeaker) to make everything seem clear and even cozy. He has a way of personalizing. At the blackboard, he would say, for example, "Now, since Don Carr and I went to Berkeley, we'll write this F instead of G, for free energy." And again: "Now, Don (Smith), doesn't that sound reasonable and good to you? If that isn't the truth (his liquid theory), it's the cutest pack of lies I know about."

Except for the great scientific stimulation, what can we learn from Henry the Great? Is it perhaps that, when you are born a genius, a fastidious clean and hardy life pays great dividends, whether you are a Mormon, a Catholic, a Jew or an atheist? He walks to work and back four times a day (10 miles total) and, when nobody is looking, he runs. In fact, he challenged everybody he met here to a fifty-yard dash, and had only one half-hearted taker in Bob Sears, although, unfortunately, there was no time to stage the sprint of the century.[15]

Henry Eyring lived chemistry. Even in the midst of a family gathering his mind used odd moments to work at problems. In a meeting he would pull out an envelope and start writing equations.

He took immense pride in the professional accomplishments of his three children, all sons, and equal satisfaction in their service as bishops. His son Edward was professor of chemistry at the University of Utah. Henry was professor of business administration at Stanford University, president of Ricks College, a counselor in the Presiding Bishopric, and a Seventy, as well as serving as Commissioner of Church Education. Harden, an attorney, was executive assistant to the commissioner of the Utah System of Higher Education.

As a father, he was skilled at comforting with stories of his own foibles. When Harden wrecked the family car, Eyring told him how he had once taken his father's gun down from above the fireplace and gone out on the front porch to frighten a neighbor boy who was walking past. He aimed at the boy, pulled the trigger, and the "unloaded" gun went off with a roar. "Fortunately," he said, "I was a terrible shot."[16]

Apostle Neal A. Maxwell said at his funeral, "Henry's humility and humor kept him from becoming a brilliant but irascible eccentric. Indeed the humor of great individuals is possible because they are not preoccupied with their own ego concerns. Thus they are free to observe the incongruities and inconsistencies of life and themselves. Henry was good natured and good humored because he was good—laughter did not come at the expense of others, but . . . was the self-effacing kind."[17]

With so much commitment to his career in science it would have been easy to have neglected his spiritual life, but Henry Eyring served the church with unflagging energy and openness. In Utah where he served for twenty-five years on the general board of the Sunday school, his favorite assignment was helping prepare gospel doctrine lessons for adult classes each year. A favorite anecdote concerned a meeting to plan the new church magazines:

> I got a letter from Richard L. Evans to come down to a two o'clock meeting for the new magazines, along with a great many other people. I was visiting my sister [Camilla, wife of Apostle Spencer W. Kimball,] and I said, "I am going to a meeting for the magazines." Spencer said, "I am going, too, at nine o'clock." I had forgotten in the meantime that mine was for two o'clock and assumed it was the same meeting. My secretary was not there that morning and I was a little bit late, so I hurried down to the church office building. When I got there, I went in and said to the receptionist that I was supposed to go to a meeting. He said, "Well, isn't it this afternoon?" I said, "No, it is this morning." So he took me in and there were four apostles—Spencer Kimball, Marion Romney, Brother Evans, and Brother Hunter—and the magazine editors. I was quite surprised that there was no one else from the Sunday School but I thought, well, they must regard me very highly, and so I just sat down. Everyone shook my hand so I sat down. The

discussion went around and I was willing to offer my views quite freely. I told them that the church magazines never would amount to a damn if they did not get some people with independence in there who had real ideas and would come out and express themselves. If they were going to rehash old stuff, they would not hold the young people. I told them I thought that *Dialogue* had caught the attention of more people and had more influence than our own church magazines did. It has some of the kind of independence that I think is a good thing. I think it is walking a very dangerous road and could easily go sour, but so far it has been good. And I told them that if they left out people like Brother Wheelwright, who had been working with the *Instructor*, they would be making a big mistake, and so on. I gave them quite a bit of very fine advice and I damned a little when I wanted to and when I got through, Brother Evans said, "I do not know anyone who characterizes the idea of independence any more than you do; are you applying for the job?" "No, I am not applying for the job, but I think I have given good advice." Everyone was very nice to me.

I did not have any feeling, even after I had been there, that there was anything wrong, and thought that they must have a high opinion of my wisdom. When I got back to my office, my secretary asked, "Where have you been?" I said I had been down to the church magazine meeting. She said, "That is this afternoon at two o'clock."

What is so funny is not that I made a mistake, but that I was so insensitive as to not realize it. I did not go to the two o'clock meeting. I felt I had done my work. Brother Evans got up in that meeting and, I am told, said that they had had a meeting in the morning and that very useful advice had been supplied by Brother Eyring. He did not say I had not been invited.

I am amazed at the graciousness of the brethren in making me feel I belonged, when any one of them might well have been annoyed. They are a most urbane group. On my part there was no holding back; I just tried to help them all I could.[18]

In 1969 Mildred Bennion Eyring, his wife of forty-one years, died. Two years later he married Winifred Brennan Clark, who added her four daughters to his family circle.

To the end of his life he was deeply involved in the three great loves of his life—chemistry, family, and church. From 1974 on he was a faithful high councilor. During his last year, seriously ill, he still turned out to help weed the onion field at the stake welfare farm.

During the last, painful illness, Henry Eyring asked rhetorically, "Why is God doing this to me?" He then fell asleep and when he woke up he said, "God needs men of courage. He is testing my courage."[19]

NOTES

1. Harvey Fletcher, *Autobiography* (Provo, UT: privately published, 1967), 29-36; copy in Archives and Manuscripts, Harold B. Lee Library, Brigham Young University, Provo, Utah.

2. Ibid., 42-43.

3. In Harvey Fletcher obituary, *New York Times*, 25 July 1981.

4. Harvey J. Fletcher, remarks at funeral of Harvey Fletcher, 27 July 1981.

5. Henry Eyring, "South of the Border," *Instructor*, Aug. 1967, 322.

6. As quoted by Harden Eyring at the funeral of Henry Eyring, 30 Dec. 1981, in Salt Lake City. Variations on the same conversation appear in a number of places: by Henry Eyring, "My Father's Formula," *Ensign*, Oct. 1978, 29; "Gospel Teaching I Remember Best," *Instructor*, Apr. 1957, 107 (this source also includes the conversation with his mother); "Wisdom—Human and Divine," *Improvement Era*, Mar. 1954, 146; and *The Faith of a Scientist* (Salt Lake City: Bookcraft, 1967), 66.

7. Steve H. Heath, "Henry Eyring, Mormon Scientist," M.A. thesis, University of Utah, 1980, 48-49.

8. Edward L. Kimball, "A Dialogue with Henry Eyring," *Dialogue: A Journal of Mormon Thought* 8 (Autumn/Winter 1973): 100.

9. Ibid.

10. Ibid., 107.

11. Reminiscence by John R. Morrey, *Chemical Dynamics*, eds. Joseph O. Hirschfelder and Douglas Henderson (New York: John Wiley & Sons, 1971), 318, in Heath, "Henry Eyring," 148-49.

12. Ibid., 75; Mildred Bennion Eyring, *My Autobiography* (Salt Lake City; privately published, 1969), 87. Harden Eyring has written a biography of Henry Eyring, as well, in his edition of *Reflections of a Scientist: Henry Eyring* (Salt Lake City: Deseret Book, 1983).

13. Twila Van Leer, "Fellow Scientists to Honor U's Dr. Eyring," *Deseret News*, 3 Apr. 1976, 8A.

14. Dorothy Stowe, "Science Was Art to Henry Eyring," *Deseret News*, 10 Feb. 1982, 1C.

15. D. E. Carr to J. A. Reid, 4 Oct. 1961, in Heath, "Henry Eyring," 98-100.

16. Harden Eyring, remarks at funeral of Henry Eyring, 30 Dec.

1981.
   17. Neal A. Maxwell, remarks at funeral of Henry Eyring, 30 Dec.
1981.
   18. Kimball, "Dialogue," 101-102.
   19. Harden Eyring, remarks at funeral.

8.
Agreeing to Disagree: Henry Eyring and Joseph Fielding Smith

Steven H. Heath

FEW PEOPLE IN MORMON HISTORY HAVE EXEMPLIFIED THE UNITY OF science and religion better than Henry Eyring. A devout student of science for over sixty years, a brilliant chemist, and a faithful believer, he exemplified the crucial possibility of being in the world but not of it for three decades. Despite his important scientific achievements, he may yet be remembered in Mormon history as a model for LDS scientists who wanted to stay happily and productively in the church's mainstream.

As Edward L. Kimball has noted in his biographical paper, "Harvey Fletcher and Henry Eyring: Mormon Scientists," this ability began with a strong grounding in fundamental beliefs in a Mormon home, continued with a personality that accepted these tenets, an investment in service and professionalism, and concluded with the fortunate circumstance that the LDS church used this combination of personal and professional skills in prominent and well-rewarded places.

Where Eyring was concerned, the ability to keep a foot firmly planted in both scientific and religious camps was buttressed by a determination to keep both equally legitimate, an important attitude at a time when science was seen as the enemy of faith in some quarters and when withdrawal into primitive fundamentalism was a possibility for the church.

In 1946 fresh from triumphs at Princeton, Eyring came to the University of Utah as dean of the graduate school. He brought remarkable strength to the university, and, as one colleague put it, he "was the single most important person in transforming Utah into a research institution."[1]

When Eyring moved to Utah in 1946 he was virtually unknown among members of the church except for family, some friends, and a few Mormon scientists. Within three years of his coming, he had won the respect and admiration of thousands in the church. Within months he had been appointed a member of the Sunday school general board and received such honors as the Research Corporation Award in 1948. He gave an increasing number of fireside talks to various groups and was personally charismatic. In February 1948 the church's *Improvement Era* ran a two-page biography by associate editor Marba Josephson. Eyring's address, "Science and Faith," was broadcast nationwide on CBS's "Church of the Air" program.[2] In that address he affirmed, as he would thousands of times, that for him there was no "difficulty in reconciling the principles of true science with the principles of true religion."

Eyring's arrival in Utah preceded a crisis in the relationship of Mormonism to science. Mormonism had not yet concerned itself with such fundamental questions as the fixity or immutability of species and the contention that life depends on a vital force which is immaterial and divine, or the age of the earth, which other Christian religions had defined as conflicts between science and religion. When authoritative pronouncements on organic evolution or the age of the earth had been made, Mormonism had generally supported science.[3] Beginning in 1953 that alliance with science was eroded by Joseph Fielding Smith's scriptural literalism.[4] Speaking on "The Origin of Man" to BYU students on 23 April 1953, Smith attacked the scientific mindset. By mid-1954 he had produced a full-length book, *Man, His Origin and Destiny*, which as one author recently observed, marked "a milestone. For the first time in Mormon history, and capping a full half-century of publication of Mormon books on science and religion, Mormonism had a book that was openly antagonistic to much of science."[5]

In this book Smith asserted that the temporal existence of this earth was very short, only a few thousand years; that there was no human life on this earth prior to Adam; that the so-called pre-Adamite finds of science were frauds or fakes; and that the theory of evolution espoused by biologists and geologists was irreconcilably opposed with religious views.[6]

The book was viewed by many within the church as authoritative. It even had the support of Mormon scientist Melvin A. Cook, who provided a special two-page introduction. But for many Mormon educators, scientists, and students, it represented a serious threat. Because Eyring had distinguished himself in science and was also a faithful Mormon, many turned to him for advice and support. Shortly after publication of the book, he recalls the following sequence of events: "When President Joseph Fielding Smith's book, *Man, His Origin and Destiny*, was published, someone urged it as an Institute course. One of the Institute teachers came to me and said, 'If we have to follow it exactly, we will lose some of the young people.' I said, 'I don't think you need to worry.' I thought it was a good idea to get the thing out in public, so the next time I went to Sunday School General Board meeting, I got up and bore testimony that the world was four or five billion years old, that evidence was strongly in that direction. That week Brother Joseph Fielding Smith called and asked me to come in and see him. I said, 'Brother Smith, I have read your books and know your point of view, and I understand that is how it looks to you. It just looks a little different to me.' He said as we ended, 'Well, Brother Eyring, I would like to have you come in and let me talk with you sometime when you are not quite so excited.' As far as I could see, we parted on the best of terms."[7]

President Smith's book was being considered at the highest levels. Elder Adam S. Bennion of the Quorum of the Twelve asked Eyring for his opinion of it. His letter of response amounts to a tactful but unsparing review of its scientific shortcomings:

> Dear Brother Bennion:
>   President Joseph Fielding Smith's book "Man—His Origin and Destiny" poses a variety of interesting questions. First it is an impressive compilation of scriptural references on Earth History and of statements of selected church leaders. One must say selected because our trained scientists among the general authorities are

not only not quoted but are not even mentioned. It would be
instructive to have President Smith comment on "The Earth and
Man" by James E. Talmage, delivered from the tabernacle August
9, 1931, and "published by the Church of Jesus Christ of Latter-day
Saints;" or on "Science and the Gospel" by Brother John A. Widtsoe, the Young Men's Mutual Improvement Association Manual of
1908-1909. Both those latter brethren regard the earth as having
a very great antiquity.

The consensus of opinion among the foremost earth scientists places the beginning of life on this earth back at about one
billion years and the earth itself as two or three times that old.
Whether or not these scientists are right is something which is best
discussed dispassionately on the basis of a careful weighing of the
evidence. Any other approach will not influence serious scholars.

Here I will briefly sketch a few of the more or less familiar
lines of evidence on the age of the earth. The world is filled with
radioactive clocks which can be read with varying accuracy but
usually within ten percent or so and often considerably better. The
principle involved is essentially simple. The heaviest elements such
as uranium are unstable and fly apart sending out particles which
can be counted in a Geiger Counter. From the number of counts
one can tell how much of the radioactive substance one has. As the
substance continues to decompose, the counts decrease, always
remaining proportional to the number of particles not yet decomposed. Now the particles that are shot out are helium so that if the
decomposing uranium is enclosed in a rock this helium will also be
entrapped. Thus by determining how much helium is entrapped
and how much uranium is present in the rocks, one can tell exactly
how long it has been since the rocks were laid down in their present
form, since it always takes exactly the same amount of time for a
given fraction of the uranium to decompose.

There is another check on this. Each time a uranium atom
decomposes it leaves a lead atom behind as well as ejecting the
helium atom. Thus the ratio of these residual lead atoms to uranium
is another wonderful clock. Four and one half billion years must
elapse in order that half of the uranium present will be gone. Half
of what remains will decompose in another four and a half billion
years and so on. Thorium, another radioactive clock, has a half life
of fourteen billion years and there are a variety of other long time
clocks as well as some short time ones like carbon fourteen with a
half life of five and one half thousand years. The radioactive clocks,

together with the orderly way many sediments containing fossils are laid down, prove that the earth is billions of years old.

In my judgment anyone who denies this orderly decomposition of sediments with their built in radioactive clocks places himself in a scientifically untenable position. Actually the antiquity of the earth was no problem for one of our greatest Latter-day Saint leaders and scientists, Brother John A. Widtsoe (see Evidences and Reconciliations, Vol. I.) It also offers not the slightest difficulty to me and to most of my scientific LDS friends. The Lord made the world in some wonderful way that I can at best only dimly comprehend. it seems to me sacrilegious to presume that I really understand him and know just how he did it. He can only tell me in figurative speech which I dimly understand but which I expect to more completely comprehend in the Eternities to come.

Probably one of the most difficult problems in reading the scriptures is to decide what is to be taken literally and what is figurative. in this connection it seems to me that the Creator must operate with facts and with an understanding which goes entirely outside our understanding and of our experience. Because of this when someone builds up a system of logic, however careful and painstaking, which gives a positive answer to this difficult question, I can't help but wonder about it, particularly if it seems to run counter to the Creator's revelations written in the rocks. At least can't we move slowly in such matters?

Our prophets have been given to see clearly the road we should follow and can point the path to the celestial kingdom, but being human they too must walk by faith and wait and study in order to partly understand many of God's wonderful works. I can understand "Man—His Origin and Destiny" as the work of a great man who is fallible. It contains many serious scientific errors and much ill humor, which mar the many beautiful things in it. Since the Gospel is only that which is true, this book cannot be more than the private opinion of one of our great men to be admired for the fine things in it. I find it much less satisfactory in scientific matters than the excellent writings of Brother Talmage and Brother Widtsoe with which it is in frequent disagreement. Our scientists in general have no difficulty in reconciling Earth History and the Gospel as presented by our scientifically trained general authorities. The concern of most LDS scientists is as to what extent President Smith's interpretations must replace those of Brother Talmage and of Brother Widtsoe where they fail to agree with President Smith.

I hope my opinions offered for what they are worth will not seem presumptuous. Please feel free to make such use of this letter and the enclosed material as you may choose. Both Dr. Stokes and Dr. Smith are devout active members of the Church and are representative of our thoughtful LDS scientists. Each is willing to document his opinions further if it would be helpful.[8]

Henry Eyring

This letter, obviously meant as an educational device, circulated widely and brought some interesting responses. Lowell Bennion, then director of the church's Institute of Religion at the University of Utah, wrote Eyring: "Thanks to the courtesy of Elmo [Morgan], I read a copy of your letter to Adam S. Bennion and wish to congratulate you on the clarity, integrity, and humility which are evident throughout."[9]

When Smith obtained a copy of the letter a few months later in April, he felt obligated to respond directly to Eyring. Eyring promptly answered the lengthy letter in a conciliatory way and expressed gratitude that brethren in high positions in the church were allowed to disagree. The two letters, important documents in the development of the issue as shaped by both men's personalities, are reproduced.

Dear Brother Eyring:

At the time of the General Conference of the Church a copy of your letter to Elder Adam S. Bennion was placed in my hands and I was given to understand that it had been given rather wide circulation. This letter was no doubt solicited for the purpose of obtaining scientific information that would discredit what I have written. If so, it is evident that it was not intended for Elder Bennion alone. The nature of the letter indicates the necessity on my part for a reply, although it was not written to me, and presumably not intended that it should fall into my hands. Permit me to say that I have rejoiced in your great accomplishments in your chosen field. I was present on one occasion when honors were conferred upon you and I joined in the applause which I felt was merited. Moreover, I am always pleased when members of the Church obtain honors and are rewarded whether it is in the field of science, art, or any other field. The great discoveries that have been made during the past one hundred years and more have been of inestimable value to mankind. I am firmly convinced, however, that every discovery and invention has come through the inspiration of the Spirit of the Lord which was promised by the Lord through Joel, for this dispensation of The Fullness of Times.

My contention with our scientific brethren and men of the world lies in another field. I speak frankly and to some my words may appear harsh, and even filled with "ill humor," by those who hold to the theories I have attacked. Nevertheless I feel that I am justified in referring thus to those who hold these evolutionary theories and who feel themselves to be superior in intelligence and wisdom and entitled to treat the rest of us as school boys and need disciplining and have no right to call them in question. It remains a definite fact that the majority of scientists have considered themselves to be superior in intelligence and wisdom. I am reminded of Job's answer to his brethren: "No doubt but ye are the people, and wisdom shall die with you." I am sure I have not said things more harsh than have been said by these advocates of organic evolution. We who believe in the mission of Jesus Christ have been designated as "curs," our doctrines have been ridiculed. We have been designated as ignorant, harking back to the days of "primitive savagery and ignorance," for believing the foolish doctrine of an anthropomorphic God! Surely these advocates are not immune from some harsh words when we consider their arrogance and claim to superior wisdom. Are we not justified as much as was our Lord when he referred to the wise men among the Jews as "hypocrites," "whited sepulchers," and "sons of Satan"? It may hurt when we retaliate in the same language which they use in references to the sacred beliefs of those who accept the revelations in the Bible. I have stated sincerely that these men whom I have called in question "are honorable and presumably honest in their convictions." I have also spoken in the highest terms of the many who, through their discoveries have benefitted mankind. (See Man, page 22.) No one realizes more than I that I am "a fallible man"; and I accord to every other man, including the scientists, the same compliment.

There is one place, however, where I feel that men are infallible. That is when they, as prophets, reveal to us the word of the Lord. We have four published works which have been accepted by the members of the Church as *standard* in doctrine, revelation and government. These are: The Bible, the Book of Mormon, the Doctrine and Covenants and the Pearl of Great Price. We accept of course the Bible, as far as correctly translated. It is a well established fact that the copies coming to us based on translations, more or less semi-modern, contain many errors but when the Bible is in full accord with the other records, we accept what is written, whether the things written harmonize with the teachings of science or not.

President Joseph F. Smith has stated the case clearly:

The Church holds to the definite authority of divine revelation which must be the standard, and that, so-called "science" has changed from age to age in its deductions, and as divine revelation is truth, and must abide forever, views as to the lesser should conform to the positive statements of the greater; and further, that in institutions of education, its instructors must be in harmony in their teachings with the principles of doctrine. . . .

The truth persists, but the theories of philosophy change and are overthrown. What men use today as a scaffolding for scientific purposes from which to reach out into the unknown for truth, may be torn down tomorrow, having served its purpose, but faith is an eternal principle through which the humble believer may secure everlasting solace. It is the only way to find God! (*Man: His Origin and Destiny*, p. 8.)

The following I stated at the conference in October 1952:

So far as the philosophy and wisdom of the world are concerned, they mean nothing unless they conform to the revealed word of God. Any doctrine, whether it comes in the name of religion, science, philosophy, or whatever it may be, if it is in conflict with the revealed word of the Lord, will fail. It may appear plausible. It may be put before you in language that appeals and which you may not be able to answer. It may appear to be established by evidence that you cannot controvert, but all you need to do is to abide your time. Time will level all things. You will find that every doctrine, every principle, no matter how universally believed, if not in accord with the divine word of the Lord to his servants, will perish. Nor is it necessary for us to try to stretch the word of the Lord, in a vain attempt to make it conform to these theories and teachings. The word of the Lord shall not pass away unfulfilled, but these false doctrines and theories will all fail. Truth and only truth will remain when all else has perished.

I, as a fallible man, do not claim to be able to give the answers to all the questions propounded by science; but I am convinced that if there arises any theory which is in conflict with the revelations given by the Lord, they will perish. It is a great regret to me that our scientific brethren at times take a contrary view which is, if the theories of science appear to be definite and possibly true and are in conflict with the revelations in these Standard Works, *then science is right and the revelations are wrong!* This attitude certainly gets some of our brethren in trouble. This is placing the judgment of man superior to God!

Here are a few doctrines taught by revelation which are rejected by evolutionary scientists because they are in conflict with their theories:

1. Adam was the first man on earth. This is declared in the Bible, the Book of Mormon, Doctrine and Covenants and Pearl of Great Price. In the Prophet Joseph Smith's revision of the Bible, the last verse in the lineage of Christ in Luke, reads as follows: "And of Enos, and of Seth, and of Adam, who was formed of God, and the *first man on earth.*" This is the same as recorded in the Pearl of Great Price and the Doctrine and Covenants, Section 84:16. Those who accept organic evolution contradict this doctrine.

2. The scriptures teach that Adam was the first flesh on the earth. This is the doctrine in the Bible, Book of Mormon, and Pearl of Great Price, but it is rejected by the advocates of organic evolution.

3. These scriptures teach that Adam was *not* subject to the mortal and spiritual death before the Fall, and that the fall brought these deaths into the world. This doctrine is denied by organic evolutionists.

4. These scriptures teach that Jesus came into the world to atone for Adam's transgressions and through his death redeemed Adam and all mankind from the effects of the fall. This is denied by the organic evolutionists.

5. These scriptures teach that through the death of Jesus Christ came the resurrection of the dead, and that *every soul* will be raised with spirit and body inseparably united. This is denied by organic evolutionists.

6. These scriptures teach that this earth is passing through seven days of *temporal* existence of one thousand of our years for

a day, and that it was not temporal before the fall. This is clearly stated in the Bible, the Doctrine and Covenants and the Pearl of Great Price, but it is definitely and positively denied by organic evolutionists.

7. These divine records promise us that the earth on which we dwell will be renewed and restored to its primitive beauty for one thousand years and be cleansed of all its iniquity. This is denied by most scientists.

8. These divine records declare that the earth shall die, for it is a living body, and will rise again in the resurrection through the redemption of Jesus Christ, to become a celestial globe and the abode of the righteous. Scientist[s] preach a far different doctrine.

Now, Dr. Eyring, you state that I have "an impressive compilation of scriptural references on Earth History and on statements of selected church leaders, but that I have avoided the quotations of the "trained scientists among the general authorities," and you mentioned two, Dr. James E. Talmage and Dr. John A. Widtsoe. In my defense I have to say that I quoted the Prophet Joseph Smith, Presidents Brigham Young, John Taylor, Joseph F. Smith and his counselors, Parley P. Pratt and Orson Pratt and others. Four of these held the keys of the Priesthood and revelations for the Church, the others were taught under the guidance of the Prophet Joseph Smith. Moreover, I backed what they had to say by the revelations in the Standard Works of the Church which we have received as the word of the Lord. Beyond such eminent testimony there was no need for me to go.

You also said: "It would be instructive to have President Smith comment on 'The Earth and Man,' by Dr. James E.Talmage, delivered from the tabernacle August 9, 1931, and published by the Church of Jesus Christ of Latter-day Saints." I assure you that it would have been a pleasure to have commented on that talk. No one is more familiar with it and how it came to be published than I, and I can state positively that it was not published by the Church, nor by the approval of the Authorities of the Church. There are some circumstances concerning this discourse which I think it is hardly proper for me to write inasmuch as the First Presidency, one of whom was President David O. McKay, gave the answer to Dr. Sterling B. Talmage in reply to an inquiry from him, which, in my opinion, sets forth the facts as I have stated them. I suggest that you write Dr. Sterling B. Talmage and ask him to permit you to read this communication from the First Presidency, Presidents Heber J. Grant, J. Reuben Clark, Jr., and David O. McKay, dated December 19, 1935.

I understand that some of the things taught by Dr. Widtsoe in his MIA lesson are no longer held as acceptable theories even in the scientific world. So far as his articles on "Evidences and Reconciliations" are concerned, I would be happy to discuss them with you personally, if we could do so calmly. Likewise some of the views of Dr. James E. Talmage in this memorable discourse and others of his writings. It might be of considerable interest.

So far as the evidence is concerned of the "Radio-active clocks," perhaps it might be possible for you and me to come to some common understanding as to the exceeding length of time it takes for the uranium, thorium and other elements to decompose. We might agree to change the viewpoint of their beginning. From what I have read it appears that the scientists look upon these elements as having been placed on the earth in their virgin, or creative state, when the earth was formed, and have been slowly but consistently, disintegrating ever since. The Lord revealed to the Prophet Joseph Smith, and it is recorded in the Doctrine and Covenants (Section 93:33) that the elements are eternal. I can readily believe that when the earth was formed, the Lord brought the elements together and placed them in the earth wisely, and in such a manner that they would be discovered in his own due time for the use of man. I can believe that the gold, silver, copper, tin, carbon and every other element, including lead, if you please, were brought to their respective places of deposit in the rocks and the earth and that they had been existing from untold ages, before the earth was formed. This could be true of radio-active elements which could have been brought here as well as any other elements in the condition in which they are found. I have been taught to believe that the Lord knows the end from the beginning and that these things have at times been revealed to his servants who were told to seal them up, for they were not to come forth until the due time of the Lord. It will be no surprise to me to discover that the Lord when he comes will do as he has said:

Yea, verily I say unto you, in that day when the Lord shall come, he shall reveal all things—

Things which have passed, and hidden things which no man knew, things of the earth, by which it was made, and the purpose and the end thereof—

Things most precious, things that are above, and things that are, beneath, things that are in the earth, and upon the earth and in the heaven.

I am sure that when the day comes there will be many surprises when the history recorded in the beginning by prophecy is revealed and the activities of our present day will be discovered to have been recorded many centuries ago.

Yours sincerely,
Joseph Fielding Smith

Dear President Smith:

Thanks for your letter of April 15, 1955. I am happy that you read my letter, which you refer to, as it expresses accurately my point of view.

Considering the difference in training of the members of the Church, I never cease to marvel at the degree of agreement found among believing Latter-Day-Saints. So far from being disturbed to find that Brother Talmage, Brother Widtsoe and yourself didn't always see scientific matters alike, this situation seems natural and as it should be. It will be a sad day for the Church and its members when the degree of disagreement you brethren expressed is not allowed.

I am convinced that if the Lord required that His children understand His works before they could be saved that no one would be saved. It seems to me that to struggle for agreement on scientific matters in view of the disparity in background which the members of the Church have is to put emphasis in the wrong place. In my judgments there is room in the Church for people who think that the periods of creation were (a) 24 hours, (b) 1000 years, or (c) millions of years. I think it is fine to discuss these questions and for each individual to try to convert the other to what he thinks is right, but in matters where apparently equally reliable authorities disagree, I prefer to make haste slowly.

Since we agree on so many things, I trust we can amicably disagree on a few. I have never liked, for example, the idea that many of the horizontally lying layers with their fossils are wreckage from earlier worlds. In any case, the Lord created the world and my faith does not hinge on the detailed procedures.

Thanks again for your kindly, thoughtful letter.[10]

Sincerely your brother,
Henry Eyring

Following exchange of these letters, Smith invited Eyring and
Cook to visit with him. Later Eyring recalled the substance of that
meeting: "A lively hour-long discussion [on "radioactive dating"]
ensued. As so often happens, each person brought up the argument
which supported his position and we parted each with much the same
position he held when the discussion began. But what was much more
important, the discussion proceeded on a completely friendly basis
without recrimination and each matter ended there. No one was
asked to conform to some preconceived position. The church is
committed to the truth whatever its source and each man is expected
to seek it out honestly and prayerfully. It is, of course, another matter
to teach as a doctrine of the church something which is manifestly
contradictory and to urge it in and out of season. The author has
never felt the least constraints in investigating any matter strictly on
its merits, and this close contact with President Smith bore out this
happy conclusion."[11]

In the spring of 1956, church president David O. McKay
requested information from Eyring on a paper Cook had written for
Smith questioning the reliability of radioactive time clocks. Cook had
argued that carbon dating was valid only if it was in equilibrium in
the earth as a whole, but such an equilibrium would take 30,000 years
before an overall unbalance could be detected experimentally. Cook
also cited continental drift to account for Noah's flood and the
dividing of the earth in the days of Peleg.[12] Eyring's reply was again
tactful but firm:

Dear President McKay:
    In accordance with your request, I am writing my opinion
regarding Dr. Melvin A. Cook's paper, "Geological Chronometry."
Dr. Cook has done a great deal of reading in the past few months
and has thought intensively on the subject. His manuscript points
up the accepted fact that there are pit falls in accurate radioactive
dating. He has also provided a useful bibliography for the serious
student. As he points out, the all but universal opinion of earth

scientists at present is that the earth is around 3 billion years old. Three hundred years ago the general opinion in Christendom placed the earth's age at around thirteen thousand years or less.

The change in viewpoint came as the result of intensive study by many scholars with an outlay of time and effort equivalent to many millions of dollars. One may expect to upset this river of opinion only by supplying a massive array of carefully established facts. In my opinion, Dr. Cook has not succeeded in doing this. This is likewise the opinion of his geological colleagues, who have listened to several lectures he has given recently on the campus.

In particular his argument that radioactive carbon in fact supports an age of about 12,600 years rests on very shaky foundations. His argument requires that the content of radioactive carbon in the atmosphere started at zero concentration in the beginning and has since risen to about three quarters of its final steady-state value. The basis for this is extremely tenuous. To plead that[,] he quotes the same authorities whom he finds so unreliable on other points[, which] leaves much to be desired. If in fact the radioactive carbon content of the atmosphere is presently more nearly its final steady-state value, a correspondingly greater antiquity for the earth would be given by his calculation. The usually accepted assumption is that for all practical purposes the radioactive carbon content has already reached its final steady-state value. This assumption leads to the usually accepted great antiquity of the earth.

I am sure if any of the brethren have the time and desire to listen to a scientific presentation of pertinent evidence of the great antiquity of the earth presented by believing Latter-Day Saints that such lectures could be readily arranged. In my judgment, such considerations are without bearing on the real question as to the divinity of the gospel, but are naturally of great scientific interest.

I hope you will feel free to show my letter to any person whom it might interest. If you care to talk to me further, I will be happy to call at your office any time.[13]

Sincerely your brother
Henry Eyring

It is difficult to judge what effect Eyring's letter had, but by the next spring the Quorum and First Presidency had, at least internally, expressed the view that the church had no official position on the matter of evolution and related questions and that *Man, His*

Origins and Destiny represented the personal views of its author.[14]

Interestingly enough during this controversy, Eyring and a colleague, Frank H. Johnson, wrote a paper on evolution and rate theory, Eyring's scientific specialty, called "The Critical Complex Theory of Biogenesis." This paper outlined a theory of prebiological evolution and addressed the question of why living things are optically active. Even in different species, the amino acids are all of the left-handed configuration (l). Using absolute rate theory and estimates of reactant concentrations, a reasonable rate of appearance of optically active templates was arrived at. These templates, capable of self-replication, began the era of biological evolution. But the chemistry is the same for the right-handed configurations (d) and the likelihood of a world with isomers of the latter type in living things is just as great. If analogous events occurred in nuclear evolution, it is possible to visualize a world with positive electrons rotating about negative nuclei. The result is that there are four possible evolutionary worlds: l-type and positive nuclei (as our world is), l-type and negative nuclei, d-type and positive nuclei, or d-type and negative nuclei.[15] For Eyring it was not how this earth was created nor how life was placed on it that mattered. God had created this world and the life on it the way he did it, and that could not be changed. "The Critical Complex Theory of Biogenesis" explained how it might have otherwise happened.

During the decade of the 1950s Eyring had clearly established himself as an important authority for Mormons on the subject of science and religion. He avoided being engulfed in controversy. Many encouraged him to take a more rigid stance, but he believed implicitly in the Mormon gospel and in the concept that both science and religion could provide answers to life's questions. As a result he became the church's example during the next decade of how one can achieve academically and remain devout. In 1961 he was featured in a church-sponsored film, "Search for Truth," produced by Brigham Young University. Its message was precisely what Eyring had advocated his entire scientific life: the principles of science and religion are in complete accord. The film, directed toward strengthening the youth of the church, contained dramatized scenes from Eyring's early life when he left for the university in 1919 and ended with his search for truth in "the six worlds of today": the world in which we live, the biological world, the chemical world, the astronomical world, the nuclear world, and the spiritual world.[16]

In addition to fireside talks on science, Eyring treated science and religion in articles for the *Improvement Era* and *The Instructor*. In 1958 Paul R. Green compiled *Science and Your Faith in God*, writings and talks by seven prominent Mormon scientists, including five of Eyring's early articles.[17] A good friend, Dr. Francis W. Kirkham, published *The Faith of a Scientist* in the spring of 1967. The book contained twenty-seven articles by Eyring on science and religion and two short, previously published biographical sketches. Apostle Mark E. Petersen was so impressed with the collection that he spear-headed a project to reproduce a portion of the book in paperback for official distribution. Nine essays were selected, and during 1969 and 1970, 146,000 copies were distributed principally to the youth of the church.

An LDS woman from Arizona, after reading Eyring's book and discussing the possibility of pre-Adamites with her husband, asked Eyring's opinion on the theory that this earth was created from the materials of an older one. He responded: "I was trained as a mining engineer so that the evidence seems to me to point toward an age of the earth between four and five billion years and to the existence of pre-Adamic man. I don't think that it is reasonable to explain the observed geologic formations on the theory that they were moved from some other worlds. I have no difficulty reconciling myself to the idea of life before Adam and to a great age of the earth. Our scriptural accounts are brief and don't seem to me to rule out these possibilities. The scriptural emphasis is on God's dealings with Adam and his descendants and the treatment of pre-Adamic history is sketchy, no doubt for a good reason. It seems, to me, clear that the Lord used the Prophet Joseph to restore His gospel. This is the important thing for me. Just how He runs the world, I'm obliged to leave up to Him. All I can do is find out how he does it by every means available."[18]

In 1967 N. Eldon Tanner of the church's First Presidency asked Eyring how to respond to a letter he had received asking why BYU required their teachers to acquire doctorates when higher education frequently made LDS teachers "Lose their faith." Eyring answered: "The gospel embraces all truth. Brigham Young especially emphasized the propriety of seeking all truth. The assumption that because a man understands something about the operation of the Universe, he will necessarily be less faithful is a gratuitous assumption contradicted by numberless examples. God, who understands all about the Universe, is apparently, not troubled by this knowledge. Some people drift when they study, but some people drift when they don't study. If the Church espouses the cause of ignorance, it will alienate more people than if it advises man to seek after truth, even at some risk."[19]

These two letters are typical of the many in Eyring's files, each containing a healthy dose of his commitment to science. Possibly the best summary, however, comes from an address he delivered on 4 December 1979 at the University of Utah shortly after receiving the Berzelius Gold Medal from the Swedish Academy. His intention was to give the advice he might share if it were his last lecture. For Eyring the supreme good would be to bring happiness to as many people as possible for as long as possible. How? He advised his listeners: first, be "honorable" in all their doings and "have no secrets"; second, make plans to be flexible enough to change; third, "work hard and do everything well," citing his mother who took her knitting when she visited; and fourth, "compete only with yourself" ("the reason people like you is because you're helpful, not because you're smart").[20] That philosophy made Henry Eyring a folk hero in the church.

NOTES

1. Conversation with Sterling McMurrin, 17 May 1978.

2. Marba C. Josephson, "Henry Eyring—Distinguished Scientist and Churchman," *Improvement Era* 51 (Feb. 1948): 81, 111. His speech was reprinted in pamphlet form and distributed by the church in 1956. In 1958 it was published in a compilation by Paul R. Green, *Science and Your Faith in God* (Salt Lake City: Bookcraft, 1958), 11-17, and in 1967 in Henry Eyring, *The Faith of a Scientist* (Salt Lake City: Bookcraft, 1967), 31-37.

3. For a thorough discussion, see Duane E. Jeffrey, "Seers, Savants and Evolution: The Uncomfortable Interface," *Dialogue: A Journal of Mormon Thought* 8 (Autumn/Winter 1974): 41-75.

4. See J. Reuben Clark, Jr., "The Charted Course of the Church in Education," address to LDS Seminary and Institute teachers, 8 Aug. 1938 (Salt Lake City: Church Education System, n.d.).

5. Jeffrey, "Seers, Savants," 65-66.

6. Joseph Fielding Smith, *Man, His Origin and Destiny* (Salt Lake City: Deseret Book, 1954). For a concise view of his position, see Bruce R. McConkie, comp., *Doctrines of Salvation—Sermons and Writings of Joseph Fielding Smith*, 3 vols. (Salt Lake City: Bookcraft, 1954), 1: chaps. 5, 9.

7. Edward L. Kimball, "A Dialogue with Henry Eyring," *Dialogue: A Journal of Mormon Thought* 8 (Autumn/Winter 1973): 102.

8. Henry Eyring to Adam S. Bennion, 16 Dec. 1954, in possession of Henry Eyring family; photocopy in Steven H. Heath, "Henry Eyring, Mormon Scientist," M.A. thesis, University of Utah, 1980, appen. 11.

9. Lowell Bennion to Henry Eyring, 15 Jan. 1955, in possession of Mrs. Winifred Eyring, Salt Lake City, Utah.

10. Joseph Fielding Smith to Henry Eyring, 15 Apr. 1955, in possession of Mrs. Winifred Eyring; Henry Eyring to Joseph Fielding Smith, 18 Apr. 1955.

11. Henry Eyring, "A Tribute to President Joseph Fielding Smith," *Dialogue: A Journal of Mormon Thought* 7 (Spring 1972): 15-16.

12. See Melvin A. Cook and M. Garfield Cook, *Science and Mormonism* (Salt Lake City: Deseret Book, 1968).

13. Henry Eyring to David O. McKay, 26 Mar. 1956, in possession of Mrs. Winifred Eyring.

14. Jeffrey, "Seers, Savants," 66-67.

15. Henry Eyring and Frank H. Johnson, "The Critical Complex Theory of Biogenesis," in *The Influence of Temperature on Biological Systems* (Washington, D.C.: American Physiological Society, 1957), 1-8.

16. Dorothy O. Rea, "Church Sponsors Film 'Search for Truth' on Science, Religion," *Church News*, 23 Dec. 1961, 47, 7, 8. See also Henry Eyring, "Our Five Worlds," *The Instructor*, June 1953, 171-72. This article was revised and published as "Our Six Worlds" in 1967 in Eyring's *The Faith of a Scientist*.

17. The other scientists were Carl J. Christensen, Harvey Fletcher, Joseph F. Merrill, Frederick J. Pack, John A. Widtsoe, and Franklin S. Harris.

18. Rosemary Kutch to Henry Eyring, 22 Jan. 1971, and Henry Eyring to Rosemary Kutch, 27 Jan. 1971, in possession of Mrs. Winifred Eyring.

19. N. Eldon Tanner to Henry Eyring, 16 Oct. 1967, and Henry Eyring to N. Eldon Tanner, 19 Oct. 1967, in possession of Mrs. Winifred Eyring.

20. From notes taken by Harold Bauman, history professor, University of Utah, who was present at the lecture.

9.
Seers, Savants, and Evolution: The Uncomfortable Interface

Duane E. Jeffery

EVER SINCE HIS GREAT SYNTHESIS, DARWIN'S NAME HAS BEEN A SOURCE of discomfort to the religious world. Too sweeping to be fully fathomed, too revolutionary to be easily accepted, but too well documented to be ignored, his concepts of evolution[1] by natural selection have been hotly debated for well over a century.[2] I do not propose here to consider the validity of Darwin's propositions but instead focus on a more immediate concern: What is the doctrine of the Mormon church on the subject of evolution? For statements on church doctrine, we are traditionally referred to the four standard works. But scripture is not of itself sufficient, and authoritative statements can originate from the president of the church.[3] Also counselors in the First Presidency share with the president in governing the affairs and doctrines of the church.[4] Statements by other authorities will be discussed only as needed for perspective, since they are not binding or fully authoritative.

The researcher faces an interesting problem: utterances on the subject in the nineteenth century are scattered and few. Compared with the output of other religious groups, Mormonism produced a tiny body of literature dealing directly with the matter of evolution.[5] The most likely explanation appears to be that LDS doctrines central to the evolution issue were not well developed. They were still in a sufficient state of flux that no direct confrontation was

155

really possible or necessary. Simply put, the church had no defined basic doctrines directly under attack.

On some matters nineteenth-century Mormonism was clearly on the side of science. In no real way could the church have been classed as party to the literalistic views of more orthodox Christian groups. Indeed Mormonism was a theologic maverick to Christian orthodoxy. The differences were deep and profound, and on several issues Mormonism was much more closely aligned with the prevailing concepts of science.[6]

For all intents and purposes, the modern story of evolution began 24 November 1859, the date of the release of Darwin's classic *On the Origin of Species*. The earlier announcement of the theory of evolution by natural selection presented as joint papers by Darwin and A. R. Wallace on the evening of 1 July 1858 to the Linnaean Society had caused little stir. Not so the 1859 publication. Public response was immediate and heated. The following five concepts are useful for comparing Mormonism to the doctrinal positions taken by science and prevailing Christian theology of the last century.

1. *Belief in an ex nihilo creation*. The Christian doctrine meant literally creation out of nothing. More recent attempts to cast it in the light of matter-energy conversions are distortions that betray the earlier meaning. The doctrine, of course, finds little place in contemporary science, which deals with conversions of matter and energy but is generally foreign to the idea of something coming from nothing.

It is difficult to find in Mormonism a philosophical doctrine that has been more consistently denounced. The concept is usually derived from Genesis 1:1: "In the beginning God created the heaven and the earth." It is here that Joseph Smith chose to set the theologians straight: "Now I ask all the learned men who hear me, why the learned men who are preaching salvation say, that God created the heavens and the earth out of nothing, and the reason is they are unlearned; they account it blasphemy to contradict the idea, they will call you a fool.—I know more than all the world put together, and the Holy Ghost within me comprehends more than all the world, and I will associate with it. The word create came from the word *baurau*; it does not mean so; it means to organize; the same as a man would organize a ship. Hence we infer that God had materials to organize the world out of chaos; chaotic matter, which is element, and in which dwells all the glory. Element had an existence from the time he had. The pure principles of element, are principles that can never be destroyed. They may be organized and re-organized; but not destroyed."[7] This view of Smith has been affirmed ever since. Brigham Young continually preached it as did his contemporaries among Mormon church authorities.[8]

Creation *ex nihilo* also means that all things were created directly by God and therefore have contingent being.[9] In this view only God had necessary being; all else depends (is contingent) on him for its existence and maintenance. This concept leads to a morass of theological difficultes, not the least of which are resposibility for evil and denial of the free agency of humanity.[10] Mormonism, while it does not escape from some of these difficulties, begins from a different base. God is not the creator of matter—nor ultimately of humanity. According to Joseph Smith, "Element had an existence from the time [God] had. . . . it had no beginning, and can have no end." He continued: "I must come to the resurrection of the dead, the soul, the mind of man, the immortal spirit. All men say God created it in the beginning. The very idea lessens man in my estimation; I do not believe the doctrine, I know better. . . . The mind of man is as immortal as God himself. I know that my testimony is true, hence when I talk to these mourners; what have they lost, they are only seperated from their bodies for a short season; their spirits existed co-equal with God, and they now exist in a place where they converse together, the same as we do on the earth. Is it logic to say that a spirit is immortal, and yet have a beginning? Because if a spirit have a beginning it will have an end. . . . I might with boldness proclaim from the house tops, that God never did have power to create a spirit of man at all. God himself could not create himself: intelligence exists upon a self existent principle, it is a spirit from age to age, and there is no creation about it."[11] Thus both matter and the basic identity of humanity share necessary existence with God. The doctrines have been taught continually by Smith's successors.[12]

2. *Belief that the earth was created in six twenty-four hour days, and is only about 6,000 years old.* Not all Christian theologians were as extreme as John Lightfoot, vice-chancellor of the University of Cambridge, who insisted that the creation of the earth took place "on the

twenty-third of October, 4004 B.C., at nine o'clock in the morning." Views of the earth's age generally ranged from about 4,000 to 6,000 years before Jesus Christ.[13] Science, of course, could not agree. Darwin in the first edition of *Origin* had opted for an age of several hundreds of millions of years. Even devoutly religious scientists who opposed him, such as the physicist Lord Kelvin, produced estimates for the earth's age in the neighborhood of twenty million years. Estimates this small were painful to Darwin, since they seemed far too short for natural selection to have played the role he postulated for it. The age of the earth has since been pushed ever further back. Current estimates range from 4.5 to 5 billion years.

Mormon speakers have ranged widely on this subject. Statements from the presiding quorum kept the church non-committed but open to the possibility of a long age. There seems to have been no one who opted for twenty-four hour creation days, unless one wishes to so interpret Oliver Cowdery's statement, published while he was assistant (associate) president of the church, that he believed the scriptures "are meant to be understood according to their *literal* reading, as those passages which teach us of the creation of the world" (emphasis his).[14] Joseph Smith left no clear statement on the matter. On the Christmas day after Smith's death, his associate W. W. Phelps wrote a letter to Smith's brother William. Therein he refers among other things to the contributions of Smith and to the eventual triumph of truth and Mormonism. One of Smith's accomplishments was the Book of Abraham, an incomplete text produced in conjunction with some Egyptian papyri. Phelps exulted: "Well, now, Brother William, when the house of Israel begin to come into the glorious mysteries of the kingdom, and find that Jesus Christ, whose goings forth, as the prophets said, have been from of old, from eternity: and that eternity, agreeably to the records found in the catacombs of Egypt, has been going on in this system, (not this world) almost *two thousand five hundred and fifty five millions* of years: and to know at the same time, that deists, geologists and others are trying to prove that matter must have existed hundreds of thousands of years;—it almost tempts the flesh to fly to God, or muster faith like Enoch to be translated."[15]

This reference has been cited many times in Mormon literature. Some have used it to indicate that the planet earth is 2.55 billion years old. Others, taking careful note of the phrase in parentheses, insist that it has no such meaning, that it refers to a much larger physical system and has no bearing on the age of the earth. Phelps never clarified the statement. However, the context of Phelps rejoicing over the developing agreement between this statement and the efforts of geologists to establish long time spans gives support to those who interpret the statement as applying to the planet earth.

After Smith's death one can find other beliefs by nineteenth-century Mormon authorities pertaining to the age of the earth. A prominent one, taught by certain apostles, was that the seven days of creation were each 1,000 years in duration, and the earth was therefore approximately 13,000 years old, calculating approximately 6,000 years since Adam's fall. This concept received limited support from members of the First Presidency. Their statements generally carried the sentiment that the age of the earth was really not known and did not matter. Brigham Young thus commented:

"It was observed here just now that we differ from the Christian world in our religious faith and belief; and so we do very materially. I am not astonished that infidelity prevails to a great extent among the inhabitants of the earth, for the religious teachers of the people advance many ideas and notions for truth which are in opposition to and contradict facts demonstrated by science, and which are generally understood. Says the scientific man, 'I do not see your religion to be true; I do not understand the law, light, rules, religion, or whatever you call it, which you say God has revealed; it is confusion to me, and if I submit to and embrace your views and theories I must reject the facts which science demonstrates to me.' This is the position, and the line of demarcation has been plainly drawn, by those who profess Christianity between the sciences and revealed religion. You take, for instance, our geologists, and they tell us that this earth has been in existence for thousands and millions of years. They think, and they have good reason for their faith, that their researches and investigations enable them to demonstrate that this earth has been in existence as long as they assert it has; and they say, 'If the Lord, as religionists declare, made the earth out of nothing in six days, six thousands years ago, our studies are all in vain; but by what we can learn from nature and the immutable laws of the Creator as revealed therein, we know that your theories are incorrect and consequently we must reject your religions as false and vain, we must be what you call infidels, with the demonstrated truths of science in our possession; or, rejecting those truths, become enthusiasts in, what you call, Christianity.'

"In these respects we differ from the Christian world, for our religion will not clash with or contradict the facts of science in any particular. You may take geology, for instance, and it is a true science; not that I would say for a moment that all the conclusions and deductions of its professors are true, but its leading principles are; they are facts—they are eternal; and to assert that the Lord made this earth out of nothing is preposterous and impossible. God never made something out of nothing; it is not in the economy or law by which the worlds were, are, or will exist. There is an eternity before us, and it is full of matter; and if we but understand enough of the Lord and his ways, we would say that he took of this matter and organized this earth from it. How long it has been organized it is not for me to say, and I do not care anything about it. As for the Bible account of the creation we may say that the Lord gave it to Moses, or rather Moses obtained the history and traditions of the fathers, and from these picked out what he considered necessary, and that account has been handed down from age to age, and we have got it, no matter whether it is correct or not, and whether the Lord found the earth empty and void, whether he made it out of nothing or out of the rude elements; or whether he made it in six days or in as many millions of years, is and will remain a matter of speculation in the minds of men unless he gives revelation on the subject. If we understood the process of creation there would be no mystery about it, it would be all reasonable and plain, for there is no mystery except to the ignorant. This we know by what we have learned naturally."[16]

3. *Fixity or immutability of species; that all species were created originally in Eden by the Creator and do not change in any significant way.* Theologians bought a bad deal when they adopted the notion of fixity of species. The irony of the matter is that the notion is not a religious one at all but an idea prematurely bought from science. The Genesis scriptures speak only of "kind."[17] Indeed no one worried much about it until about the seventeenth century when John Ray (1627-1705) and Carl Linné (Linnaeus) (1707-78) laid the foundations of modern taxonomy and systematics.

Linné's case is particularly instructive. Few people have ever so completely dominated the intellectual thought of their time. His gift and passion for cataloging organisms was unmatched and contagious; plants and animals were brought to him from all over the world for proper naming and classification. His passion was to name everything, to pigeonhole all living things into the neat compartments he attributed to the Genesis creations. He thus declared a fixity of species, unchangeable entities each descended from a specific Edenic stock, by whose analysis one caught a glimpse of the Creator at work. But the concept was an illusion, one which tragically escaped his control. For it caught the human fancy, and when in his maturity Linné realized that it was worthless, he was powerless to change its hold on the human mind. By then it had been seized on as a classic demonstration of the neatness of creation. Science, self-correcting as it eventually is, finally grew openly beyond the strictures of Linné's early concepts. Species obviously could change and did. The battle with theology was joined after Darwin proposed a mechanism (natural selection) for such change.

What position on species fixity was being articulated by the leaders of Mormonism up to and during this critical time? The subject hardly ever caught their attention. Casual statements that God and humankind are of the same species occur periodically, but beyond that the treatment is sketchy. Speaking on divine decrees, Joseph Smith commented: "The sea also has its bounds which it cannot pass. God has set many signs on the earth, as well as in the heavens; for instance, the oak of the forest, the fruit of the tree, the herb of the field—all bear a sign that seed hath been planted there; for it is a decree of the Lord that every tree, plant, and herb bearing seed should bring forth of its kind, and cannot come forth after any other law or principle."[18] No mention here of species at all, just the generic "kind," and no definition of that. For all its looseness, however, a certain sentiment is evidenced which tends to favor some sort of fixity.

Eighteen years later in 1860 Brigham Young touched the subject. In a sermon launched upon the matter of death and the resurrection, he asserted: "The whole Scriptures plainly teach us that we are the children of that God who framed the world. Let us look round and see whether we can find a father and son in this congregation. Do we see one an elephant, and the other a hen? No. Does a father that looks like a human being have a son like an ape, going on all fours? No; the son looks like his father. There is an endless variety of distinction in the few features that compose the human face, yet children have in their countenances and general expression of figure and temperament a greater or less likeness of their parents. You do not see brutes rising from human beings. Every species is true to its kind. The children of men are featured alike and walk erect."[19] As it is, this does not constitute a statement against the scientific version of changes in species. Modern evolution texts carry many statements concerning developmental canalization and genetic homeostasis which express these same concepts. But still Young's words express a sentiment towards fixity.

These are virtually the only authoritative statements during the early Darwinian period. Although such comments take on the flavor of the theology of their day, a doctrine of species fixity was not of prime concern in the nineteenth-century LDS church.

4. *Belief that life depends on an activating vital force which is immaterial and divine, the spirit or soul.* While not strictly a product of the Darwinian revolution and in many ways antedating it, the question of the existence of a vital force became an important part of the discussion surrounding Darwinism. Particularly was this true in later years of the furor, when vitalism was offered in various forms as an alternative to the causalistic theories which were more in vogue.[20]

Mormon speakers on this matter glimpsed a view different from the usual Christian positions, but their tenets are poorly appreciated in the church today. In fact the general concept in the church today is essentially standard Christian.

A recent treatment outlines the basic positions of vitalism and mechanism: "Life, the subject matter of biology, is a phenomenon intimately connected with matter. Biology, therefore, must be concerned with the relationship between matter and the phenomenon we call life. Animate and Inanimate things have matter in common, and it is in their materiality that the two can best be compared. In this comparison, two theories, vitalism and mechanism, compete for the mastery. The vitalist sees in a living organism the convergence of two essentially different factors. For him matter is shaped and dominated by a life principle; unaided, matter could never give rise to life. The mechanist, on the other hand, denies any joint action of two essentially different factors. He holds that matter is capable of giving rise to life by its own intrinsic forces. The mechanist considers matter to be 'alive,' the vitalist considers that something immaterial lives in and through matter."[21] To Mormons the divergence between the two approaches is seen in two basic issues: whether an outside force is necessary to make a body "alive," and whether such an outside force is material. The popular nineteenth-century theological view of course was that life is due to a non-material force. Science, profiting from a long series of investigations on spontaneous generation dating primarily from Redi in the seventeenth century to Pasteur and Tyndall in the 1870s, became associated with mechanism (materialism). The reason for this latter association is not that either view has been rigorously proved. It is rather that the materialistic view allows experimentation whereas the vitalist view does not, since one is hard pressed to experiment with immaterial things.

Teachings of the church in the nineteenth century on the issues of spirit, life, vital force, and so on were in a state of flux. B. H. Roberts pointed out that Joseph Smith sometimes used the terms "intelligence," "mind," "spirit," and "soul" interchangeably—"life" and even "light" could be added to the list as well.[22] That Mormonism accepts the view that living things possess spirits is well known. Our spirit is said to be the result of spirit birth in a pre-mortal state. That "spirit," "spirits," and so on are material is likewise clear: "There is no such thing as immaterial matter. All spirit is matter, but it is more fine or pure, and can only be discerned by purer eyes; . . . it is all matter" (D&C 131:7-8). This canonized statement has been the justification for a long series of missionary tracts and doctrinal assertions spelling out that Mormonism is a materialistic system. There can be no identification whatever with sentiments of immateriality. To early Mormons immateriality was virtually synonymous with atheism.

Beyond this, the thinking becomes less clear. Brigham Young in an 1856 discourse described spirit or life as a property of matter itself. Speaking of "natural, true philosophy" and developing the idea that the processes associated with death are a manifestation of inherent life in matter, he continued: "What is commonly called death does not destroy the body, it only causes a separation of spirit and body, but the principle of life, inherent in the native elements, of which the body is composed, still continues with the particles of that body and causes it to decay, to dissolve itself into the elements of which it was composed, and all of which continue to have life. When the spirit given to man leaves the body, the tabernacle begins to decompose, is that death? No, death only separates the spirit and body, and a principle of life still operates in the untenanted taberna- cle, but in a different way, and producing different effects from those observed while it was tenanted by the spirit. There is not a particle of element which is not filled with life, and all space is filled with element; there is no such thing as empty space, though some philoso- phers contend that there is.

"Life in various proportions, combinations, conditions, etc., fills all matter. Is there life in a tree when it ceases to put forth leaves? You see it standing upright, and when it ceases to bear leaves and fruit you say it is dead, but that is a mistake. It still has life, but that life operates upon the tree in another way, and continues to operate until it resolves it to the native elements. It is life in another condition that begins to operate upon man, upon animal, upon vegetation, and upon minerals when we see the change termed dissolution. There is life in the material of the fleshly tabernacle, independent of the spirit given of God to undergo this probation. There is life in all matter, throughout the vast extent of all the eternities; it is in the rock, the sand, the dust, in water, air, the gases, and, in short, in every description and organization of matter, wether it be solid, liquid, or gasesous, particle operating with particle."[23]

Elsewhere Young repeatedly referred to "organization" as a key in determining differences in life quality.[24] Taken with the concepts above, such teachings resemble those of the mechanists- materialists. To the mechanist life is an expression of a unique combination or organization of matter. At this most fundamental level, differences between science and Mormonism as taught by Young are reduced to mere semantics. The points of agreement are profound. Young's entire philosophy, to be sure, ranges far beyond matters that are in the realm of science, but at the fundamental level, at the point of contact, they are in essential agreement.

5. *Special creation of humanity; that God literally molded Adam's body from the dust of the ground and blew into it the breath of life, the spirit.*

Here we venture into the hottest point of discussion. In *The Origin* Darwin marshalled one powerful argument after another for the evolution of plant and animal species from earlier forms. Only one sentence, on the penultimate page, was directed to humankind: "Much light will be thrown on the origin of man and his history." Though Darwin was not yet ready to tackle this problem, others were not so retiring. The issue was quickly joined. Huxley and others insisted that the human body was related to and derived from other life forms; theologians of the day insisted with equal vehemence that the body was the result of a special creative act, independently developed from the dust of the ground by the shaping hand of the Creator, and activated by "the breath of life." Mormons accept as part of their canon the same scripture-text utilized by orthodox theologians, Genesis 2:7 in the King James rendition. The Book of Abraham, first published in the *Times and Seasons* in 1842 and canonized in 1880, expresses the same thought (compare 5:7). The Book of Moses, proclaimed as a revealed restoration of the Genesis text in 1830 and canonized in 1880, is the most explicit of the three: "And I, the Lord God, formed man from the dust of the ground, and breathed into his nostrils the breath of life; and man became a living soul, the first flesh upon the earth, the first man also" (3:7). A literal reading of the passage lends credence to special creation. The fascinating point, however, is that with the possible exception of Apostle Orson Pratt, no Mormon leader seems to have taken the full passage literally.[25] The intense scriptural literalism with which some current writers try to paint LDS presidents falls apart on this and related passages.

No president or member of the First Presidency has ever accepted the idea of special creation of the human body or of anything else for that matter. An examination of Joseph Smith's teachings reveals an idea, never expressed in detail, that humans came via an act of natural procreation. That sentiment runs generally through the teachings of his successors.[26] Smith's clearest statement on the matter is: "Where was there ever a son without a father? And where was there ever a father without first being a son? Whenever did a tree or anything spring into existence without a progenitor? And everything comes in this way."[27]

Under Brigham Young's administration more specific teachings were developed. Beginning in 1852, the same year that plural marriage was acknowledged, Young served public notice of a distinctive Mormon doctrine: that Adam and Eve were resurrected beings, exalted to Godhood from a mortality on another and older sphere. They had produced the spirits of all men and women and had then come to this earth, degraded their "celestial" bodies so that they could produce the bodies of Abel, Cain, Seth, and so on.[28] In short, Adam in Young's view occupied essentially the same place that modern church members reserve for Elohim; Elohim was regarded as the Grandfather in Heaven, rather than the Father. We need not concern ourselves here with the details of the doctrine, only that Adam was purported to have had a resurrected body and to have begun the family of humankind by direct sexual union and procreation.

The response of church members to the doctrine is of importance to us. With most the concept does not seem to have been well received. Indeed Young's public sermons on the matter began to skirt the issue, referring to it continually but obliquely. In private he and his colleagues taught it affirmatively. With rare exceptions the writings and sermons of Mormons in general avoided the entire issue or couched it in vague terms.

There was one notable exception: Apostle Orson Pratt. On this matter at least he seems to have accepted the scriptures literally and could not reconcile them with Young's doctrine. Beginning in 1853 he published a periodical entitled *The Seer* and in its pages promulgated a doctrine that sounded like special creation. Articles from *The Seer* were republished in England in the pages of the *LDS Millennial Star*, a situation not pleasing to the church presidency. As early as January 1855, Young requested the editor of the *Star* to refrain from any further publication of material from *The Seer*, citing "erroneous doctrine" as the reason.[29]

Five years later Pratt brought the matter into the open in a dramatic sermon during the regular Sunday morning worship service in the Salt Lake Tabernacle, 29 January 1860. Confessing the errors of his ways, Pratt sued for reconciliation. A few months later a "carefully revised" version of his speech was published in the *Deseret News* followed by a formal statement from the First Presidency, listing explicit errors in Pratt's writings.[30] The first item cited was Pratt's teaching that Adam had been formed "out of the ground." The refutation states that with regard to Adam "it is deemed wisest to let the subject remain without further explanation at present, for it is written that we are to receive 'line upon line,' according to our faith and capacities, and the circumstances attending our progress."

Where in the early days of debates between science and theology did Mormonism find its closest affinites? On the doctrine of *ex nihilo* creation Mormonism was clearly allied with science. The matter of the earth's age was an open one, the fixity of species was virtually ignored, the issue of materialism and vital forces was in a state of flux but showed fundamental agreements with science. Only on the subject of special creation could Mormonism be tied to orthodox Christianity, and even that was tenuous. Darwin's book was published 24 November 1859. Less than a year later Pratt again pleaded special creation, but he was refuted by the First Presidency.

In 1882 church president John Taylor published *Mediation and Atonement* in which he made the strongest statement by any president favoring the fixity of species,[31] thus inching the church toward the orthodox theologians' position. But during the following year his first counselor, George Q. Cannon, twice reaffirmed the sentiment of Brigham Young that the creation periods were "periods of time" and that Joseph Smith had anticipated science on the matter of the earth's age. Happy that science was bolstering the prophet, Cannon summarized: "Geologists have declared it, and religious people are adopting it; and so the world is progressing."[32] But Cannon was eclectic in his beliefs. Acceptance of an old earth was not to be taken as an acceptance of Darwinism—at least so far as it applied to humankind. In an editorial in 1883 he made it clear that he regarded belief in "Darwin's theories concerning the origin of man" as evidence of spiritual apostasy.[33] This sentiment is not surprising, since Cannon had often expressed himself in similar vein before being called to the First Presidency[34] and was a firm believer in Young's Adamic doctrines.[35]

The general feeling of the church in the latter 1800s, however, was that science would continue to demonstrate the validity of Mormon positions. Indeed a heady flirtation with science affixed itself on the church. Church hierarchy seems to have rejoiced at the goodwill generated by James E. Talmage's reception in scientific circles, his participation and membership in esteemed societies, and his trips to England and Russia. In 1896 Talmage became holder of

Mormonism's first real doctorate degree. He was joined in this distinction in 1899 by John A. Widtsoe and Joseph F. Merrill. All three of these physical scientists later became prominent apostles and articulate spokesmen in the church.

Davis Bitton has rightly focused on the turn of the century as a period critical in Mormonism when the prevailing optimism toward science and reason began to erode.[36] But this cooling must not be overstated. The antagonism of recent times towards science can be seen more correctly as a product of only the last couple of decades.

In the early years of the century, the *Improvement Era* regularly ran articles by Talmage, Widtsoe, Frederick Pack, and others extolling areas of agreement between science and Mormon theology. These articles show a degree of caution and sensitivity toward evolution that is commendable. The distinction between evolution *per se* and Darwinism was periodically noted, a point which many later writers seem to have missed. The then recent rediscovery of Mendel's paper and principles of genetics and the question of their compatibility with Darwinism were watched with interest. But the concept that science and Mormonism were a basic unity formed the dominant theme.

The year 1909 marked the fiftieth anniversary of publication of *The Origin of the Species*. Debates on the "current status of Darwinism" abounded in scientific and lay literature alike. In Mormonism the question was not ignored. The YMMIA manual for the year (Widtsoe's *Joseph Smith as Scientist*[37]) reaffirmed ideas taught by Brigham Young and others that the earth was very old and that the creative days were indefinite periods. The manual evoked a series of questions on the matter, which were discussed in a special column of the *Improvement Era*. The managing editor, Edward H. Anderson, defended the manual. He contended that the verses of D&C 77:12, cited by questioners in support of a young-earth theory, did not apply to the subject and turned the column over to Widtsoe for further discussion. Widtsoe proceeded to dismiss the twenty-four-hour-day view, the 1,000-year-day concept, the D&C 77 argument, and the theory attributed to Joseph Smith that the earth had been formed of fragments of others worlds.[38] The following month's issue published as its lead article an essay by Apostle Charles W. Penrose entitled,

"The Age and Destiny of the Earth," which also argued for an old earth of indefinite age.[39]

In November 1909 the first formal statement on evolution from the First Presidency was published. It was signed by Joseph F. Smith, John R. Winder, and Anthon H. Lund.[40] Entitled "The Origin of Man," it is cited by some individuals as "the official pronouncement against evolution." A more honest appraisal of the text, its background, and meaning to later presidents indicates that such a judgment is inaccurate. The document is carefully worded. Its message is an affirmation that we are spirit children of divine parentage, are in the image of God both in body and spirit, and that we are all descendants of a common ancestor, Adam. Lengthy scriptural passages are cited in affirmation of humankind's divine spiritual pedigree. Three paragraphs are relevant to discussion of the origin of physical bodies: "Adam, our great progenitor, 'the first man,' was, like Christ, a pre-existent spirit, and like Christ he took upon him an appropriate body, the body of a man, and so became a 'living soul.' The doctrine of the pre-existence,—revealed so plainly, particularly in latter days, pours a wonderful flood of light upon the otherwise mysterious problem of man's origin. It shows that man, as a spirit, was begotten and born of heavenly parents, and reared to maturity in the eternal mansions of the Father, prior to coming upon the earth in a temporal body to undergo an experience in mortality. It teaches that all men existed in the spirit before any man existed in the flesh, and that all who have inhabited the earth since Adam have taken bodies and become souls in like manner.

"It is held by some that Adam was not the first man upon this earth, and that the original human being was a development from lower orders of the animal creation. These, however, are the theories of men. The word of the Lord declares that Adam was 'the first man of all men' (Moses 1:34), and we are therefore in duty bound to regard him as the primal parent of our race. It was shown to the brother of Jared that all men were created in the *beginning* after the image of God; and whether we take this to mean the spirit or the body, or both, it commits us to the same conclusion: Man began life as a human being, in the likeness of our heavenly Father.

"True it is that the body of man enters upon its career as a tiny germ or embryo, which becomes an infant, quickened at a certain stage by the spirit whose tabernacle it is, and the child, after being born, develops into a man. There is nothing in this, however, to indicate that the original man, the first of our race, began life as anything less than a man, or less than the human germ or embryo that becomes a man."[41]

The anti-evolutionary sentiment is evident though guarded. The likelihood that the article constitutes an authoritative pronouncement against evolution as a possibility for the origin of the human body was strengthened by a statement in the 1910 manual for the priests of the Aaronic priesthood: "descent has not been from a lower form of life, but from the highest Form of Life; in other words, man is, in the most literal sense, a child of God. This is not only true of the spirit of man, but of his body also. There never was a time, probably, in all the eternities of the past, when there was not men or children of God. This world is only one of many worlds which have been created by the Father through His Only Begotten."[42]

But the statement continues in a markedly less definitive vein: "Adam, then, was probably not the first mortal man in the universe, but he was likely the first for this earth." And two pages later the tone of indefiniteness is further continued as a matter of reasoning: "One of the important points about this topic is to learn, if possible, how Adam obtained his body of flesh and bones. There would seem to be but one natural and reasonable explanation, and that is, that Adam obtained his body in the same way Christ obtained his—and just as all men obtain theirs—namely, by being born of woman. 'The Father has a body of flesh and bones as tangible as man's; the Son also.' (Doc. & Cov., 130:22). Then what is more natural than to conclude that the offspring of such Beings would have bodies of flesh and bones? Like begets like."[43]

Such sentiments further evoked questions from church members, which were again answered by an editorial in the *Improvement Era*. Joseph F. Smith, as president of the church, and Edward H. Anderson, were the editors: "*Origin of Man.*—'In just what manner did the mortal bodies of Adam and Eve come into existence on this earth?' This question comes from several High Priests' quorums.

"Of course, all are familiar with the statements in Genesis 1:26, 27; 2:7; also in the Book of Moses, Pearl of Great Price, 2:27; and in the Book of Abraham 5:7. The latter statement reads: 'And the Gods formed man from the dust of the ground, and took his spirit (that is, the man's spirit) and put it into him; and breathed into his nostrils the breath of life, and man became a living soul.'

"These are the authentic statements of the scriptures, ancient and modern, and it is best to rest with these, until the Lord shall see fit to give more light on the subject. Whether the mortal bodies of man evolved in natural processes to present perfection, through the direction and power of God; whether the first parents of our generations, Adam and Eve, were transplanted from another sphere, with immortal tabernacles, which became corrupted through sin and the partaking of natural foods, in the process of time; whether they were born here in mortality, as other mortals have been, are questions not fully answered in the revealed word of God. For helpful discussion of the subject, see *Improvement Era*, Vol. XI, August 1908, No. 10, page 778, article, 'Creation and Growth of Adam'; also article by the First Presidency, 'Origin of Man,' Vol. XI, No. 1, page 75, 1909."

The August 1908 article was a response to a question raised about an earlier article. The author of the two pieces, William Halls, had contended that Adam could not have been created full-grown but must have gone through a natural childhood and adolescence. When pushed for documentation by *Era* readers who felt that such a view was incompatible with scriptural literalism, he answered in the article that he could not document it but that "When a passage of scripture taken literally contradicts a fundamental, natural law, I take it as allegorical; and in the absence of divine authority, put a construction on it that seems to harmonize with my experience and reason."

Thus ended the matter so far as Joseph F. Smith was concerned: the editorial listed three options, and it is evident that not one of them agrees with a literal interpretation of Moses 3:7 or other such creation passages. The *Improvement Era* continued to publish articles on science and the gospel (mostly articles by Frederick Pack, a University of Utah geology professor) until April 1911. A few months before, the touchy matter of academic freedom in the church school system had reared its head, specifically the propriety of teaching "the theories of evolution as at present set forth in the text books, and also theories relating to the Bible known as 'higher criticism.'" President Smith in a special editorial[44] reported to the church on the matter. He indicated that "it is well known that evolution and the 'higher criticism'—though perhaps containing many truths—are in conflict on some matters with the scriptures, including some modern revelation." He concluded: "it appears a waste of time and means, and detrimental to faith and religion to enter too extensively into the undemonstrated theories of men on philosophies relating to the origin of life, or the methods adopted by an All-wise Creator in peopling the earth with the bodies of men, birds and beasts. Let us rather turn our abilities to the practical analysis of the soil."

A companion editorial from Smith was aimed at the youth of the church and appeared in *The Juvenile Instructor*.[45] Though more general in its approach, it makes a finer distinction between the president's personal feelings and the church position. His private views seem to be embodied in the following passage: "They [students] are not old enough or learned enough to discriminate, or put proper limitations upon a theory which we believe is more or less a fallacy. In reaching the conclusion that evolution would be best left out of discussion in our Church schools we are deciding a question of propriety and are not undertaking to say how much of evolution is true, or how much is false. We think that while it is a hypothesis, on both sides of which the most eminent scientific men of the world are arrayed, that it is folly to take up its discussion in our institutions of learning, and we cannot see wherein such discussions are likely to promote the faith of our young people." He then clearly spelled out the church position on the matter: "The Church itself has no philosophy about the *modus operandi* employed by the Lord in His creation of the world, and much of the talk therefore about the philosophy of Mormonism is altogether misleading." Here Smith let the matter rest.

Two years later in a conference address in Arizona, Smith delivered himself of one further comment: "Man was born of woman; Christ, the Savior, was born of woman and God, the Father, was born of woman. Adam, our earthly parent, was also born of woman into this world, the same as Jesus and you and I."[46] This statement is consistent with all three of the 1910 options. Clarification of further questions such as when, how, and of whom can only be answered by extensive and tenuous proof-texting. Smith, one of the most scripturally committed of all LDS presidents, remained consistent with his predecessors, leaving the matter open and unresolved.

No further authoritative statements were made until 1925 during the administration of Heber J. Grant. That was the year of the famous Scopes trial in Dayton, Tennessee. Young John Scopes, charged with teaching evolution forbidden by state law, was the defendant, but the trial became a classic confrontation between theology and science. Correspondents from around the world converged on the town for the great showdown.[47] During the post-trial period, the document "'Mormon' View of Evolution" appeared, published over the signature of the First Presidency—Heber J. Grant, Anthony W. Ivins, and Charles W. Nibley.[48] This document consists of several paragraphs with only a few minor word changes from the 1909 statement. The anti-evolution paragraphs quoted above are absent. The statement affirms the spiritual pedigree of humanity and the common descent of all people from an ancestor named Adam, who had taken upon himself "an appropriate body." As with the 1909 document, this text uses the word evolution or its derivatives only once, affirming that humankind formed in the image of God "is capable, by experience through ages and aeons, of evolving into a God." Seen against the theological ferment and rhetoric of the day, this is an amazingly temperate document.

The next episode involving evolution occurred in 1930 but was kept within the closed circle of the church leaders. The relatively young apostle, Joseph Fielding Smith, delivered a lecture to the genealogical conference on 5 April. In his enthusiastic style, he spoke of the creation of humankind, acknowledging that "The Lord has not seen fit to tell us definitely just how Adam came for we are not ready to receive that truth." But he also spelled out clearly a disbelief in "pre-Adamites," peoples of any sort upon the earth before Adam. He affirmed that "the doctrine of 'pre-Adamites' is not a doctrine of the Church, and is not advocated nor countenanced in the Church." Then he went further: "There was no death in the earth before the fall of Adam. . . . All life in the sea, the air, on the earth, was without death. Animals were not dying. Things were not changing as we find them changing in this mortal existence, for mortality had not come."[49]

Shortly after publication of the speech, B. H. Roberts challenged the legitimacy of the remarks in a letter to the First Presidency. Both Roberts and Smith were given opportunity to present their positions, orally and in writing, to the Twelve and First Presidency. Roberts developed his ideas from scripture, science, and the sermons of Apostle Orson Hyde and President Brigham Young. Smith used scripture and the teachings of Orson Pratt and the anti-evolution language of the 1909 statement of the First Presidency. Finally convinced that continued discussion would be fruitless, the First Presidency issued a seven-page directive to all general authorities, reviewing the entire discussion and then stating: "The statement made by Elder Smith that the existence of pre-Adamites is not a doctrine of the Church is true. It is just as true that the statement: 'There were not pre-Adamites upon the earth' is not a doctrine of the Church. Neither side of the controversy has been accepted as a doctrine at all. Both parties make the scripture and the statements of men who have been prominent in the affairs of the Church the basis of their contention; neither has produced definite proof in support of his views. . . . Upon the fundamental doctrines of the Church we are all agreed. Our mission is to bear the message of the restored gospel to the people of the world. Leave Geology, Biology, Archaeology and Anthropology, no one of which has to do with the salvation of the souls of mankind, to scientific research, while we magnify our calling in the realm of the Church."[50]

In addition to this written directive, the First Presidency called a special meeting of all general authorities the day after general conference to discuss the matter. Apostle James E. Talmage records the following account of the meeting: "Involved in this question is that of the beginning of life upon the earth, and as to whether there was death either of animal or plant before the fall of Adam, on which proposition Elder Smith was very pronounced in denial and Elder Roberts equally forceful in the affirmative. As to whether Pre-adamite races existed upon the earth there has been much discussion among some of our people of late. The decision reached by the First Presidency, and announced to this morning's assembly, was in answer to a specific question that obviously the doctrine of the existence of races of human beings upon the earth prior to the fall of Adam was not a doctrine of the Church; and, further, that the conception embodied in the belief of many to the effect that there were no such Pre-adamite races, and that there was no death upon the earth prior to Adam's fall is likewise declared to be no doctrine of the Church. I think the decision of the First Presidency is a wise one in the premises. This is one of the many things upon which we cannot preach with assurance and dogmatic assertions on either side are likely to do harm rather than good."[51]

The two contestants, Roberts and Smith, were thus directed to drop the matter. Publication of a major manuscript already written by Roberts dealing with the subject was as a result proscribed.

But this proscription left the public record with only one side of the story, Smith's speech, which in many ways is an avowal of the position of nineteenth-century Christian theologians. Not everyone in the governing quorums of the church was content with such a situation. On Sunday, 9 August 1931, Apostle Talmage took the stand in the Salt Lake Tabernacle worship service and there delivered his address, "The Earth and Man."[52] In light of the restrictions proposed by the First Presidency, Talmage's position was carefully worded. Affirming his belief in the ultimate synthesis of God's word in both the rocks and the scriptures, Talmage promulgated a clear message of sensitivity to and reception of science and the scientific method.

From certain quarters in the Twelve, opposition developed to the speech's publication. The subject was a matter of consideration in at least four meetings of the Twelve and First Presidency. Eventually the First Presidency directed Talmage to send it to the "Church News." They also instructed him to have it published as a separate pamphlet to be available upon request. Both publications were released to the public 21 November 1931.[53]

The resulting stalemate continued for over two decades. Cognizant of the fact that writings and expressions of general authorities, no matter how intended, tend to become canonized by elements within the church community, the First Presidency continued the proscription against publication of the Roberts manuscript. In 1933 both Roberts and Talmage died. Their philosophical legacy was continued by apostles Widtsoe and Merrill. In the ensuing years, Apostle Smith also completed a book-length manuscript, which outlined his objections to evolution. The record indicates that his manuscript was subjected to the same publication injunction as that of Roberts.[54] Widtsoe and Merrill also continued to resist what they saw as Smith's overly-literalistic interpretation. Their deaths in 1952 marked the end of an era.

Smith began an open exposition of his views on 22 April 1953 in a speech at Brigham Young University entitled "The Origin of Man."[55] His June 1953 Mutual Improvement Association conference address continued the same theme: scriptural literalism on scientific matters coupled with a disregard for scientific data.[56] A rapid though minor updating of his book manuscript followed, and by mid-1954 it was made available to the public under the title *Man: His Origin and Destiny*.[57]

The work marked a milestone. For the first time Mormonism had a book openly antagonistic to much of science.[58] The long-standing concern of past church presidents was realized: the book was hailed by many as an authoritative church statement which locked Mormonism into direct confrontation with science and sparked a wave of religious fundamentalism showing little sign of abatement. Others, mindful of the embarrassment which other Christian churches had suffered on issues of science and fearful of the consequences for their own church if the new stance was widely adopted, openly expressed consternation. Church president David O. McKay abhorred controversy. The difference in philosophy between the book's author and himself could hardly have been more disparate within the church framework. But in his public capacity McKay reacted cautiously.

Smith vigorously presented his basic thesis to seminary and Institute teachers gathered at Brigham Young University on 28 June 1954.[59] Exactly nine days later, President J. Reuben Clark, Jr., second counselor in the First Presidency, delivered (by invitation) his speech, "When are the Writings or Sermons of Church Leaders Entitled to the Claim of Scripture?" His message was clear and hard-hitting; it has no peer in Mormon literature. Emphasizing that only the president of the church may declare doctrine, interpret scripture, "or change in any way the existing doctrines of the Church," he proceeded to examine the scriptural affirmation that whatever holders of the priesthood speak "when moved upon by the Holy Ghost shall be scripture." He acknowledged that the scripture applied with special force to general authorities but that "They must act and teach subject to the over-all power and authority of the President of the Church. . . . Sometimes in the past they have spoken 'out of turn,' so to speak. . . .

"There have been rare occasions when even the President of the Church in his preaching and teaching has not been 'moved upon by the Holy Ghost.' You will recall the Prophet Joseph declared that a prophet is not always a prophet. . . . [E]ven the President of the Church, himself, may not always be 'moved upon by the Holy Ghost,' when he addresses the people. This has happened about matters of doctrine (usually of a highly speculative character) where subsequent Presidents of the Church and the people themselves have felt that in declaring the doctrine, the announcer was not 'moved upon by the Holy Ghost.'

"How shall the Church know. . . ? The Church will know by the testimony of the Holy Ghost in the body of the members . . . and in due time that knowledge will be made manifest."

In his final paragraphs he moved from trying to define what is scripture to identifying what is not scripture. When anyone other than the president of the church attempts to proclaim any new doctrine, unless acting specifically under the president's direction, the church may know that the utterances are not scripture. "When any man, except the President of the Church," Clark concluded, "undertakes to proclaim one unsettled doctrine, as among two or more doctrines in dispute, as the settled doctrine of the Church, we may know that he is not 'moved upon by the Holy Ghost,' unless he is acting under the authority of the President."

McKay himself avoided any direct public statement on the matter. His closest approach to public commentary came from his beginning-of-the-school-year speech to Brigham Young University faculty, 17 September 1954.[60] He discussed various categories of knowledge and touched briefly on science and religion. He averred that it is a "stern fact of life" that all living things obey fixed laws of nature and divine commands. He referred to the creation of human-kind thus: "When the Creator 'breathed into his nostrils the breath of life,' (and never mind when it was), 'and man became a living soul' God gave him the power of choice." In his closing sentence, he moved to "bless you [the faculty] with wisdom to know the truth as it is given by revealed word in the authorized books of the Church, bless you with the power to discern between truth and errors as given by individuals."

This public response by the First Presidency did not satisfy the members. Over the years inquiries were made about the doctrinal soundness of Smith's book and similar teachings. The response from the First Presidency has been consistent: an avowal that the church has taken no official position on evolution and related subjects, that it has made no official statement on the subject, that the book in question is neither "authorized" by the church nor "published" by the church, that it "is not approved by the church," and that it contains only the author's personal views. On occasion the inquirer has been sent two documents, the 1909 First Presidency statement and Talmage's 1931 speech, with the admonition that the matter should be dealt with by "suspending judgment as long as may be necessary" until the complete truth is perceived.[61]

Here the matter rests as far as authoritative statements are concerned. There has been no further official response. The 1931 First Presidency's observation that these matters do not relate to "salvation" is astute as well as practical. Darwin perceived that his views bore no necessary antagonism to religion,[62] and a nineteenth-century commentator phrased the same sentiment in the following way: "Evolution, if rightly understood, has no theological or antitheological influence whatever. What is evolution? It is not an entity. It is a mode of creation. It leaves the whole field of Christian faith where and as it found it. Its believers and advocates may be theists, pantheists, or atheists. The causes of these radically different religious views cannot be sought in the one theory. They are to be found elsewhere."[63]

At the same time there can be no denying the fact that the polemics of the theology-biology debate have polarized people into opposite camps. This opposition is detrimental to the cause of both camps. Mormonism is committed to the concept of a lawful, loving, orderly Deity to whom capriciousness and deceit are anathema. The concept that God works through universal law, that he is obedient to law, is fundamental. This gives Mormonism a basis for synthesis of the two camps that exists in few if any other Western religions.

Teachers in the church cannot be honest in their teachings if they present only one point of view as the position of the church. Rather we must insist on greater honesty and scholarship in our gospel discussions. Perhaps the sentiments of Apostle John Taylor are relevant: "I do not want to be frightened about hell-fire, pitchforks, and serpents, nor to be scared to death with hobgoblins and ghosts, nor anything of the kind that is got up to scare the ignorant; but I want truth, intelligence, and something that will bear investigation. I want to probe things to the bottom and to find out the truth if there is any way to find it out."[64]

And further: "[O]ur religion . . . embraces every principle of truth and intelligence pertaining to us as moral, intellectual, mortal and immortal beings, pertaining to this world and the world that is to come. We are open to truth of every kind, no matter whence it comes, where it originates, or who believes in it. . . . A man in search of truth has no peculiar system to sustain, no peculiar dogma to defend or theory to uphold; he embraces all truth, and that truth, like the sun in the firmament, shines forth and spreads its effulgent rays over all creation, and if men will divest themselves of bias and prejudice, and prayerfully and conscientiously search after truth, they will find it wherever they turn their attention."[65]

NOTES

1. By "evolution," I refer only to the general concept that living things as we know them today have over a long period of time been developed by differentiation from a single or several primordial entities, i.e. descent by modification. Other tighter or more specialized definitions do not generally apply here. I will be content with just the very general concept portrayed by Darwin in his closing sentence to *The Origin of Species* (2d and all subsequent editions): "There is grandeur in this view of life, with its several powers, having been originally breathed by the Creator into a few forms or into one; and that . . . from so simple a beginning endless forms most beautiful and most wonderful have been, and are being evolved."

2. Cf. I. M. Lerner, "The Concept of Natural Selection: A Centennial View," *Proceedings of the American Philosophical Society* 103 (1959): 173-82; reprinted in W. M. Laetsch, ed., *The Biological Perspective* (New York: Little, Brown & Co., 1969). An excellent statement of what natural selection is and is not is Th. Dobzhansky, "Creative Evolution," *Diogenes* 60 (1967): 62-74. Materials pertinent to the current level of acceptance of the main body of evolutionary concepts are: H. J. Muller, "Biologists' Statement on Teaching Evolution," *Bulletin of Atomic Scientists* 23 (1967): 39-40, and S. Tax, ed., *Evolution After Darwin* (Chicago: University of Chicago Press, 1960), which encompasses in three volumes the proceedings of the Darwin Centennial Celebration (symposium) at the University of Chicago in 1959. A rather

critical but factually reliable appraisal of the current status of evolutionary knowledge, particularly as it applies to invertebrate animals, is G. A. Kerkut, *Implications of Evolution* (New York: Pergamon Press, 1960). Review of this work by J. T. Bonner, *American Scientist* 49 (1961): 240-44, and Th. Dobzhansky, *Science* 133 (1961): 752, will also prove valuable. The review by W. Bullock, *J. Am. Sci. Affil.* 16 (1964): 125-26 will be of particular interest to those interested in religious correlations.

    3. First Presidency (Joseph F. Smith, et. al.) *Deseret News*, 2 Aug. 1913; also in James R. Clark, ed., *Messages of the First Presidency* (Salt Lake City: Bookcraft, 1968), 4:284-86; H. B. Lee, *Improvement Era* 73 (1970): 63-65; *Ensign* 3 (Jan. 1973): 104-108.

    4. The best statement on the intimacies of this relationship is Joseph F. Smith's pledge to the church upon assuming its presidency, 10 Nov. 1901, *Conference Reports*, 82; also in Clark, *Messages of First Presidency*, 4:4-6.

    5. An introduction to non-LDS literature can be gained from A. D. White, *A History of the Warfare of Science with Theology in Christendom*, 2 vols. (1869; New York: Dover Publications, 1960), and B. J. Loewenberg, *Darwinism Comes to America, 1859-1900* (Philadelphia: Fortress Press, 1969).

    6. Cf. O. K. White, Jr., "Mormonism—A Nineteenth Century Heresy," *Journal of Religious Thought* 26 (1969): 44-55. That Brigham Young perceived these deep distinctions is evident: "We differ from the Christian world in our religious faith and belief; and so we do very materially. I am not astonished that infidelity prevails to a great extent among the inhabitants of the earth, for the religious teachers of the people advance many ideas and notions for truth which are in opposition to and contradict facts demonstrated by science, and which are generally understood," *Journal of Discourses*, 14:115 (hereafter JD).

    7. *Times and Seasons* 5 (1844): 615 (hereafter T&S). An expanded and variant version of this statement appears in B. H. Roberts, *History of the Church*, 6:308-309 (hereafter HC). The same quote is given in Joseph Fielding Smith, ed., *Teachings of the Prophet Joseph Smith* (Salt Lake City: Deseret Book, 1958), 350-52. Though Smith cites the *Times and Seasons* as his source, he actually gives the HC account.

    8. See, for example, JD 11:120, 13:248, 14:116, 16:167, 18:231-32.

    9. A good discussion of creation *ex nihilo* as it applies to Mormon thought is found in O. K. White, "The Social-Psychological Basis of Mormon New-Orthodoxy," M.S. thesis, University of Utah, 1967, 87ff; also "The Transformation of Mormon Theology," *Dialogue: A Journal of Mormon Thought* 5 (1970): 9-24. White maintains that Mormon authors consistently miss the deeper or even essential meanings of the doctrine, that of necessary versus contingent being. Cf. Truman Madsen, *Instructor* 99 (1964): 96-99, and ibid., 236f. For the most detailed treatment available in Mormon literature on the subject, see S. M. McMurrin, *The Theological Foundations of the Mormon*

Religion (Salt Lake City: University of Utah Press, 1965).

10. Cf. B. H. Roberts, *Comprehensive History of the Church* (Salt Lake City: Deseret News Press, 1930), 2:404-406.

11. T&S 5 (1844): 615. An expanded version is in HC 6:310-11. It is Roberts who equates the term "co-equal" with "co-eternal." Once again Joseph Fielding Smith follows Roberts's version (352-54). Cf. also Joseph Smith, T&S 3 (1842): 745. Any errors are in the original.

12. Cf. JD 1:116, 3:356, 7:285, 8:27, and W. O. Rich, *Distinctive Teachings of the Restoration* (Salt Lake City: Deseret News Press, 1962), chap. 3.

13. Suggestions were made occasionally that the "days" were periods of indefinite length, but such views were lost in the melee; see J. C. Greene, *Darwin and the Modern World View* (New York: Mentor Books, 1963), 18-19.

14. *Latter Day Saints Messenger and Advocate*, 1 (Feb. 1835): 78.

15. T&S, published 1 Jan. 1845. Emphasis and parentheses in original.

16. JD 14:115-16. Lest LDS geologists become overly smug, however, I point out that they too could share Young's disdain; cf. JD 13:248-29; *Deseret News*, 18 June 1873, 308.

17. There is no legitimate discussion of the word "kind" (Hebrew=*min*) in biological terms in Mormon literature. For a beginning discussion, not LDS, see A. J. Jones, "A General Analysis of the Biblical 'Kind' (Min)," *Creation Research Society Quarterly* 9 (1972): 53-57; and "Boundaries of the Min: An Analysis of the Mosaic Lists of Clean and Unclean Animals," ibid. 9 (1972): 114-23. Most current writers consider "kind" to represent a biological grouping at approximately the Family level in the taxonomic hierarchy; few indeed are those who still try to equate it with "species."

18. From Wilford Woodruff's notes in HC 4:554 from a speech delivered 20 March 1842; see also Roberts's qualifying comments on the notes (556), which must be kept in mind regarding all such speech texts. We have not been able to locate any earlier published accounts.

19. JD 8:29-30.

20. See G. G. Simpson, *The Meaning of Evolution* (New Haven, CT: Yale University Press, 1949), 124-29, 263-79. Simpson, usually pictured as quite insensitive to religious viewpoints, develops some concepts of the limitations and implications of materialism that have considerable interest to Mormons.

21. R. Schubert-Soldern, *Mechanism and Vitalism, Philosophical Aspects of Biology*, ed. P. G. Fothergill (South Bend, IN: University of Notre Dame Press, 1962), 10-11.

22. Roberts, *Comprehensive History*, 2:392. A close friend of Joseph Smith, Benjamin F. Johnson, makes the "light-life-spirit" equation in his 1903

letter to Elder George F. Gibbs, 5, typescript, Harold B. Lee Library, Brigham Young University, Provo, Utah. There is no satisfactory synthesis of the subject, and it is doubtful that one could be produced. Andrus's imaginative treatment is as wide-ranging as any available and should be consulted for its references; see H. L. Andrus, *God, Man and the Universe* (Salt Lake City: Bookcraft, 1968), 144-92. Roberts's brief discussion is valuable (*Comprehensive History*, 2:381-42, especially 399-401).

    23. JD 3:276-77. Benjamin F. Johnson, letter, indicates that essentially this same doctrine was taught by Joseph Smith.

    24. JD 1:349; 3:354; 7:2-3, 285; 9:242.

    25. In H. B. Lee, "Find the Answers in the Scriptures, *Ensign* 2 (Dec. 1972): 2-3, there does appear a passage which seems to imply acceptance of the literal interpretation of Moses 3:7. Correspondence which I am not at liberty to release, however, indicates that this should not be construed as a pronouncement of any particular interpretation or doctrinal position.

    26. From Brigham Young, JD 3:319; 4:216-18; 7:285; 15:137.

    27. HC 6:476, a speech by Joseph Smith dated 16 June 1884, from notes by Thomas Bullock. I have not been able to locate any earlier published sources. Cf. n49.

    28. I am aware of the intense arguments and deeply held opinions revolving around this doctrine and the current propensity to deny that it was ever taught. There can be no justification for denying its historical reality; it is too well documented and was taught by Young from 1852 until his death in 1877. See R. Turner, "The Position of Adam in Latter-day Saint Scripture and Theology," M.A. thesis, Brigham Young University, 1953. A more recent and thorough account is O. Kraut, *Michael/Adam* ([1972], n.p.). Both sources discuss reactions of church members to the doctrine, which include problems with scriptural reconciliation. Those who attempt to prove that Young taught only doctrine that is currently orthodox are driven to considerable freedom in interpreting and even doctoring his sermons; for example, J. A. Widtsoe, comp., *Discourses of Brigham Young*, (1925), 159. These errors are compounded and further promulgated by Joseph Fielding Smith, *Answers to Gospel Questions* (1966), 5:121-28, excerpted in the 1972-1973 Melchizedek Priesthood manual, 20-22. Compare, for example, the quote from JD 9:148 in its original form and as printed by Widtsoe, by Smith (124), and in the priesthood manual (22).

    I do not contend that Young's concepts concerning Adam are an accurate representation of the concepts of other LDS presidents or that they are to be accepted as church doctrine. That to Young, Adam was a resurrected being is clear: "The mystery in this, as with miracles, or anything else, is only to those who are ignorant. Father Adam came here, and then they brought his wife. 'Well,' says one, 'Why was Adam called Adam'? He was the first man on the earth, and its framer and maker. He, with the help of his brethren, brought it into existence. Then he said, 'I want my children who are in the spirit world to come and live here. I once dwelt upon an earth something like this, in a mortal state, I was faithful, I received my crown and exaltation. I have the privilege of extending my work, and to its increase there will be no end. I want my children that were born to me in the spirit world to come here and take tabernacles of flesh, that their spirits may have a house, a tabernacle or a dwelling place as mine has, and where is the mystery?" (*Deseret News*, 18 June 1873, reporting a speech of 8 June 1873)

Later presidents did not share this view. A request for more information on the subject from Bishop Joseph H. Eldredge of Myron, Utah, to President Heber J. Grant was answered: "If what is meant is that Adam has passed on to celestial glory through a resurrection before he came here, and that afterwards he was appointed to this earth to die again, the second time becoming mortal, then it is not scriptural or according to the truth.... Adam had not passed through the resurrection." The letter, signed by President Grant and dated 26 February 1931, is published in Clark, *Messages of the First Presidency*, 5:289-90. Such differences in viewpoint should serve as a caution to all who are tempted to teach any given doctrine about Adam as "the church view."

29. *LDS Millennial Star*, 17 (1855): 297-98.

30. *Deseret News*, 25 July 1860, 162-63. The First Presidency's statement was reprinted as part of the 1865 refutation also, cf. n50. The "revised" version of Pratt's sermon may also be found in JD 7:371-76.

31. J. Taylor, *Mediation and Atonement* (Salt Lake City: Deseret News Co., 1882; Salt Lake City: Stevens and Wallis, Inc., 1950), 163-65; 159-60.

32. JD 24:61, cf. 24:257.

33. *Juvenile Instructor* 18 (15 June 1883): 191. President Cannon appears to have addressed essentially the same theme in his Founder's Day speech at Brigham Young Academy in 1896. The best account I have been able to locate of this speech quotes Cannon only "in substance," however, so it is impossible to determine his exact statements. The basic stance, however, is anti-evolutionary, at least with respect to human origins; cf. *Daily Enquirer* (Provo, Utah), 16 Oct. 1896, 1.

34. See for example, *LDS Millennial Star* 23 (12 Oct. 1961): 651-54.

35. Cf. Turner and/or Kraut, n57, and Journal of Abraham H. Cannon, 10 Mar. 1888, 23 June 1889, in Archives and Manuscripts, Harold B. Lee Library.

36. Davis Bitton, "Anti-Intellectualism in Mormon History," *Dialogue: A Journal of Mormon Thought* 1 (1966): 111-34.

37. J. A. Widtsoe, *Joseph Smith as Scientist, A Contribution to Mormon Philosophy* (Salt Lake City: General Board Young Men's Mutual Improvement Associations, 1908).

38. Editor's Table, *Improvement Era* 12 (Apr. 1909): 489-94.

39. *Improvement Era* 12 (May 1909): 505-9, a reprint from the 11 Feb. 1909 *LDS Millennial Star.*

40. *Improvement Era* 13 (Nov. 1909): 75-81; also in Clark, *Messages of the First Presidency*, 4:199-206. Actually this statement is the work of a special committee appointed for its production. James E. Talmage, not yet one of the general authorities, records meeting with the committee to consider the document; cf. James E. Talmage Journal, 12:91-92, Archives and Manuscripts, Harold B. Lee Library.

41. When this statement was reprinted in Joseph Fielding Smith, *Man: His Origin and Destiny* (Salt Lake City: Deseret Book Co., 1954), the phrase "primal parent of *our* race" was changed to read "primal parent of *the* race" (354). And it continues to be quoted thus incorrectly in other Mormon works. To some students this represents an alteration in meaning. Whether it would have been so interpreted by the 1909 First Presidency, however, is moot.

42. *Divine Mission of the Savior*, "Course of Study for the . . . Priests (2d year), prepared and issued under the direction of the general authorities of the Church" (1910), 35. The statement to this point was reprinted in the "Church News" section, *Deseret News*, 19 Sept. 1936, 8, and is often quoted as though complete in itself.

43. Ibid., 37. The manual at this point cites three statements, one each from Brigham Young (JD 1:50); Parley P. Pratt (*Key to Theology*); and Orson Pratt (JD 21:201). No attempt is made in the manual to capture the complete thought of these statements, particularly the sermons of President Young and Orson Pratt which reveal fundamental differences in concept. It must also be remembered that major sentiments in both these sermons were severely compromised by statements of subsequent presidencies.

44. *Improvement Era* 14 (Apr. 1911): 548-51. Further details of the case are found in R. V. Chamberlin, *Life and Philosophy of W. H. Chamberlin* (Salt Lake City: Deseret News Press, 1925), 140f. In this rather trying incident, three BYU faculty members, Henry Peterson, Joseph Peterson, and Ralph V. Chamberlin, were fired or resigned under pressure.

45. *Juvenile Instructor* 46 (Apr. 1911): 108-109.

46. *Deseret News*, 24 Dec. 1913, 7; reprinted in the "Church News" section of *Deseret News*, Sept. 1936, 2, 8.

47. The best single account is L. S. de Camp, *The Great Monkey Trial* (Garden City, NY: Doubleday and Co., 1968).

48. *Improvement Era* 28 (Sept. 1925): 1090-91. The sympathy of LDS people for the general religious position in the 1925 Scopes episode is reflected in the remarks of varous speakers, both general authorities and otherwise, during the October General Conference of 1925. Of the First Presidency, however, Charles W. Nibley made no reference to the matter; President Heber J. Grant went no further than to recall favorable impressions

of William Jennings Bryan, the chief religious spokesman (and prosecutor) at the Scopes trial, who died shortly after the trial. Anthony W. Ivins, first counselor, addressed the topic of evolution directly and at some length, articulating a middle-of-the-road position, with too many hypothetical statements and qualifiers to be easily categorized (*LDS General Conference Reports,* Oct. 1925, 19-28).

49. Joseph Fielding Smith, "Faith Leads to a Fulness of Truth and Righteousness," *Utah Genealogical and Historical Magazine* 21 (Oct. 1930): 145-58.

50. Typescript copy in my possession, 7 pp.

51. James E. Talmage Journal, 7 Apr. 1930; cf. entries of 2, 7, 14, and 21 Jan. 1931.

52. J. E. Talmage, "The Earth and Man," "Church News" section of *Deseret News,* 21 Nov. 1931, 7-8. In pamphlet form it was "published by the Church of Jesus Christ of Latter-day Saints" (16 pp.). The speech was republished various times, including by Brigham Young University Extension Publications by the *Instructor* 100 (Dec. 1965): 474-77, and 101 (Jan. 1966): 9-11, 15.

53. Elder Talmage discusses the matter in his journal: "Many of our students have inferred from Elder Smith's address that the Church refuses to recognize the findings of science if there be a word in scriptural record in our interpretation of which we find even a seeming conflict with scientific discoveries or deductions, and that therefore the 'policy' of the Church is in effect opposed to scientific research.

"In speaking at the Tabernacle on August 9 last I had not forgotten that in the pronouncement of the First Presidency mentioned under date of April 7 last it was advised and really required that the General Authorities of the Church refrain from discussing in public, that is preaching, the debatable subject of the existence of human kind upon the earth prior to the beginning of Adamic history as recorded in scripture; but, I had been present at a consultation in the course of which the First Presidency had commented somewhat favorably upon the suggestion that sometime, somewhere, something should be said by one or more of us to make plain that the Church does not refuse to recognize the discoveries and demonstrations of science, especially in relation to the subject at issue. President Anthony W. Ivins, of the First Presidency, presided at the Tabernacle meeting, and three members of the Council of the Twelve were present—Elders George F. Richards, Joseph Fielding Smith and Richard R. Lyman. Of course, Elder Smith, and in fact all of us, recognize that my address was in some important respects opposed to his published remarks, but the other brethren named, including President Ivins, expressed their tentative approval of what I had said.

"I am very grateful that my address has come under a very thorough consideration, and I may say investigation, by the First Presidency and the

Council of the Twelve. The discussions throughout as relating to the matter have been forceful but in every respect friendly, and the majority of the Twelve have been in favor of the publication of the address from the time they first took it under consideration. I have hoped and fervently prayed that the brethren would be rightly guided in reaching a decision, and, as the Lord knows my heart, I have had no personal desire for triumph or victory in the matter, but have hoped that the address would be published or suppressed as would be for the best. The issue is now closed; the address is in print" (Talmage Journal, 21 Nov. 1931; see comments under 9 Aug., 5, 16, and 17 Nov. 1931).

54. Roberts's manuscript, "The Truth, The Way, The Life: An Elementary Treatise on Theology," consists of nearly 600 manuscript pages. Roberts considered it "the most important work that I have yet contributed to the Church, the six-volumed *Comprehensive History of the Church* not omitted" (letter of 9 Feb. 1931 to the First Presidency). Though it is in many critical ways contrapositive to the theology championed by Elder Smith, it does not advocate acceptance of evolution *per se.*

55. Joseph Fielding Smith, "The Origin of Man," 22 Apr. 1953 (Brigham Young University Extension Division).

56. Joseph Fielding Smith, "Entangle Not Yourselves in Sin," *Improvement Era* 56 (Sept. 1953): 646f.

57. Joseph Fielding Smith, *Man, His Origin and Destiny* (Salt Lake City, Utah: Deseret Book, 1954).

58. So far as I am aware, the first book in Mormonism that can really be said to be directed to a discussion of science and religion is *Scientific Aspects of Mormonism* by Nels L. Nelson (New York: G. P. Putnam's Sons, 1904). Others followed sporadically over the years, by Widtsoe, Nelson, Pack, and Merrill. All of these exhibit a deep recognition of the validity of scientific knowledge. *Man: His Origin and Destiny* is a clear break with that long tradition, opting as it does for schism rather than synthesis.

59. Speech published in the "Church News" section, *Deseret News*, 24 July 1954, under the caption, "Discusses Organic Evolution Opposed to Divine Revelation."

60. David O. McKay, "Some Fundamental Objectives of a Church University," "Church News" Section, *Deseret News*, 25 Sept. 1954, 2f.

61. I have photostatic copies in my files of several of these inquiries and responses and know of additional oral discussions of the matter. Before his death President McKay gave formal permission for the publication of at least one of the written responses.

62. As it is expressed in the conclusion to *Origin*: "I see no good reason why the views given in this volume should shock the religious feelings of any one." Though Darwin, once a candidate for the ministry, came to feel that the entire question of rational evidence for design and/or the existence

of God was "insoluble," he was clear that religious commitment was a matter separate and distinct from belief or disbelief in either evolution or natural selection.

63. W. R. Thompson, *Catholic World* 34 (1882): 692.
64. JD 11:317.
65. Ibid. 16: 369-70.

10.
Organic Evolution and the Bible

Eldon J. Gardner

PREFACE. THIS DISCUSSION IS WRITTEN FOR PEOPLE, PARTICULARLY university students, who are already acquainted with the principles of biology and who are interested in an attempt at rationalization between evolution and theology. It is intended as a fair and sympathetic, but objective appraisal of both sides of the issue. The presentation for science students seems to justify a more detailed treatment of scientific than of theological aspects. In another situation the proportion of detail might well be reversed.

The position taken in this paper is that the Bible is a valuable and important document with primarily religious significance, that it is not a scientific treatise, nor a complete and detailed history. The Bible was written by many different authors, each telling his own story and reflecting the cultural background available to him. Scientific accomplishments, on the other hand, are based on an objective method for seeking truth. The scientific method of observation and experimentation can be practiced by anyone who is willing to be objective and who knows how to use the tools of science. It has done much to influence the trend of thought in the modern world and promises to be an even greater force in the future. Science is here to stay and must be allowed to speak in areas where it can contribute. It is a challenging field, worthy of the best minds in our society.

Science has limitations that are well recognized. The methods of science apply only in areas where tangible materials and relations can be investigated and where objective data can be obtained and verified. As science has developed, the insight of scientists has been sharpened and tools useful to scientists have been improved. There is every reason to expect that this trend toward more effectiveness in the use of the scientific method will continue. A review of history reminds us that viewpoints have changed as new developments have occurred. Current views are not necessarily final and conclusive. New interpretations will be required as new data are accumulated by the scientific method.

Evolution Defined. The first consideration is our attitude and approach to a scientific problem. Interpretation and evaluation of information from books and tradition, compared with that from observations in nature and deductions from experiments, present real challenges, especially to university students. The question "What is truth?" is still with us. As children at home and in our churches we have heard versions of how the earth and man [meaning all men and women] were created. At the university we may hear an entirely different story. This is often an unsettling experience, especially when it involves people in whom we have confidence and the book that forms the principal document of Christianity. In the light of scientific discoveries must we discard the Bible? and with it our religion? On the other hand, if we choose to keep a place for religion in our lives, are we unfit to pursue science with complete objectivity? The first step in analyzing the immediate problem of evolution and the Bible is the definition of terms. This is necessary because some people have spoken of evolution as if it were synonymous with atheism or materialism and some have spoken of religion as if it were synonymous with emotion or superstition.

In the broadest sense, evolution is change. It occurs virtually everywhere and is associated with the largest and the smallest objects known to man. On the one hand the vast universe with some 10^{20} (100,000,000,000,000,000,000) suns, many of which are surrounded by planets like our solar system, is undergoing change. Young, middle- aged, and mature systems are known to astronomers. Of the vast number of planets some 10^8 (100,000,000) are considered by some astronomers to be capable of supporting life in some form. Presumable living things in all these creations are evolving in their particular environments. At the other extreme in size range, atoms and molecules are also undergoing change in nature. Our whole earth, despite its seemingly rigid and stable construction, has evolved over long periods of geological time and continues to undergo change.

Another kind of evolution has occurred within very recent history. Man-made objects such as the automobile, airplane and space ship have evolved because of man's activity and inventive genius. In the brief period of human history, man has been able to accomplish countless remarkable developments through his acquaintance with the laws of nature and his ability to direct them toward his purposes. The rate of developments for some of these products of human enterprise has been so rapid that their entire span of evolution has occurred within the memory of living people. Yet one must bring together and compare the different successive models to realize the full extent and trend of evolution of a given man-made device. It is infinitely more difficult to visualize the grand sequence of evolutionary change that has occurred during long periods of the earth's history.

Organic evolution is the aspect of the broad subject that deals with changes among living organisms, i.e., plants and animals. This kind of change is different from that in the non-living world. It is based on a dynamic system in nature through which variation, selection, and isolation occur. Not only individuals but whole populations are involved in organic evolution. The unit that must be visualized whenever evolution is considered is the population rather than the individual.

Although the idea of evolution has been expressed repeatedly in the early history of biology, Charles Darwin and Alfred Russel Wallace in 1858 were the first clearly to describe the process and to suggest a mechanism for its accomplishment. Darwin described organic evolution as descent from a common ancestor with modification. Members of present day animal and plant species are alike because of their common inheritance, and different because hereditary variations have accumulated since their separation from a common ancestral stock. This concept implies an actual biological relation among individuals and species. It follows that plants and animals now living on the earth are modified descendants of somewhat different plants and animals that lived in times past. Their ancestors in turn descended from predecessors from which they differed, and so on, back to the early periods of biological history.

Species formation is a part of evolution. There are several kinds of species and many factors involved in their origin. One kind may be formed when segments of a breeding group become separated by physical or geographical barriers from other segments of the breeding unit. Through random mutations and chromosome modifications that accumulate over long periods of time in isolated populations, and selection favoring local environmental conditions, members of sub-groups become different enough to make interbreeding with members of other segments of the former breeding population impossible. Reproductive isolation makes the sub-group independent. Because the species is a basic biological unit, species formation is an important aspect of evolution.

The word "evolution" denotes the grand over-all process by which physical and biological changes were (and are being) accomplished in nature. Darwinism is the theory of evolution by natural selection. This was the first attempt in modern times to account for the mechanics of organic evolution. As would be expected (and as Darwin himself recognized) this factor alone is inadequate for a complete explanation, but it represents one of the major processes now known to direct evolution. Selection operates on inherent variations which occur ultimately from change or mutation in the hereditary material called germ plasm. People who do not believe in evolution should have no fear concerning the effects of "fallout" on man and other living things.

Sources of Evidence of Evolution. During the past one hundred years evolution has been widely investigated and discussed by biologists. It has now emerged as the basic theme of biological science and has become not only the most far-reaching principle in that area of science but the common meeting ground for all the life sciences. As a biologist observes the distribution of fauna and flora, he is impressed with the fact that closely related species are living in near proximity, suggesting common ancestry. This observation impressed both Darwin and Wallace, and biogeography thus became the first supporting field for evolution. Comparative anatomists of the last century observed that common patterns are followed in the anatomy of related groups of organisms, and comparative physiologists found functional similarities among related biological units suggesting that they had their origin from a common source. Serological tests supported the physiological evidence and showed similarities in antigenic response among closely related groups. The phylogenetic sequence that is reflected to a large extent in present day taxonomy of plants and animals also suggests common ancestry.

Embryology has contributed a share of evidence supporting evolution by demonstrating relations among individuals in developmental stages as well as in their adult forms. Embryos of some animals have proved more valuable than adults in placing the group in its proper phylogenetic sequence with other groups. This indicates that developmental stages, as well as final products, reflect ancestral relations. Ecological relations among plants and animals also suggest evolution. The mechanism of adaptation that must have occurred over long periods of time to account for the present intimate relation between organisms and their environment provides support for the evolution concept. The most tangible evidence for evolution has come from paleontology. Actual fossil remains representing animals and plants living in past eras of the earth's history can be studied and thus provide a pattern of the history of animals and plants upon the earth. Although many details are lacking in the series of fossils now available, the general evidence favoring evolution is remarkably clear. New evidence from genetics has contributed much to the present understanding of the mechanics of evolution.

All of these lines of evidence support a view of common ancestry among animals and plants. Presumably the processes responsible for the production of the various forms now living on the earth will continue and will result in other forms in future generations unlike those now upon the earth.

Man's Place in the Biological World. The word "Darwinism" has been used by some as if it were synonymous with "evolution." In this connotation it has been restricted by laymen to include only human evolution and equated with the theory that man descended from a "monkey." Evolution is a broad biological principle of change occurring among all living things. It was known and discussed long before the time of Darwin and the theory has been refined considerably since Darwin's time.

Physical man, as a part of nature, has evolved from mammalian ancestry but not from a modern monkey. It is inaccurate to speak of man as having descended from any kind of monkey now living but there is abundant evidence to show that man received his body from more generalized mammals of the taxonomic order Primate, the order to which man and monkey belong. It makes little difference, actually, whether the physical ancestors are called apes or monkeys or given a more precise scientific name.

Where does present-day man fit into the biological picture of evolution? Evidence cited above along with that from other lines of investigation indicates that man obtained his body from animal ancestors. There are no close relatives of man upon the earth at present and the "near men" from which man may have descended are all extinct. Although man and his immediate ancestors were not good fossil-formers and have lived for the most part in environments where fossils are not readily found, there is now a fairly complete fossil record of man's physical ancestry.

Darwin speculated in *The Descent of Man* (1871, 240-42) that man's ancestry would eventually be traced to Africa because the higher primates native to Africa (gorilla, chimpanzee) are more like man that those native to other parts of the world. An important discovery supporting this speculation was made in East Africa on July 17, 1959, by Dr. L. S. B. Leakey. Remains of a "near man," *Zinjanthropous boisii*, were found with very crude tools and other evidences of a level of culture representing one of man's possible physical ancestors that lived some 600,000 years ago. This creature was a plains animal and not a tree dweller like the gorilla and chimpanzee that now inhabit Africa. Another "man-ape," Australopithecus, was discovered in South Africa a few years before (Dart 1956; 1959).

In 1891 the Dutch anthropologist, Dubois, found fossil remains of a prehuman primate in Java. He considered this to be an "ape-man" capable of walking erect and names him *Pithecanthropus erectus* (renamed by Mayr, *Homo erectus erectus*). Other Java men have been found since, and dated in the Pleistocene epoch at about 500,000 years ago. More recently (1927-29) remains of the Peking man called *Sinanthropus pekinensis* (Homo *erectus pekinensis* in Mayr's terminology) were found in China by D. Black and F. Weidenreich. Some forty specimens of Peking men are now known. They were cave dwellers and hunters who lived about 360,000 years ago according to the estimate of B. Kurtin made in 1959.

In 1859 when the *Origin of Species* was published, the fossil record on man's ancestry was meager, indeed. The Neanderthal man was the only well-established example. Perhaps this is one reason Darwin did not make reference to man's ancestry in the *Origin*. When the *Descent of Man* was published in 1871, the fossil evidence was still very limited, but Darwin felt secure on other grounds and devoted some 240 pages to man's physical ancestry. Now there is a considerable amount of evidence from fossils to document the ancestral history of man.

Darwin had nothing against the Bible story of Man's origin and history and was surprised by the reaction that his writings brought forth among theologians. The reaction was largely due to the threat that the natural explanation seemed to pose for the literal interpretation of the scriptures. Another reason for the conflict was Darwin's interpretation of natural selection that was based on the "tooth and claw" principles emphasizing the destructive powers in nature. This was basically against Christian fundamentalism and did not conform to the kind of human relations that nineteenth-century Christians hopefully were striving toward. Darwin had neglected the elements of enlightenment and cooperation in human society that have since been woven into the evolution theme by some of Darwin's followers.

Chemical Theory of the Origin of Life. Darwin made no attempt to explain how life began on the earth. Spontaneous generation was the common view at the time and there was no reason to question this explanation. Church people did not oppose spontaneous generation because it seemed both logical and proper that the earth itself should be endowed with the ability to bring forth living things as a continuing process of creation. If life was being created spontaneously all the time, there was no problem concerning the ultimate origin of living things. As shown in the following pages, Pasteur along with his predecessors and contemporaries showed that sterile nutrient media protected from outside contamination remained free from living organisms and that under the conditions of the experiments spontaneous generation did not occur. These experiments represented a triumph of reason over speculation, but they left no alternative other than special creation for the origin of life.

The ultimate origin of life on the earth is a problem in which many present-day biologists are interested. Chemical mechanisms have been discovered that will explain the most fundamental physical properties and requirements of living things such as self duplication (reproduction), protein synthesis, use of energy, and change (mutation). Common chemical elements known to be present in the early stages of the earth's history have been put together under suitable environmental conditions in the laboratory, and crude nucleic acids, amino acids, and acetic acid have been synthesized. These compounds are essential to living systems, and it is possible that they represent all of the basic requirements for life processes. Their synthesis in the laboratory suggests that life may actually be created in a test tube. Nine leading scientists making up a panel at the Darwin Centennial held at Chicago in November 1959 agreed that the production of life in a test tube is a real possibility and that it will probably be accomplished before the end of the present century. This stimulating biological problem is occupying the attention of many present-day biologists and biochemists.

If life can be created in a test tube, a mechanism through which life was originally created on the earth may be suggested. A type of spontaneous generation may have taken place in the remote past (a billion years or more ago) from which the forms presently living on the earth may have descended. Several theories have been advanced to account for the chemical origin of living things. The most productive hypothesis is that of A. I. Oparin, based on the gradual origin of hydrocarbons and other organic substances from hydrogen, ammonia, methane, hydrogen sulfide, and water vapor in a reducing atmosphere. From these simple organic substances polypeptides and polynucleotides were postulated to have developed and eventually colloidal systems to have been built up.

An energy source would be required to bring chemicals together and form the compounds necessary for living systems. Lightning, known to occur in the early stages of the earth's history could represent the required energy source. Some such reactions have been actually carried out in the laboratory by H. C. Urey, S. L. Miller, and S. W. Fox under conditions simulating as nearly as possible those which were likely present at the time when life was first created on the earth. The possibility of the appropriate elements, energy and suitable environment coming together by chance seems remote, indeed, but in tremendously long periods of time the "impossible" becomes inevitable.

Such an event could occur and life arising from it could be perpetuated only once in a particular location. After life was created and living things became widespread and diversified, any new elementary form of life, occurring in a place where conditions suitable for such an origin are present, would be immediately devoured by one of the numerous organisms occupying such places. Furthermore, the increased amount of oxygen through photosynthesis, after plant life became established, would bring about the oxidation of such an elementary, unprotected form before it could become established.

This naturalistic explanation of the creation of life does not exclude a creator but only suggests a method by which the creation of life may have been accomplished. The word "spontaneous" is not used here to imply that something came from nothing but rather to suggest that the origin came about by natural processes. The actual steps in the process have been suggested, and the scientific method now being applied to such problems seems appropriate and capable of supplying answers to questions concerning the "what" and "how" of creation.

Anyone really interested in the mechanics of the origin of life may ask himself *how* it might have been accomplished. Some would say simply that God did it. Although this does not answer the question, it would be acceptable to many, but *how* was it done? The idea that a creator took mud from a pond and shaped it into man (or a lower animal or plant) is, to a person with some understanding of nature, ridiculous. Some would say that life came from another planet through "floating spores" or living organisms transported on meteors, but that merely postpones the ultimate question. *How* was life created in the place from which it came? And how did it get from a distant planet through space, intense cold, and irradiation to this earth.

Experiments Concerning the Origin of Life. Throughout the history of biology there has been much interest in the origin of life, both the ultimate origin of living things and the immediate origin of individuals. A brief review of history will illustrate man's struggle with meager tools to answer profound questions. It will also show the changing attitude toward the idea of spontaneous generation. Spontaneous generation implies an origin of living things by processes other than the reproduction of parent organisms. A favorable combination of non-living materials was considered sufficient to account for the origin of living things. Spontaneous generation was a common explanation from the earliest periods of biological history until the middle of the last century.

Aristotle, like many of his contemporaries, considered flies and frogs to be formed spontaneously from the mud in the bottom of streams and pools. He was able to observe other animals such as the cuttle fish and octopus engaged in the reproductive process. These he recognized as being formed from eggs produced by the female and activated by the "milt" from the male. Higher organisms were considered by Aristotle to develop from eggs even though they had not been observed, but lower organisms whose reproduction was entirely unknown, were believed to arise spontaneously.

From the time of Aristotle through the Middle Ages, many people expressed themselves favorable toward spontaneous generation. Diodorus Siculus in the first century B.C. claimed that the mud of the Thebes region was capable of generating mice and other organisms. This belief survived the rebirth of inquiry in the twelfth century and persisted without serious question until the eighteenth century. J. B. van Helmont (1577-1644), Belgian alchemist, physician and philosopher, was outspoken in promoting this explanation for the origin of life. He was specific in prescribing a technique for producing mice. It was only necessary, he said, to place moist soiled rags in a dark attic and surround them with kernels of wheat or pieces of cheese. Within a reasonable time mice would invariably appear, and there seemed to be no doubt that they were actually produced spontaneously. Cause and effect relations have been troublesome throughout history. Many authors described the spontaneous origin of frogs, eels, and snakes from the mud in river bottoms. In Shakespeare's *Anthony and Cleopatra*, Lepidus says that crocodiles are produced from the mud of the Nile under the influence of the warm summer sun.

One of the first men to question the spontaneous origin of living things was the Italian physician and naturalist, Francesco Redi (1626-97?). After studying medicine at the University of Pisa, he became court physician to Ferdinand II (1610-70), the Medici Grand Duke of Tuscany. He was a member of the famous Academy of Experiments that was organized in 1657 at Florence, Italy.

Redi set out to determine by experimentation whether flies could be developed spontaneously. His procedure followed an experimental method. He began by killing three snakes and placing them in an open box where they were allowed to decay. Maggots appeared on the decaying flesh, fed on the meat, and grew rapidly. During the growth period of rapid and continuous growth, they became dormant (pupated) and after a few days emerged into flies. Several varieties of pupae were identified by size, shape, and color, and each was observed to give rise to a particular type of adult fly.

Redi continued his experiments, testing different kinds of flesh, both raw and cooked. He used the meat of oxen, deer, buffalo, lion, tiger, duck, lamb, kid, rabbit, goose, chicken, and swallow and also studied several kinds of fish, including sword fish, tuna, eel, and sole. Particular types of maggots developed on the meat and emerged in due course to become particular types of adult flies. Sometimes the maggots were all of the same type, and Redi observed that only one type of fly emerged; whereas in other cases several different types were identified. Each type of maggot was later isolated and found to give rise to a particular kind of fly. Adult flies of the same kinds that emerged from the maggots were observed to hover over the decaying meat and Redi noticed that the flies dropped tiny objects on the meat. Some flies would remain quiet on the meat and deposit several units in one place, whereas others would deposit single objects while hovering above the decaying meat. Redi theorized that the flies might be developed from the objects dropped by the adult flies on the putrifying meat.

An experiment was carefully designed to test this hypothesis. Portions of fish and eel were placed in flasks. The openings were completely sealed off, and the meat was observed through the glass as it underwent decay while other comparable flasks were prepared in the same way but left uncovered. Flies were soon attracted to the opened flasks, and in a few days maggots appeared on the meat. Flies were also observed hovering over the sealed flasks but no maggots developed on the meat inside. Occasionally maggots appeared on the top of the sealed flasks. They would wriggle on the surface and appear to be trying to get through the glass to the putrifying meat inside. This indicated that the maggots were developed from the elements dropped from the adult flies and were not derived spontaneously on the decaying meat.

Even though the results seemed conclusive, Redi was not content with these experiments. He tried variations of different kinds to see if the results could be repeated. The experiments were repeated at different seasons of the year with various kinds of vessels and different kinds of meat. He even buried meat underground and observed that no maggots were developed in the covered meat, but at the same time maggots that emerged into flies were formed on meat that was exposed to the air. There was one difficulty with the experiments; the sealed containers and the soil covering could exclude some vital force necessary for the spontaneous generation of life. To obviate this uncertainty, Redi designed a further experiment in which air was permitted to enter, but flies were excluded.

For this experiment, Redi covered glass containers with a fine gauge veil which allowed air to enter but through which flies were unable to reach the decaying meat. He found that the covered meat would not produce maggots but that the unprotected containers provided for the controls were well supplied with maggots and in due time adult flies. Thus, he had demonstrated that under conditions in which air was not excluded, but when the flies were merely prevented from laying their eggs on the meat, no life was created. Redi observed carefully the activities of flies during the different phases of the experiment. Flies were attracted to the meat as soon as it showed the first signs of decay and laid eggs on the outside surface of the unprotected meat. Some eggs were deposited on the veil, and the larvae that emerged would have wriggled their way through the mesh work and entered the containers, but Redi removed them as fast as they appeared. He observed closely the method of egg deposition and noted that in a few cases active young were deposited by adult flies. The eggs had apparently hatched in the body of the mother. Some adults would remain quiet on the surface and deposit several eggs at one time, but others would drop single eggs or larvae from the air without lighting.

Redi, through these simple but ingenious experiments, was able to demonstrate that flies do not develop spontaneously on putrifying meat but that they must come from other flies through the medium of eggs. In his book, *Experiments on the Generation of Insects*, published in 1668, Redi recorded the results of his experiments that dispelled spontaneous generation as it applied to animals as complex as flies. With the advent of microbiology, however, the whole controversy flared up again and required further and more critical experiments. In dealing with minute organisms that could not be readily observed, scientists found that more elaborate tools and refined techniques were necessary.

One of the earliest experiments on microorganisms that produced evidence against spontaneous generation was performed by the French microscopist, Louis Joblot (1645-1723). He observed in 1710, as did Leeuwenhoek in an earlier period, that hay when infused in water and allowed to stand for a few days gave rise to countless microorganisms that were called "infusoria." According to present day taxonomic arrangement, the organisms included in a hay infusion would mostly fall into the groups of bacteria and protozoa. Only a small portion would represent the class of protozoa, now known as infusoria.

Joblot's contemporaries, and many who followed, considered the presence of microorganisms in a hay infusion as conclusive evidence for spontaneous generation, but Joblot was critical of the interpretation and carried out an experiment to test the prevalent idea. He boiled the material to be used for a hay infusion and divided the boiled material into two parts. One was placed in a container that was sealed off completely and then protected from air, whereas the other was left open. The open container soon had numerous microorganisms, but the material in the closed container was free from all living things. By this experiment, Joblot showed that the boiled infusion alone was not capable of producing life anew. Something in the air was required for organisms to become established in the originally sterile infusion.

In 1745 a report on a similar study, but with different results, was published by John T. Needham (1712-82), an English Catholic priest who was interested in science. In his experiments, organisms developed in the heated and closed hay infusions as well as in those left open, supporting spontaneous generation. Obviously, there were technical differences in the way the two experiments were conducted by the two investigators. Hay is now known to carry resistant spores that are not killed by ordinary boiling. Needham apparently did not heat his cultures to a temperature sufficiently high to kill the spores.

On the strength of his contribution, Needham was elected a member of the Royal Society of London, and later he became one of the eight foreign associates of the French Academy of Science. One of the main reasons for the wide recognition accorded Needham's results was the support and exposition provided by Buffon (1707-88). In his enthusiasm for Needham's work, Buffon gave it considerable space in his own *Natural History* and added comments favoring spontaneous generation. Needham was invited to Paris as the guest of Buffon, and he collaborated with Buffon on the second volume of Buffon's encyclopedia of scientific knowledge. The distinguished London churchman and the famous French encyclopedist thus formed a strong team favoring spontaneous generation.

At this same time, a slightly different idea concerning the origin of life was presented by another distinguished French naturalist, Charles Bonnet (1720-93) who spoke of a pre-existence of germs. This idea was speculative, like many others of that period, but it supported the existence of microorganisms and the stability of the living processes. The pre-existence of organisms was never demonstrated, and the idea suffered for want of experimental support. A heated discussion, however, followed the presentation of Bonnet's speculation. It has since been shown that neither the view of Bonnet nor that of Needham and Buffon was correct.

Many experiments followed and different interpretations were made, but the question was still unresolved in the middle of the nineteenth century. Recognizing the uncertainty existing on this fundamental question, the French Academy of Sciences offered a prize for the best dissertation on the subject "Attempts by Well-Conceived Experiments to Throw New Light on the Question of Spontaneous Generation." Louis Pasteur (1822-95) entered the contest and performed a series of well-known experiments demonstrating that microorganisms did not develop spontaneously under the conditions of his experiments.

Then came discoveries of viruses and questions as to their origin arose. Spontaneous generation is now being considered in a more restricted sense, not to explain the immediate origin of individuals but rather to account for the first origin of life on the earth that may have given rise over long periods of time to particles such as "free-living" viruses. As new problems arise, more refined tools must be devised in the continuing search for truth.

To many people, questions concerning the origin of life are among the mysteries that are not supposed to be explored; but to the scientist they are legitimate questions. They may not be answered immediately, but they can at least be asked and experiments may be designed to suggest possible answers. It is doubtful that a more logical tentative explanation than the natural one involving the chemical origin could be suggested to answer the question of *how* life was created.

Curious scientists are interested in problems concerning the physical construction of the earth and living things, even though such questions may seem foolish or outside the limits of authorized knowledge to some other people. My good friend, for example, in commenting on a newspaper release of Dr. Leakey's archeological discovery of the African "near-man" reported to carry the history of man's ancestry back 600,000 years said, "I don't see why they want to discover things like that." He is not a scientist, and although he frequently says that he accepts all truth no matter what the source might be, he does not share the scientist's enthusiasm for the discovery of new truth.

Some theologians have been dogmatic in denouncing scientists and their discoveries, and have advised their followers against science for fear of losing faith. Actually many scientists find that their activities probing into nature strengthen their faith in wholesome religion. In this age of science when capable scientists and men of strong character and integrity are needed desperately in the free world, a farsighted approach is recommended. Science must be taught effectively and qualified students must be counseled wisely in making proper preparation for careers in science.

Religion, to be of any value, must be sincerely believed. It must satisfy the reason as well as the emotions and must be consistent with the person's knowledge of nature and man. Religious beliefs and doctrines cannot stand still when all other knowledge is moving ahead. Damage has come to religion itself by pious attempts on the part of its supporters to oppose science with unscientific methods.

Students are especially prone to lose confidence in religious leaders who are not abreast of the times. Thoughtful people with deep personal convictions, worthy aspirations, and high ideals have been driven to indifference or even hostility to established religion because of the narrowness and extreme literal interpretation on the part of some theologians.

Religion supplies meaning and purpose for many people and for them it answers questions that cannot yet, at least, be answered from scientific data. It should find a legitimate place for itself even in an age dominated by science. Educational, social, and scientific agencies alike are stressing the need for building character and integrity in individuals and the absolute necessity of developing brotherhood and understanding among peoples and nations. Few, if any, of these agencies have found a way to accomplish this important function. Church organizations devoted as they are to the premise that man is important and to the objectives of building better men and improving human relations may be in a better position than other agencies to realize the projected goals.

The Bible, A Book of Religion. When the mechanism of creation is considered, two possibilities are available for evaluation: (1) the evolution concept supported by an impressive body of observations and deductions; and (2) the Bible story of creation that has been preserved with other scriptural documents. How can apparent conflicts be reconciled? If there are conflicts, it may be because some people try to use the Bible in ways for which it was never intended. It is a book of religion and not a book of science. When this fact is established most of the difficulty will be obviated. As stated in the preface, the Bible, as we know it, is the work of many authors, writing at widely different periods of human history. In current editions, the books by various authors are not always in chronological sequence, but Bible scholars have done much to date the various contributions. One thing seems evident: all the biblical writers were primarily interested in religion rather than science. Furthermore, they wrote long before anyone knew anything about modern science. It is true that some sections, such as Job 39, deal extensively with natural subjects: "Knowest thou the time when the wild goats of the rock bring forth? or canst thou mark when the hinds do calve? Canst thou number the months that they fulfill? or knowest thou the time when they bring forth? They bow themselves, they bring forth their young ones, they cast out their sorrows" (vv. 1-2), and, again: "Gavest thou the goodly wings unto the peacocks or wings and feathers unto the ostrich? Which leaveth her eggs in the earth, and warmeth them in dust, and forgetteth that the foot may crush them, or that the wild beast may break them, she is hardened against her young ones, as though they were not hers: her labour is in vain without fear; because God hath deprived her of wisdom, neither hath he imparted to her understanding" (vv. 13-17).

These lines deal with the mechanics of natural phenomena, but their greatest significance is in their beauty and religious feeling rather than in their scientific accuracy. The underlying purpose is apparently to show the grandeur of God's creations. Biblical writers were writing about religion. When they had occasion to refer to natural objects and processes, they spoke in terms of common beliefs of their day. If scattered references to the physical world are pieced together, the resulting picture represents the world and solar system as these people thought them to be. They relied on their senses for descriptions of physical things and visualized the universe as it seemed to be.

Some biblical writers thought the earth was flat and a sea lay under it. For example, the writer of Psalms praised Him, "that stretched out the earth above the waters" (Ps. 136:6; see also 24:1-2 and Gen. 7:11). The heavens were pictured by the author of Genesis as a tent or an upturned bowl above the flat earth with a sea above the sky and windows in the sky through which the rain came down, "And God said, let there be a firmament in the midst of the waters, and let it divide the waters. And God made the firmament and divided the waters which were under the firmament from the waters which were above the firmament . . ." (Gen. 1:6-7; see also 7:11, Job 37:18, Ps. 104:2, 148:4, Isa. 40:22). This is now known to be good Babylonian "science"—the science of that day.

In other references the earth was considered to be stationary, "the world also is established, that it cannot be moved" (Ps. 93:1; also 104:5). The sun, moon and stars were thought to be moved through the heavens for the special purpose of illuminating the earth: "And God made two great lights; the greater light to rule the day, and the lesser light to rule the night: he made the stars also" (Gen. 1:16; see also 1:14-15 and 17-18).

The above descriptions of the physical world are now known to be scientifically incorrect, but they were incidental to the writer's main purpose in writing. Biblical references to "life sciences" like those to the "physical sciences" are dated. For example, the writer of Psalms 139:13-14, was obviously not informed in modern obstetrics, "For thou hast possessed my reins: thou hast covered me in my mother's womb. I will praise thee; for I am fearfully and wonderfully made; marvellous are thy works . . ." Lack of technical accuracy should not obscure the value of a beautiful religious poem. Obviously, these writers were intent in getting over their message of religion. If in doing so, they made inaccurate allusions to the nature of the universe, of the living things therein, it is of no real importance. Their writings must be evaluated on the basis of their worth to religion or philosophy rather than their worth to modern science.

The controversy on the matter of the earth's being stationary may be cited as an example of misuse of the Bible. When Nicolaus Copernicus (1473-1543 A.D.) established his proof (*On the Revolutions of the Heavenly Bodies*, 1543) that the earth revolves (instead of the sun, moon and stars), various religious leaders were extremely upset. Father Inchofer commented that, "the opinion of the earth's motion is of all heresies the most abominable, the most pernicious, the most scandalous; the immovability of the earth is thrice sacred; argument against the immortality of the soul, the existence of God, and the incarnation should be tolerated sooner than an argument to prove that the earth moves" (Moody 1953, 427). Martin Luther attacked Copernicus in these words: "People gave ear to an upstart astrologer who strove to show the earth revolves, not the heavens, or the firmament, the sun and the moon. Whoever wishes to appear clever must devise some new system which of all systems is, of course, the very best. This fool wishes to turn the whole science of astronomy upside down, but sacred scripture tells us that Joshua commanded the sun to stand still and not the earth" (Tischreden, ed. Walch 1743, 2260). We ask now what was the matter with such people? These critics failed to recognize that the Bible is a book of religion but not a book of science.

Evolution is a relative newcomer in the history of science. Most people before 1859 had thought little about it. When Darwin published his *Origin of Species* the storm broke all over again. Religious leaders who were entirely reconciled concerning astronomy despite its contradiction of scripture maintained that the theories of creation in Genesis must be accepted as literal history. They showed a peculiar inconsistency in considering the Bible not to be scientific in matters of astronomy but refusing to recognize that it is not scientific in matters of biology.

The Threat of Evolution to Religion. Evolution was considered by many religious leaders to represent a more serious threat than earlier scientific advances to established religion. It seemed to challenge the trustworthiness of the scriptures more directly than even the work of Copernicus. The place of God in the universe was shaken and the efficacy of faith was brought into question. Darwin had cut the line between man and Adam. The doctrine of the "Fall" seemed untenable with Darwinian biology. The most seriously threatened of all Christian teachings was the role of God as creator as told in the Bible story of creation. To religious leaders of the last century, there seemed to be no middle ground and no possibility for reinterpretation on this issue: if evolution was right, the Bible was wrong, and vice versa.

The nineteenth-century background that made Darwin's work a severe shock can be appreciated only in the perspective of history. As stated earlier, ideas of natural relations and creation in natural ways were considered by the Greek philosopher-scientists and perhaps by even earlier students of nature. The early Chinese, for example, are now known to have had a crude concept of evolution.

The book of Genesis is not world history, but the history of "God's people." In any case the writers were thinking in terms of historical and not cosmic creation. The words "make" and "create" used in Genesis 1 and 2 have been at the base of interpretations of creation. These words are used elsewhere in the Old Testament with different connotations, sometimes with broad and sometimes with restricted meaning. In some places they refer to the coming of Christ or other divine activity as in Psalms 104:30, "Thou sendest forth thy spirit, they are created; and thou renewest the face of the earth." The word was not intended to indicate actually when and how creations occurred. Early writers apparently did not intend to state how things began but rather how they were. The story of the creation was the story of God's dealings with his chosen people. There was no reason to present a full and detailed account of the creation of the universe. A passing reference to the creation of "all things" was adequate for the writer's purpose.

In the New Testament, creation was presupposed and correlated with redemption. Some early Christians discussed the possible method followed by God in the creation of the world and man. Conspicuous scriptural passages provided the theme that the creator molded directly with his hands all things living and dead. The first of the early Christian fathers to discuss creation in detail was Theophilus of Antioch (second century A.D.) who developed the idea of instantaneous creation of something from nothing. Tertullian, also in the second century, was first to use the phrase "creator of heaven and earth." Other early fathers of the church were critical of this point of view and found little support for it in either the Old or New Testament. Saint Augustine (354-430) urged an allegorical interpretation of Genesis 1, particularly the reference to the six-day periods. In one of his writings he said, "to suppose that God formed man from the dust with bodily hands is very childish. God neither formed man with bodily hands nor did he breathe upon him with throat and lips" (Chamberlin 1911, 12).

St. Thomas Aquinas (1225-74) developed a more natural interpretation of theology than his predecessors and contemporaries. In his view all things were created by God in the beginning, but the original creations were endowed with the capacity for change. Once created, the world and living things were set up to run themselves without further intervention. St. Basil declared in the fourth century A.D. that in the beginning, at the command of God, the waters were gifted with productive powers and that "from the slime and muddy places frogs, flies and gnats came into being" (Chamberlin 1911, 11). This is spontaneous generation. St. Basil concluded that the same command that gave this generative power to the earth in the beginning should be effective until the end of the world.

Later Christians were more dogmatic about the specific act of creation by God, called special creation, and it became heresy to advocate any other view. The trend of church leaders was toward a literal interpretation of the scriptures. James Ussher (1581-1656), an Irish prelate, constructed a chronology of the Bible and on the premise that the earth was created instantaneously on the first day mentioned in Genesis 1, set the date of creation at 4004 B.C. At the time Bishop Ussher made his calculation and through the two centuries that followed, there was little reason to question this chronology.

The question of the time required for the creation of the earth, the origin of life, and the development of man has been one of more recent controversy. Few people now believe that the earth and all its inhabitants were created in six twenty-four hour days but, it is argued, that the "days" could well represent longer periods or perhaps six impulses of God's creative activity and not definite time periods. One interpretation in terms of definite time periods is that each "day" represents 1,000 years. This would allow a total of some 6,000 years for the entire process of creation. A realistic perspective of time is difficult to establish. One student recently insisted that the dinosaurs, extinct for some 75 million years, were destroyed in Noah's flood. Another student explained an Indian legend describing transportation by water from one location to another in Western America as relating to Lake Bonneville times. The student dated this event at 300 years ago but Lake Bonneville dates back more than 25,000 years.

One scientific concept essential to an appreciation of evolution is that of geological time. The familiar units of time such as days, years, and centuries are inadequate to describe the long periods required for evolution to occur. Members of the human species, *Homo sapiens*, for example, have been present on the earth in substantially their present physical form for some 25,000 to 50,000 years. Man's entire history on the earth covers only a very small part of the earth's history which goes into the billions of years.

Pre-Darwinian Biologists. Not only church people but most scientists as well found no place for evolution in the two centuries preceding the time of Darwin. Biology and other sciences during this period were dominated by systematists.

New knowledge had been accumulated during the Renaissance and the next logical step was to classify it into useful systems. Movements to systemize and classify were promoted in the cultural areas such as literature, theology and art as well as in science. The key to the period was characterized in Newton's book *Principia* (1687) in which mathematical principles of natural philosophy were presented. Newton viewed the universe as fixed and static with the earth and heavenly bodies precisely arranged and moving in mathematical harmony. The same fixed and rigid pattern developed for the physical world was carried over to biology. Attempts were made to classify animals and plants according to a prearranged fixed system.

The English naturalist and theologian, John Ray (1627-1705), was one of the leading biologists of his time. He accepted the biblical explanation of creation. In the preface to the third edition of his *The Wisdom of God Manifested in the Works of the Creation* (1701), he wrote, "by the Works of Creation . . . I mean the Works created by God at first and by him conserved to this Day in the same State and Condition in which they were first made." Ray devoted his life to discriminating, defining, and arranging plants and animals systematically. He insisted that distinctions should be based on structure rather than color, size or habit of plants and animals. His system of classification was a natural one in spite of his rigid view of creation.

Carl V. Linnaeus (Linné Latinized) (1707-78) was the greatest systematist in the history of biology. He spent his early life in the modest home of a pastor who was a nature lover. Linnaeus was educated in his native Sweden and later in Holland. At twenty-eight years of age he published the first edition of his *Systema Naturae* (1735). Later editions, along with *The Classes of Plants* (1738), *Botanical Philosophy* (1751), and *The Species of Plants* (1753), presented the binomial (two-term naming) system of nomenclature which became the method for classification of plants and animals.

Although Linnaeus was a special creationist, he followed inadvertently the natural system of classification. There is evidence that later in life Linnaeus considered the evolution concept more favorable. When he tried to hybridize plants of different species, he became aware of natural mechanisms which serve as isolating factors. During the Linnean period in the eighteenth century, however, the fixity of species was firmly established and any ideas of evolution were crowded into the background. Only a few biologists gave the subject much consideration.

The French naturalist, politician, and writer, Buffon (1707-88) who was contemporary with Linnaeus, discussed evolution extensively, but he took different positions on this subject at different times in his life. During his early life, he took an extreme view in favor of special creation, much like that of Linnaeus. He did not, however, agree with Linnaeus in other respects. Linnean classification was depicted as trifling and artificial. Buffon considered nature as a whole and looked for large likenesses rather than trivial differences. This led him to a consideration of broad natural relation and evolution.

Later in life Buffon developed an extreme view in favor of inheritance of acquired characteristics. The factors that he visualized as influencing evolutionary change were: (1) direct influences of the environment, (2) migration, (3) geographical isolation, and (4) overcrowding and struggle for existence. These factors would result in a gradual development of new forms of life rather than abrupt changes. When he was more involved in politics at a later stage in his career, he adopted a more liberal, middle-of-the-road position and wavered between the extremes of his earlier views. He compromised the position of special creation and evolution with a number of wild speculations. The pig, for example, was described as a compound of other animals, the ass was a degenerate horse, and the ape a degenerate man. Buffon was a prolific writer and an interpreter of contemporary thought, but he was not an original investigator.

Erasmus Darwin (1731-1802), English philosopher and free thinker, was somewhat clearer than Buffon on the subject of evolution. The name of his best known book *Zoonomia*, was coined to represent the laws of organic life. In this book Darwin developed the theme of the inheritance of acquired characteristics. The age of the earth was described in millions of years, and life was considered to have originated from a primordial protoplasmic mass. The struggle for existence that was elaborated by Charles Darwin, grandson of Erasmus, was suggested in *Zoonomia*.

In the preface to *Zoonomia*, Darwin wrote, "The Great Creator of all things has infinitely diversified the works of his hands but has at the same time stamped a certain similitude on the features of nature, that demonstrate to us that the whole is one family of one parent. On this similitude is founded all rational analogy." Erasmus Darwin independently concluded that species descend from common ancestors. He speculated on the variation in animals and the reasons for such variations; for example, the tendency for the strongest to reproduce themselves in greater proportion, and the struggle for existence constantly occurring among animals. It is now evident that

Charles Darwin received more from his grandfather than was previously supposed. For every volume written by Charles, there was a corresponding chapter by Erasmus. Charles, in one of his treatises, expressed his disappointment in finding *Zoonomia* more speculative than scientific.

The most important of the eighteenth-century evolutionists was Jean Baptiste Lamarck (1744-1829). In the years 1781-82, Lamarck traveled across Europe studying plants and taking notes for his *Dictionary of Botany*. Later he wrote *Flora of France*, a work published by the French government. Through the assistance of Buffon, he obtained a job in the Museum of Natural History where he contributed further to botanical literature. During the French revolution when he was becoming a good botanist, he changed his field to invertebrate zoology, and over a period of years prepared a seven-volume, systematic study of the invertebrates. His best known work is *Philosophical Zoology* (1809).

Lamarck's contribution to evolution was a substantial one, even though it has not always been fully appreciated. Lamarck described the animal kingdom as a graded series from simple to complex forms. In his view, no group became extinct through abrupt catastrophes as his contemporary Cuvier contended, but one form changed into another. Lamarck was not as well trained and disciplined as Cuvier, but he gave the first detailed defense of evolution. When he came to an explanation of the mechanics of evolution, he made use of the theory of inheritance of acquired characteristics that had come from the Greeks and had been developed by Erasmus Darwin and Buffon. Lamarck made bold speculations and carried the subject to great detail, and, even though he did not originate the view, his name has become associated with the inheritance of acquired characteristics. Briefly, he held that (1) the environment modifies plants and animals; (2) new needs modify old organs and bring new ones into use; (3) use and disuse modify development; and (4) these modifications are inherited.

Lamarck made other contributions to evolution that are more sound but are not as well remembered as his speculation on the inheritance of acquired characteristics. He appreciated the factor of isolation in forming new species and recognized the influence of proximity in destroying differences between varieties within species.

He saw unity existing in nature and provided the first diagram of an evolutionary tree. He understood, at least in a general way, the physiological balance maintained in nature. Lamarck was first to use the word "species" correctly, as a term to describe a natural unit of related animals or plants. Aristotle had used the term, and in the years that followed the word was used extensively in logic. It had been applied to groups of animals and plants by Ray and other early systematists, but Lamarck gave the word its modern usage.

Georges Cuvier (1769-1832) was noted primarily for his work in systematics, comparative anatomy, and paleontology. Although he greatly improved the geological time table and possessed the fundamental knowledge on which evolution is now based, his personal influence on the theory of evolution was negative. He openly opposed evolution and supported the alternative view of fixity of species. His theory of catastrophism and successive new creations was popularized at the expense of the alternative theory of the gradual change supported by Lamarck. Cuvier belittled Lamarck and was largely responsible for the unpopularity of Lamarck in his later life. Geoffry St. Hilaire (1772-1844), a contemporary and colleague of Cuvier, opposed Cuvier's views and defended evolution. He advocated the direct effect of environment as Buffon and Lamarck had done to explain small variations, recognized the evolutionary effects of isolation, and visualized physiological as well as geographical isolation as a factor in species formation.

A well-known incident of this period arose from a controversy between Cuvier and St. Hilaire concerning the origin of the squid. Instead of discussing the matter privately and objectively the two men held a public debate which was announced and widely publicized, making the issue more emotional than scientific. St. Hilaire, who had an idea of evolution, but based only on meager and crude observations, was tight in principle but poorly prepared and perhaps wrong in detail. Cuvier explained the origin of the squid on the basis of special creation. He was wrong in general principle but well prepared with supporting details and won the debate by a better argument and a dramatic show. The effect was to retard the study of evolution.

Nineteenth-century Conflict. It must be remembered that developments in science were meager indeed during the Middle Ages and that the broad natural relations now fundamental to biology were not widely appreciated even until the last century. In a background devoid of science, the scriptures provided the only available information, and they were interpreted to answer questions that ordinarily would be considered within the province of science. Although attacks had been made on Genesis 1 as far back as the seventeenth century, there was no well established reason for not taking Genesis 1 literally until the time of Charles Darwin (1809-82). When Darwin came on the scene, the traditional interpretation of creation was so well established that even the suggestion of an alternative explanation met resistance. Darwin's conclusions, which probably would not have surprised thinking people in earlier periods of history, caused a major intellectual revolution in the middle nineteenth century. Perhaps nothing since the Reformation has had such a profound influence on men's thinking.

During the five years (1831-36) while Darwin traveled around the world on the *Beagle* he observed and collected plants, animals and fossils. On the Galapagos Islands he was impressed with the gigantic tortoises and large crabs not like those on the shores of the South American mainland some 600 miles away. Among the armored animals he noted transitional forms from island to island. Different islands sometimes had entirely different species. He kept notes on all these observations and pondered over the strange relations. As his observations were accumulated, his faith in the fixity of species was shaken. On his return to England, he published the *Journal of Researches* and took care of other matters of immediate importance. When these tasks were completed, he returned to his notes on species formation and took time to reflect on the significance of his observation.

The problem to be solved was: do species of living creatures really change or become modified, and if so, how? A few observers had postulated that existing species were descended from other species and had gradually become modified in the process. But why should modification occur? It was common knowledge that man could "select" certain types of domestic animals and alter the characteristics of a breed. But how selection could be applied to organisms living in nature was a mystery.

At first Darwin was merely collecting and classifying facts.

Then a theory dawned on him, and he began working with a purpose. The key to the problem apparently came to him when he read an essay by Thomas Malthus on the *Principle of Population*. Briefly, the theme of the essay was that man multiplies more rapidly than does his supply of food; therefore, competition occurs for the requirements of existence. The prize for which the competitors struggled was life itself and the success of one animal meant the failure of the others. Darwin pondered over the problem and decided that if he could demonstrate that favorable variations would tend to be preserved in living populations and unfavorable ones destroyed, he could show how new species came into being.

Darwin spent some twenty years working over this theory. In the early part of this period (1842), he prepared a small paper outlining the theory that he sent to his biologist friends for criticism. With the help they provided, he strengthened each point and improved the theory. He read, discussed, observed, and spared no effort in making the case as clear and well documented as possible. A book was planned in which all of his data would be presented. In the meantime, while the great book was taking form, he undertook the writing of an abstract. This was about half written when Darwin suffered a shattering blow. He received for review a short manuscript written by the explorer-naturalist Alfred Russel Wallace (1823-1913) entitled *On the Tendency of Varieties to Depart Indefinitely from the Original Type.*

So closely did the paper by Wallace agree with his own theory, he commented later, that it might have been an abstract of his own work. Twenty years of work and thought had apparently been wasted. Darwin generously recognized the contribution of his then obscure, young colleague and suggested that Wallace's paper be published immediately. Friends of Darwin, however, who knew of his work, intervened and suggested a joint publication by the two pioneers, summarizing the new theory of evolution. This seemed a fair solution to the problem of priority. A joint paper was read in June, 1858, before the Linnean Society and published in the *Transactions* of the society later the same year.

The two authors of the evolution theory arrived at their conclusions through different paths. Darwin had pondered the matter for some twenty years and had collected volumes of data. Al-

though Wallace had undoubtedly given the general subject considerable thought during the preceding three or four years, he apparently
arrived at the conclusion in a single flash of insight. In February 1858,
during an attack of yellow fever, Wallace had time and inclination to
think about the problem of how living populations have arrived at
their present status. He remembered the thesis of Malthus on population that he had read many years before and hit upon the idea of
"survival of the fittest" as it applied to animals and plants. He thought
out the theory in a few hours and by the evening of the same day had
prepared a rough outline of the idea. Two days later he had written
the paper that was sent to Darwin.

The detailed book that Darwin had planned was never written. After seeing Wallace's paper he changed from his usual methodi-
cal way and moved into high gear on his abstract, completing it in
thirteen months. It was published in 1859 under the title, *On the
Origin of Species by Means of Natural Selection, or the Preservation of
Favored Races in the Struggle for Life.* Every single copy of the first
edition was sold on the day of publication.

The conflict during the latter part of the nineteenth century
was bitter and is not yet completely dead. There are many controversial points that become obvious when philosophical and theological
implications are considered. For the most part, religious leaders are
now recognizing the Bible for what it is, a book of religion, but not
a book of science. Speaking at the Darwin centennial held at Chicago
in November 1959, Dr. J. Pelikan of the Federated Theological
Faculty of the University of Chicago, said, "Even the most reactionary
theologian today must give some consideration to the scientific
explanation of creation. Most theologians agree that essential theology is but little affected by the adjustment necessary to accommodate
modern science. Both science and religion have a place and each
should respect the other's position and method." Actually they need
each other. Science without religion may become materialism as it
has in some parts of the world. Religion without science may become
superstition, as in earlier periods of history. Together they contribute
to wholesome human activity based on intellectual, emotional, and
spiritual experience.

Biblical Accounts of Creation. Since some people regard the
creation stories in Genesis as literal history, let us consider them more

critically. Two different stories of the creation appear in Genesis. The transmission of the records of early writings to us has involved many devious pathways. The Bible in its present form represents a composite production made from several sources that have been blended, brought up to date, and supplemented by the various authors. One of the sources was the Judahite, J narrative (Yahoistic or Jehovistic document) written as the religious book of the Kingdom of Judah. The northern kingdom of Israel also had its narrative, usually called the E (Elohist) narrative. There are also other documents such as the Book of the Covenant, the Law, the Priestly Code (P), and Deuteronomy (D). Although neither the J nor the E narrative was written earlier than the ninth century B.C., both tell of the founding of the Hebrew nation centuries before.

The E narrative starts with Abraham, but the J narrative begins with the creation. This most ancient account of the creation is now found in the King James Bible in the second chapter of Genesis (vv. 4-23). According to this account God made the earth suitable for life and formed man from the dust of the ground. A garden was planted for the man Adam to live in with a variety of trees for his use. God then created the beasts of the field and the fowls, and brought them to Adam to name. Afterward, God created woman from one of Adam's ribs. Note that in this account man was created before the lower animals and that the time of creation was not divided into separate days.

When the J and E narratives were united and added to, the ancient Judahite account of the creation was left intact but ahead of it was placed another and differing account of the creation (Gen. 1 and 2:1-4). This latter account is the familiar one divided into six days. The entire story is told in some 600 words. In this narrative plants were created on the third day, and then the sun, moon and stars were created on the fourth day; certainly an improbable sequence. The process of photosynthesis, essential for plant nutrition, would be difficult to maintain for even a day before the sun was created. According to this account, water dwelling animals and fowls were then created, followed on the next day by the beasts and the creeping things. Finally on the sixth day man was created male and female (no mention here of Adam and his rib). The taxonomy and phylogeny suggested in this account indicate again that the Bible is not intended as a text of modern science. The classification represents a mere lumping of individuals for convenient reference. In some cases the mode of movement is used (e.g., walking or swimming), in other cases the habitat (e.g. water, air or land) or the presumed origin (e.g. from water or earth), or the mode of propagation (e.g. fast breeding insects).

In the first two chapters of Genesis two entirely different stories of creation are recorded, conflicting in detail and chronology. Both cannot be a literal history of what actually occurred, so why regard either of them as being literal? Why were these accounts of the creation written? Their emphasis is religious, not scientific. "In the beginning God created the heavens and the earth." Early biblical writers were intent upon impressing the idea of God and only one God, not many gods as most other people at that time believed. Later writers were showing that God was trustworthy, merciful and just in dealing with those bound to Him, but the mechanics of creation were incidental.

The first chapters of Genesis record great religious concepts. Acceptance of the religious message they carry should not be dependent upon the scientific allusions they contain. Is it not just as possible to worship a God who works through natural laws, slowly evolving life on this planet, as it is to worship a God who creates by sudden command? To many thinking people the concept of the creator becomes more satisfying as they become more familiar with the intricate workings of the universe. Such a creator is to many people far greater in stature than a miracle worker who created things once and for all in 4004 B.C.

Evolution and God. The next question is: does not science prove that there is no creator? Science deals with phenomena that can be studied by the physical senses, particularly the sense of sight aided by methods available for extending these senses, such as the microscope or telescope. These methods have not thus far yielded any evidence concerning a creator. If they ever do, science may then be in a position to prove whether or not there is a creator; but that time seems far removed from the present. Science can neither prove that there is a creator nor prove that there is not a creator.

To the next question, do not many scientists believe that there is not creator? one must answer, "yes," but this is quite another matter. Scientists, like other human beings, believe many things not proved by science. Some bankers, some machinists, and some farmers do not believe in a creator. What people believe to be true is determined by numerous factors, many of which have nothing to do with scientific demonstration. This statement is as true of scientists as it is of other people. Scientists are not a distinctive race of mankind. Each scientist has had an impressionable childhood molded by varied influences. The scientist leads his private life as do other people. Accordingly, in matters of belief scientists are much like other people. Many of them believe in a creator; some of them do not. But if they are thoughtful and honest they readily recognize that their belief one way or another is not equivalent to scientific demonstration.

It is true that the phenomena which can be observed in evolution operate by chance with no apparent direction or design. Many students of evolution conclude that there is no purpose, that the whole process is opportunistic. They point to many blind alleys through which animals have gone only to become extinct; they emphasize the fact that evolution, as evaluated by common standards, is not progressing, that apparent progress is frequently followed by obvious retrogression; and that animals do not seem to evolve according to any established pattern. How animal populations evolve depends upon the opportunities that chance to befall them. These are matters of observation, yet they may not in themselves represent the whole pattern. Why should we assume that the laws of the universe, including those of evolution, must be so organized to reach our chosen goal by what seems to us the proper or most direct route? And why should we conclude that if the natural laws do not seem to be leading toward a goal, that there is no goal at all? A chance mechanism on the surface could obscure guiding lines on the inside. Natural selection could be a part of a plan of creation.

As an example of a scientist who was honest and objective in his search for scientific truth but deeply sensitive to religion, Charles Darwin, himself, might be cited. In the final paragraph on the *Origin of Species*, Darwin said, "There is a grandeur in this view of life, with its several powers, having been originally breathed by the creator into a few forms or into one; and that, whilst this planet has gone cycling on according to the fixed law of gravity, from so simple a beginning endless forms, most beautiful and most wonderful, have been, and are being evolved." Darwin considered his theory of evolution to be quite compatible with a belief in God. In one of his last letters he wrote, "I have never been an atheist in the sense of denying the existence of God."

At the conclusion of the introduction to the first edition (1859) of the *Origin of Species* Darwin wrote: "I see no good reason why the views given in this volume should shock the religious feeling of anyone. It is satisfactory, as showing how transient such impressions are, to remember that the greatest discovery ever made by man, namely, the law of the attraction of gravity, was also attacked by Leibnitz, 'as subversive of natural and inferentially of revealed religion.' A celebrated author and divine [sic] has written to me that 'he has gradually learnt to see that it is just as noble a conception of the Deity to believe that He created a few original forms capable of self-development into other and needful forms, as to believe that He required a fresh act of creation to supply the voids caused by the action of His laws.'"

Any new development in science may appear as a threat to some orthodox interpretation. On the other hand close observations in nature may suggest new ways to interpret cherished phrases in line with knowledge and reason.

Man is More than an Animal. The next question, then, is whether or not it makes a difference to man and his feeling of importance to recognize his animal ancestry. If it does, what adjustments are necessary for him to maintain his self-esteem and yet to accommodate scientific facts? It may require a change in viewpoint to regard man as having received his body from the animals rather than from an especially created perfect state. It should be emphasized here that only the physical body is involved in the evolution concept. Whatever else goes into the makeup of a man is totally unknown from scientific data. People who on occasion speak of man as a dual being made of body and soul, or "breath of life," are sincerely distressed at the thought that man's body is an animal body. For them there is comfort in the thought that the body once was perfect and that man's principal task is to regain that perfect state.

All scientific evidence available on man's physical history indicates that he was on the average less perfect in times past than now. Anthropologists can demonstrate that early men as a whole were crude and barbaric. Certain individuals, however, were more highly developed than others. Man, as he has developed from the dawn of civilization down to the present, represents the finest fruit of the evolutionary process. This does not mean that no finer fruit will be produced, but if superior physical types of man do arise they will undoubtedly represent a new development, not a reversion to a "perfect state" once existing but subsequently lost. Accordingly, evolution provides an optimistic viewpoint from which to look at man. We may well believe that the great days for humanity are ahead, not behind. Man *is being* created in the image of God. An extreme view of evolution came from religion, not science, and is embodied in the phrase "as God now is, man may become," implying that man may become a god. In a theological sense this is tremendous progress. Theologians who propound this doctrine consider both body and spirit to be making progress and to be endowed with the capacity for eternal progression.

The word "animal" has been used in describing the physical ancestry of man. This does not mean necessarily that man is only an animal. Although the obvious uniqueness of man may not support the authenticity of the Bible or the existence of God, it should be pointed out that man has achieved heights attained by no other inhabitant on this planet. His development of spoken and written language has made possible the social inheritance which forms a unique addition to his biological inheritance. Through this social inheritance ideas and achievements of past generations are handed on so that members of one generation build upon the achievements of their predecessors in a manner unlike anything possible among other animals. Because one generation does build on the achieve-ments of its predecessors, there is a continued social evolution independent of the biological evolution that has brought man to his present physical state. This is a unique achievement of man and it enables him increasingly to control his own destiny. Man's ability to make and use tools has enabled him increasingly to adopt his envi-ronment to himself instead of adapting himself to his environment, as other animals have done.

Moral and ethical values are important to a free society and religion is one agency for perpetuating such values. It would be unfortunate for students and scientists to lose sight of such values because of a conflict between science and religion that is actually more apparent than real. Scientists must remember that everything need not be scientific to be important. Great issues of life are determined by emotional and ethical criteria rather than by cold intellectual decisions: "Out of the heart are the issues of life" (Prov. 4:20). Theologians on the other hand should recognize their debt to the critical attitude that has come with the age of science. Much of the superstition and superficial emotion that has grown up with religion has been removed by science. A new and more intellectual approach has greatly strengthened religion.

Science with its objective methods is prepared to work on questions of "what," "how," and "when." Its function is to provide knowledge. Questions of "why" and "by whom" are for the most part within the province of philosophy and religion. During a period when there was no science, some questions such as how and when the earth was created got over into theology. The day is long since past when scientific questions can be resolved by theologians not trained in science. Subjective methods of religion such as faith may be inappropriate when applied to physical problems but they have a place in developing security, love, and improved human relations.

A great message of the Bible is that man has dignity and is important. Biology, in its present state of development, does little for man's dignity but it shows that man is the only creature on the earth with ability to think, reflect, make and use tools, and cooperate intelligently with his fellows.

11.
Fossils and the Scriptures

Morris S. Petersen

THERE IS MUCH WE DO NOT KNOW ABOUT THE CREATION AND EARLY history of the earth. The scriptural record is sketchy, and the record of science is incomplete. Indeed, what we imagine to be true now about the history of the earth may prove to be only partially true in the light of greater knowledge. We are assured in the Doctrine and Covenants, however, that the day will come when the Lord "shall reveal all things—Things which have passed, and hidden things which no man knew, things of the earth, by which it was made, and the purpose and the end thereof—Things most precious, things that are above, and things that are beneath, things that are in the earth, and upon the earth, and in heaven" (101:32-34). Until that day comes, we must rely on what we are taught in the scriptures and what we assume to be true based on the evidence gathered and examined by science.

We are, in fact, encouraged to obtain both scriptural and secular knowledge in striving to learn about God and his creations: "Teach ye diligently and my grace shall attend you, that you may be instructed more perfectly in theory, in principle, in doctrine, in the law of the gospel, in all things that pertain unto the kingdom of God, that are expedient for you to understand; Of things both in heaven and in the earth, and under the earth; things which have been, things which are, things which must shortly come to pass; things which are at home, things which are abroad; the wars and the perplexities of nations, and the judgments which are on the land; and a knowledge also of countries and of kingdoms" (D&C 88:78-79).

Latter-day Saints share Elder James E. Talmage's conviction

that "within the gospel of Jesus Christ there is room and place for every truth thus far learned by man, or yet to be made known."[1] With these ideas in mind, let us examine briefly what we currently know from the fossil record and compare it with the scriptural record.

God is creator of our earth and of all life on the earth. "In the beginning God created the heavens and the earth. . . . And God created . . . every living creature that moveth . . . And God saw every thing that he had made, and, behold, it was very good" (Gen. 1:1, 21, 31).

Among the life forms God created were many species now extinct. Fossil-bearing rocks are common on the earth, and these fossils represent once-living organisms, preserved now as part of the earth's rocky crust. Paleontology is the branch of science that studies these fossils to collect information about the past. But one does not need to be a paleontologist to find fossiliferous rocks—they are more common than most people imagine, and almost anyone can find fossils near home. These fossils may include microscopic invertebrate and plant remains, a myriad of fossilized bones of large terrestrial animals, the dinosaurs. Local and national laws generally protect fossil deposits, and would-be-collectors should be aware of these restrictions. People are free, however, to examine fossils in place without removing them, thus preserving their scientific value and meeting the intentions of the protective laws.

As one examines the rock layers, it becomes evident that there is a highly ordered pattern in the occurrence of fossils. As Elder Talmage wrote: "Geologists say that these very simple forms of plant and animal bodies were succeeded by others more complicated; and in the indestructible record of the rocks they read the story of advancing life from the simple to the more complex, from the single-celled protozoan to the highest animals, from the marine algae to the advanced types of flowering plant—to the apple tree, the rose and the oak."[2]

The sequence in the occurrence of fossils repeats itself in sedimentary rocks throughout the world. Furthermore, whether they were in Australia, Africa, the Americas, or elsewhere, the various forms of life on earth appeared and disappeared at the same time. To the student of scripture, this precision reflects the ordered processes of God. The sequence of creation of life on earth recorded in

Genesis 1—first plants (vv. 11-12), then animals (vv. 20-23)—is dupli-
cated in the fossil record: plant fossils precede the appearance of
animal fossils.

This agreement should not be surprising because the God
who created this earth is the same God who inspired the prophets. A
conflict arises only when we assume that God has revealed all he is
going to reveal on the subject or forget that scientific theories change
as new discoveries are made.

We also need to remember both the purposes for which the
scriptures were given and the objectives of the scientific method.
Foremost, the scriptures testify of Jesus Christ and how we may
receive the blessings of salvation and exaltation through his atonement. They reveal why (not necessarily how) the earth was created,
and what laws and principles a person must follow to obtain eternal
life. The goal of science, on the other hand, is to learn how (not why)
the world was made and to understand the laws and principles
governing the physical world.

The different roles science and religion play is illustrated in
a study of dinosaurs. From the fossil record we learn that the
dinosaurs were the dominant animals on earth between 225 and 67
million years ago. Some were carnivorous, others herbivorous. Some
were small, while others were gigantic, weighing up to 80 tons and
growing to lengths of more than 90 feet.

The existence of these animals is indisputable, for their
remains have been found in rocks all over the earth. What eternal
purpose they played in the creation and early history of the earth is
unknown. The scriptures do not address the question. We can only
conclude, as Elder Talmage did, that "the whole series of chalk
deposits and many of our deep-sea limestones contain the skeletal
remains of animals. These lived and died, age after age, while the
earth was yet unfit for human habitation."[3]

The findings of science and the statements made in the
scriptures are not exclusive of each other. Often the one augments
knowledge supplied by the other. A case in point is an event in LDS
history when a prominent paleontologist, through his study of fossils,
seemed to support statements made in the Book of Mormon. A story
published by the *New York Tribune* on 17 November 1873 relates a
meeting in Salt Lake City between President Brigham Young and

Professor O. C. Marsh of Yale University. Marsh was one of the leading paleontologists of his time in America. His specialty, fossil horses, was the subject of the two men's conversation.

President Young sought information concerning the occurrence of horse fossils, especially in America. His purpose was to answer questions regarding the mention of horses on this continent in the Book of Mormon. Everybody knew, said some scholars, that there were no horses in America until the Spaniards introduced them. Marsh's research, however, clearly established the presence of modern horses in America long before the appearance of Spanish people in America.

The *Tribune* article concluded with the following: "So, while most theologians are regarding the developments of the natural sciences with fear and trembling, the chiefs of the Mormon religion are prepared to hail the discoveries of paleontology as an aid in establishing their peculiar beliefs."

The relationship between scripture and what is currently understood in science is ever changing. Science continually learns more about the history of life on earth, and we have every reason to believe that much more will be learned as research continues.

The struggle to correlate a passage in scripture with a specific portion of scientific research has been a challenge for centuries. But experience has shown that what a person understands today will be modified by tomorrow's discoveries. Patience and humility eventually resolve questions, though some will probably not be fully answered in our lifetimes.

Fortunately, we need not know all the details of creation to take advantage of the essential saving ordinances of the gospel. The scriptures and the inspired counsel of the prophets are sufficient to lead us back to God.

But this does not mean that science has no place in our pursuit of truth. The more we learn of God's handiwork, the more we come to know him and love his works. As a Latter-day Saint geologist, I consider myself fortunate indeed to have the opportunity to study rocks and fossils as evidence of God's creations. Everything I have learned of the grandeur of creation has strengthened my resolve to learn more and to live as God would have me live.

NOTES

1. James E. Talmage, "The Earth and Man," *Deseret News*, 21 Nov. 1931.

2. Ibid.

3. Ibid.

12.
Adam's Navel

Keith E. Norman

A FEW YEARS AGO ON A CROSS-COUNTRY TRIP, MY BROTHER PAUL AND I detoured from Interstate 70 in western Missouri for some sightseeing. After stopping at the Far West temple site and the town square at Gallatin, we trekked a few more miles north. Our goal was that most esoteric of spots on the Mormon tour, Adam-ondi-Ahman.

The country road ended in the woods, where a marker identified a pile of stones as the spot where the Ancient of Days himself built the first sacrificial altar after his expulsion from paradise. Rumor had it that local Saints replenished the heap each spring, but I pocketed a souvenir anyway.

Several paths wandered through the trees among the rubble of early Mormon homes, and we soon found ourselves in an oval-shaped clearing. Another, cruder sign affixed to a beech tree was no longer legible, but this, we surmised, must be the place where the great patriarch gathered his posterity to bestow his final blessing exhortation. The late afternoon sun burnished the already dry grass, and the atmosphere was hushed, inviting reverence.

I could not hold back. "I walked today where Adam walked," I sang, "in days of long ago . . ." Paul rebuked me for the sacrilege but could not altogether stifle a snicker of his own.

Latter-day Saints who interpret the scriptures literally must exercise great faith when reading the first chapters of Genesis. Although the account of Adam and Eve in the Garden of Eden makes for a great read and is the one Bible story that is known the world over, even a true-blue literalist must swallow hard to accept it as a

229

documentary of how the world and the human race really began. Heaven and earth in six days? A talking snake? Fruit that can make you wise or immortal? In the words of Alice, "there's no use trying, one can't believe impossible things."

"I dare say you haven't had much practice," replied the White Queen. "When I was your age, I always did it for half an hour a day. Why, sometimes I've believed as many as six impossible things before breakfast."[1] Today of course an early-rising Saint can get in two sessions before a late breakfast and thus easily top Her Majesty from Wonderland's prodigious feat.

An unquestioning biblical literalism was the norm in Mormonism's formative years. For some time now and especially since Darwin, the debate has raged over whether the biblical version of creation and fall is history. Was Adam a real person, the first man on earth? Or is this all just a myth, the product of a primitive mind trying to explain how things came to be? I think it was Mark Twain who wondered whether Adam had a navel. It does give one pause.

I contend that these questions of science versus creation and history versus myth obscure the real meaning of the Genesis text, because they are set up as alternatives with the assumption that only one version can be true. On the one hand, some contend, if the scientific theory of evolution over eons of time is accurate, then the Genesis account of the origins of humankind cannot be true. If it does not recount actual historical events, the story of Adam and Eve is myth or fable. The opposite view holds that because the biblical account is inspired by God, it is necessarily true history. God cannot lie. Modern science is mistaken in this case and should be ignored.

Of course a third alternative attempts to resolve the tension by compromise. Proponents of this view would reconcile the scientific and biblical accounts by explaining away the differences as arising from misinterpretations. They often express confidence that future discoveries or better analysis will show that both versions are saying the same thing: the order of creation in Genesis 1 follows the broad outlines of the scientific version; the "days" are not twenty-four-hour periods but seem to correspond to geological eras (or at least should be understood as 1,000 years each according to the Lord's calendar); Adam was the first man with a full-sized brain, or perhaps the first man to hold the priesthood . . . and so on. This approach requires its proponents to dismiss a disturbingly large number of specific details as mistranslations or corruptions of the original text.

All three positions—the literal, the scientific, or some blend of the two—suffer from the attempt to impose modern standards of science and history on a text written thousands of years before those standards were invented. Our value system insists that for something to be true it must correspond to objective reality. Indeed such correspondence is the classical philosophical definition of truth. Consequently we equate myth with the false, the made-up, the naive, and the superstitious. Because we prefer our history sanitized and documented, we refuse to acknowledge the obvious mythological elements in the opening chapters of Genesis in order to protect its authority.

Such cultural chauvinism is unfortunate, because it tends to obscure the deeper meaning and richness of the text. Focusing on the particularity of historical incidents not only restricts our vision to a surface, superficial understanding but also distorts the message of Genesis. Recognizing the function of myth removes those blinders and opens us to the universal, symbolic truths crucial to the text's spiritual import.

The first step in getting past misconceptions about the biblical creation story is to recognize the setting in which the first chapters of Genesis were written. Chapters 1 and 2 offer two differing accounts of the creation story with conflicting details. Further analysis of style, vocabulary, theology, and purpose has allowed scholars to date Genesis 1 through 2:4a to the time during or immediately after the exile in Babylon. The writer is concerned with preserving and restoring the religion of Israel in a time of great uncertainty, and his themes are stability, legitimacy, and the proper performance of ritual. He is known anonymously as the priestly (P) writer or writers. P's magnum opus was the book of Leviticus, but he contributed to other parts of the Bible, including the genealogical lists of Genesis.[2] It is not surprising that P ends his account of creation with the summary statement, "These are the generations of the heavens and of the earth" (Gen. 2:4). Even the ground we stand on has a pedigree.

The King James version of Genesis, following the manuscripts available at the time, obscures the transition to the second account by running P's conclusion into the new statement, which is now numbered 2:4b. A better translation of this opening might read, "In the day that the Lord made the earth and the heavens, before there were any plants in the earth or herbs growing in the fields. . . ."[3] This is another way of saying, "In the beginning," but this dry, barren world awaiting the Creator is a very different scenario from the chaotic deep P describes. We note right off that this second writer calls the deity "Lord," while P referred to him as "God" (Hebrew *Eloheim*). Lord is the English equivalent of *Adonai*, the Hebrew circumlocution used to avoid pronouncing the sacred name of God, YHWH, from which we derive the name Jehovah (scholarly consensus now vocalizes this as Yahweh). According to P's version, this name was first revealed to Moses (Ex. 6:3), and any use before then would be an anachronism. The liberal use of the name Yahweh (or Jehovah) has earned for the author of Genesis 2:4b-4:27 the designation of J. He[4] is a masterful storyteller but a less careful scholar. J's is actually the earlier of the two creation accounts by several hundred years. He reflects the national self-confidence and less restrictive theology of David's and Solomon's reigns.[5]

Conspicuous by omission from this discussion of authorship is Moses. Although the traditional ascription of the Pentateuch, the first five books of the Bible, to the great Hebrew prophet is no longer tenable among scholars, much of the oral, if not written, tradition used by the later authors can be traced back to Moses' time or even earlier. Nowhere, however, does the text itself claim Moses as the author, and it tells his story in the third person, including an account of his death. Several passages in Genesis, for instance the phrase "even to this day" (19:38) or the list of the kings of Edom down to the time of David (36:31), clearly point to a much later author.

Latter-day Saints have a tougher time than most dismissing Moses as the author of Genesis. Joseph Smith's revision of the opening chapters is now canonized by the church as the book of Moses in the Pearl of Great Price, and the Reorganized Church of Jesus Christ of Latter Day Saints uses the revised or inspired version as their standard text. However, I regard the prophet's work here as a primarily doctrinal correction rather than textual restoration or historical reconstruction. The Mormon canon adds significant dimensions to the creation accounts, but it is important to deal with Genesis on its own terms first.

Close examination of the background to these creation stories precludes a simplistic, literalistic view. While the evolutionary theory of human origins has been developing, new discoveries and analyses of ancient Near Eastern documents and artifacts have illuminated the cultural background of the Genesis text. Scholars now recognize that the biblical creation stories contain numerous allusions and parallels to earlier myths from Mesopotamia, Babylon, Egypt, and Canaan. Virtually every detail in Genesis 1-3 has some reference to these tales.6 Understanding these similarities will help us appreciate what is distinctive and inspired about Israel's recounting of the beginning.

One of the most widespread mythic motifs refers to the dark and chaotic watery element out of which the world was formed. The battle between the life-giving god and the serpent monster of the deep was the principal feature of the annual or seasonal renewal/fertility festivals that dramatized and revalidated the original creation: in Canaan, Baal fought the sea serpent Lotan; in Babylon, Marduk slew Tiamat. *Tiamat* is thought to be a cognate with the Hebrew *tehom*, translated as "the deep" in Genesis 1:2. P sees creation out of chaos (formless and void) as a process of separation: light is separated from darkness, land from water, and plants and animals from the earth. Chaos and darkness are pushed back but not destroyed, and the chaotic floods surround the earth above and below as well as on all sides.[7] In the Old Testament conception of the world exemplified in P, the sun, moon, and stars are suspended under the firmament, a solid barrier resting on the pillars of the sky to hold back the waters above. Sheol, where shades of former mortals dwell, is encased in a kind of underground island. The whole cosmic structure is designed to protect against the breakout of the chaos represented in the surrounding waters.[8]

The mythic personification of chaos as a sea monster, although only hinted at by P, is perhaps the most widespread creation motif in the Bible. It is variously referred to as Rahab, Leviathan, Tehom, or Yam in the Psalms (18:5; 74:12-14; 77:16-19; 89:9-10; 104:5-9), Isaiah (44:27; 50:2; 51:9-11), Job (9:8; 26:11-13; 38:8-11), and elsewhere (Nahum 1:4; Habbakuk 3:8, 10). This formless monster from the deep is capable of breaking out in a destructive rampage at any time. When God loses patience with his creatures, he need only step back to loosen the floods from above and below (Gen. 7:11). Israel celebrates its victory over Pharaoh in the "Song of the Sea" (Ex. 15:1-18) after *tehomot* (compare with Tiamat), the floods, covers the Egyptian army. Jesus Christ affirms his creative power in calming the raging sea (Mark 4:39-41) and compares his coming death to Jonah being swallowed by the monster of the sea (Matt. 12:40). When God's work is finally complete, the sea will be no more (Rev. 21:1); the dragon will be slain at last (Isa. 27;1). It is significant that in the creation cycle of the opening chapters of Genesis, the forces of disorder or chaos return in the form of a serpent to undermine the Creator's work. This animal was considered particularly cunning because of its seemingly effortless mobility. The snake's ability to shed its skin and perpetually renew itself appeared to give it the secret of immortality.[9] Casting the serpent as villain may also reflect a polemic against the Canaanite fertility cult, in which the snake as a phallic symbol represented life, death, and wisdom. The cult long held a certain fascination and temptation for Israel.[10]

Another widespread myth is that of a god forming the first humans from mud or clay. This ancient motif often involves breathing life into the creature. Creation in the image of the god is also common in oriental myths. In Egypt and Babylon, the king was regarded as the image and thus the representative or viceroy of God on earth.[11] The creation of humanity in God's image in Genesis 1 is followed by the commission to subdue and have dominion over the rest of creation: the royalty metaphor is transferred to all humankind (compare with Ps. 8:4-6).

A number of the mythical features in Genesis 1-3 are conspicuous because they seem superfluous to the narrative. The tree of life recalls one of the most common myths in ancient cultures.[12] Here it is mentioned but briefly and is connected only to other overtly mythological motifs—the jealous god who prevents man from grasping immortality and the guardian creatures or magical weapon that cut off access to the treasure. These elements would hardly be missed from the story. On the surface their inclusion seems arbitrary, as if J were juggling the contents of a creation grab bag.

One of the most fascinating parallels to Genesis is found in the Babylonian Gilgamesh epic from about 2000 B.C.E.—long before even the time of Moses.[13] Enkidu, the prototype human hero, is created as a wild man, naked and uncivilized. He lives with animals until the god Ana sends a woman to seduce him. This encounter results in the loss of his superhuman agility and strength but gives him wisdom and understanding "like a god." He thus becomes fully human, dons clothes, and the animals flee from him. When Enkidu faces death he curses the woman who brought him awareness of his mortality. In a later episode his companion Gilgamesh is in quest of the plant of life, but just as the means of immortality is within his grasp, he loses it to a serpent. If J was not directly familiar with the Gilgamesh cycle, he was certainly influenced by similar tales.[14] Sumerian literature contemporary with the Gilgamesh epic speaks of a blissful paradise garden where there is no sorrow. Some versions specify that the garden is watered from a source that divides into four streams flowing into the four corners of the world, strongly suggesting the later geographical description in Genesis 2:10-14.[15]

Although the authors of the Israelite creation stories drew upon the mythic cultural background of the ancient Near East, their focus is entirely different. In fact the thrust of the early chapters of Genesis is to demythologize this common heritage. The decided monotheistic emphasis retains only an echo of the pantheon of gods in the earlier stories. P's concluding statement, that these are the generations of the heavens and of the earth (Gen. 2:4a), seems to mock the theogonies that depict creation as a process of sexual generation from the pagan deities, as when the earth mates with the sky to produce plants and animals. Similarly the heavenly bodies are no longer astrological deities that rule human fate but which only govern the days and season under God's direction. The garden is planted to provide food for humans, not as a resort for the gods with men as their slaves.

The thrust of this demythologizing was to disassociate Israel's religion, which was grounded in God's mighty acts in history, from the ritualized mythical nature cycles celebrated by her neighbors. Creation as it functions in the Old Testament is not a timeless, mystical drama that must be repeated periodically to ensure fertility or avert the wrath of the gods. It is rather the prelude to history and establishes the basis of humanity's relationship to God.[16]

If the biblical writers wanted to ground their religious faith in history and experience, why did they make such extensive use of the myths of the surrounding cultures? Again this question falters on the modern assumption that myth and history are alternative categories, representing respectively the fanciful and the real. We need to expand our definition of myth to encompass the understanding of those cultures who created and used it.

Historians of religion define myth as a specialized category of literature which communicates otherworldly or metaphysical concepts in the language of this world. Myth uses poetry and symbolism to express truth indirectly. Thus, according to one scholar, "the dragon-killing creation myth, for example, found in so many Near Eastern mythologies, appears in the Bible too, not as a matter of belief or ritual but of poetic imagery."[17] Or in the words of another scholar, the poetic meaning of these Old Testament texts is not just "something read in later on the basis of more sophisticated philosophies. These implications are inherent in the myths and usages from the beginning."[18] In other words biblical writers used myth consciously and intentionally, not because they did not know any better. Our recognition of this literary fact adds to the value of the narrative. "Legends are not lies," as Hermann Gunkel recognized a century ago, but "a particular form of poetry," and it is this literary form that makes the stories of Genesis among "the most beautiful and profound ever known on earth."[19]

By looking beyond everyday experience, myth takes us where history dares not tread. It infuses ordinary events with a significance beyond the mundane by assimilating them to archetypal models. As one historian of religion has described this process: "Myth, or *mythopoeia* . . . envisages and expresses things in terms of their impact, not of their essence; it is impressionistic, not analytic, and it finds expression in poetry and art rather than in science. Its concern is with experience, not with categorization; it [translates] the real into the ideal."[20]

In this sense then the issue of history versus myth is not a concern of the biblical writers. Both categories are concerned with past events but view them from different perspectives. Myth is not antihistorical or ahistorical but suprahistorical. It focuses on inner reality, the meaning of the past, and on those issues which are decisive for the present. Historical accounts of actual events are subject to external criteria of truth, but a poetic form such as myth has a broader scope. According to Northrop Frye, "Poetry expresses the universal in the event, the aspect of the event that makes it an example of the kind of thing that is always happening. In our language, the universal in the history is what is conveyed by the *mythos*, the shape of the historical narrative. A myth is designed not to describe a specific situation but to contain it in a way that does not restrict its significance to one situation."[21]

Historical accuracy in this frame of thinking is not an end in itself, and events are recounted or reshaped in terms of their spiritual profundity. Nephi advocates a similar editorial bias in record keeping when he emphasizes the spiritual history of his nation in preference to political events (Jacob 1:2; 1 Ne. 19:6; 9:4). Our cultural prejudice, which devalues myth, fable, or fiction as "not really true," is directly at odds with the biblical mindset. The presence of myth in the scriptures by no means precludes inspiration or revelation in producing the text. God speaks to us according to our ability to understand, and myth can be a very powerful means of conveying truth.

Jesus understood this fact, and his own literary skill was quite sophisticated. The truths taught in the parables clearly do not depend on their historicity. Christ began the story of the Good Samaritan with the characteristic phrase, "a certain man," roughly equivalent to our "once upon a time." Although the details of this tale are realistic, acknowledging that the Good Samaritan is a fictional character does not seem to bother us. In fact the parables' non-specificity allows us to identify more closely with the characters.

Similarly by re-presenting Israel's early and prehistory in mythical terms that universalize the events of the past, Genesis involves us in the drama. Many scholars believe that the creation stories in Genesis, as well as numerous references to creation in the Psalms (24, 47, and 93-100), reflect the liturgy of the temple rites in Jerusalem.[22] In common with customs of most of their neighbors, ancient Jews used recitation or even dramatic reenactment in their New Year festival to commemorate the triumph of God over darkness and chaos. Although the Jewish version was not explicitly a fertility rite, weddings were often celebrated in this context, and the new couples participated in the blessing bestowed on the first human pair. The New Year was preceded by the Day of Atonement (Yom Kippur) with its fastings, confessions, purification rites, and purges, culminating in the expulsion of a scapegoat, which carried the community's sins off into the desert. Having thus annulled his own history, the worshipper suspended time and could return to the primal moment, free to participate in the regeneration of the cosmos and begin a pure existence each year.[23] Our own New Year's resolutions are but a watered down version of this impulse.

For Christians the real renewal festival is Easter. Not only does it herald the regeneration of the earth (in the northern hemisphere), but it celebrates the renewal and triumph of Jesus Christ, the new Adam, the first of a new humanity. Mircea Eliade points out that Easter and New Year's Day were traditionally the foremost baptismal occasions for Christians. "On the cosmic level [baptism] is equivalent to the deluge," he writes, with the water symbolizing the chaos out of which a new creation emerges.[24]

This background makes it evident that the view of creation and structure of the physical universe set forth in Genesis does not reflect an attempt to objectively document a historical or scientific creation. As Claus Westermann points out, "It is clearly not P's intention to describe creation in such a way as we can imagine how it took place." No eyewitnesses took notes. No cameras were on the scene. Hollywood's attempts to reconstruct the narrative on film are misleading precisely to the extent that they achieve realism. The biblical writers strove to universalize, not to particularize.

Both P and J support this interpretation. P does not mention an individual at all: God created humankind (Hebrew 'adam), male and female, as a species, just as the animals before them, "each according to their kind." The text in most English translations of Chapters 2 and 3 give Adam and eventually Eve as proper names. However, the Hebrew word 'adam, meaning humankind or humanity, is translated accordingly in Genesis 1:26-27. J's account in Genesis 2:7 brings out the pun on the cognate 'adamah, ground or soil: the Lord formed 'adam from the dust of the 'adamah. Furthermore the text in the Garden of Eden narration almost always uses the word in the generic form, with the article, ha-'adam, the human. Translating this as "the man Adam" is redundant and inaccurate. Not until the end of Chapter 4, relating the birth of Seth after Adam and Eve enter the world as we know it, does J drop the article, indicating a shift to a proper name. Similarly Eve is a rough transliteration of the Hebrew *hawu,* and here the author's etymology as "the mother of all living" pointedly recognizes her representative or universal status. The focus of the story is not to give us historical information about the original man and woman as individuals but to help us identify with them and so to recognize both our maker and our responsibility for our alienation from our creator. Our goal should be to restore our intended relationship and present ourselves before God in innocence, stripped of worldly concerns.

Approaching the text in this way destroys the rationale for an opposition between the Bible and scientific research into the origins of the human species. The Genesis accounts are interested in theology not science. "All efforts to reconcile biblical cosmogony with modern science," writes Theodore H. Gaster, "rest . . . on a fundamental misunderstanding of [biblical] purpose and intent, and on a naive confusion between two distinct forms of mental activity."[25] Modern scientific creationists refuse to understand this and end up being false to both science and scripture. Recognizing that Genesis uses poetic and mythical literary forms to communicate its theological message exposes the conflict between science and religion as a red herring.

Without the distraction of irrelevant concerns, Genesis 1-3 reveals a profound insight into the human condition and our relationship to God. The wisdom of the editor who combined the P and J narratives becomes apparent. The accounts are complimentary: their discrepancies fade into the background in the sweep of the tale. We can only touch on the highlights here.

In contrast to many ancient religions, biblical faith is anthropocentric. The world exists for humans; we are not mere playthings or slaves to the gods. J makes this point immediately by having the Lord form a human as the first of his works; all else is ancillary. P accomplishes the same thing by placing us at the climax or pinnacle of God's creations. To be in the image of God means that we have a familial relationship to him, as Genesis 5:1-3 makes clear. Only we among all the creatures can hold a dialogue with the Creator. We are assigned dominance and given responsibility as partners or counterparts to God on earth. Surrounding cultures make their kings or heroes the sons and representatives of God, but Hebrew thought exalted all humankind to this status.[26] We are thus freed from polytheism, materialism, and fatalism.

Such an optimistic picture, however, seems at odds with everyday existence, and Genesis gives us a striking account of how we got into our present mess. Both narratives exonerate God from the evil and imperfection in the world. At the end of the first section, God pronounces his work "very good." He had brought order and beauty out of formless chaos. The motif of creation through struggle, which lies behind P's account, is continued in J's saga of humanity and indeed throughout the Hebrew Bible. God continually must contend with the wickedness and disorder of humanity. The tempter serpent in Genesis 3 represents a new breakout of chaos, a resistance to the order and tranquility established by God. Humans compound the problem by misuse of free choice, thus increasing spiritual entropy. The blame for moral evil rests squarely on us, not on some outside force.

The ambiguity of the choice faced by Adam and Eve, however, makes this more than a simple fable of good versus evil. The woman chooses the godlike wisdom of experience over the naive innocence of a sheltered existence. The conditions of mortality are not so much a punishment as a statement of the human condition. Opposition and paradox are the terms of our existence. The joys cannot be separated from the ills. Westermann describes the woman's "punishment" in terms of the irony: "just where the woman finds her fulfillment in life, her honor and her joy, namely in her relationship to her husband and as mother of her children, there too she finds that it is not pure bliss, but pain, burden, humiliation and subordination."[27] Similarly man's work in the field, producing life-giving food, is beset with trouble, sweat, and thorns.

That the woman transgresses first does not degrade her. In fact Genesis 2 is unique among creation myths of its era in granting woman fully human status and partnership with man. The King James Bible, which describes woman as "an help *meet* for man" (v. 18), is often misunderstood as a help-mate, a subordinate maid to do his bidding. The word "meet" here means proper, suitable, corresponding to; in other words, one of his own kind—"bone of my bone and flesh of my flesh" (v. 23)—compared to the animals, who were not suitable partners.

A major theme of the Genesis myth is the sanctification of

family life and the relation between the sexes, as Jesus reiterated in Matthew 19:4-6. The text makes no suggestion that the transgression had anything to do with sex. It is true that the knowledge gained from their choice entailed an awareness of the man's and woman's sexuality—they were ashamed to be found naked—but this shame is not associated with lust or sexual sin. That Eve is granted her name or title as mother of all living after the sentence is pronounced emphasizes that the punishment did not nullify the blessing of procreation.

The foregoing description of theological motifs in Genesis 1-3 is by no means exhaustive. Many other doctrines associated with these creation stories, however, were developed by later exegetes and rely to a great extent on a literal historical interpretation. The most prominent are teachings about the fall of humanity, original sin, and the origin of death.

It is striking that the Hebrew Bible never mentions the Fall or any concept relating to it. There is no lament over a lost golden age or blame for primeval humans for spoiling things. Jewish thought tends to value humanity as good and capable of communion with God. Only in the Apocrypha and Pseudepigrapha is Adam's original stature greatly magnified and the cosmological significance of his sin emphasized.[28] This trend is continued in rabbinical literature and Philo, which also influence the New Testament, and is especially notable in Paul's writings (Luke 3:38; Rom. 5:12-21; 1 Cor. 15:22, 45-47). The development of the atonement doctrine was the major impetus for the prominence of the Fall in Christianity. If the account of the Fall is taken as a figurative expression of our alienation from God, the Atonement may need to be understood in a more subjective manner as well.[29]

Although inspired by Pauline thought, the principal features of the original sin dogma were outlined by Augustine in the late fourth century. Augustine developed a theory implying that Adam's guilt and corrupt nature are biologically passed on through the seed in procreation.[30] The logical if extreme conclusion was reached in the Calvinistic teaching of the total depravity of humankind. This classic doctrine of original sin requires a literal interpretation of Genesis 3. Recognizing the mythical nature of the account, however, exposes the absurdity of the idea that we inherit the guilt and responsibility of a progenitor's sin. Rather the mythical understanding points to our psychological affinity with the characters in the story: they represent humanity and illustrate the contradictions of our existence.

The issue of death in Genesis 2-3 is more puzzling. Traditionally Adam's transgression has been blamed for bringing death into the world, but this is never explicit in the text. The Lord's warning is not that partaking the forbidden fruit would introduce death but that it would result in death on the same day. Thus the serpent's refutation of this as an idle threat turns out to be correct. The tree of life further complicates matters, since it was not forbidden before Adam and Eve's expulsion from the garden. Understanding the story as myth rather than as a historical account makes such narrative lapses unimportant. On one level, the message is that eternal life is inaccessible to humans because they are formed out of the dust of the earth. Physical death is unavoidable. On a higher plane it tells us that disobedience or defiance of God means spiritual death, exclusion from fellowship with God, who is the source of life.

The position and contribution of Mormonism on this topic is somewhat complex and deserves separate treatment. I will only suggest some preliminary observations and conclusions here.

LDS statements on the literalness of the creation and Garden of Eden stories seem somewhat contradictory. Adam is almost always seen as a historical figure, however, and the historicity of Genesis is intensified for Mormons by such peculiar features in their tradition as Adam-ondi-Ahman, the temple endowment, and the Adam-God theory. On the other hand, Mormons are told in the temple that the formation of the man from the dust and of woman from the man's rib is only figurative. In addition there is a strong impulse in Mormonism to universalize the Adam and Eve story—to invest it with mythical dimensions. The temple ritual instructs participants to consider themselves to be Adam or Eve as the drama unfolds. Mormon scriptures also seem to recognize that Adam is more than a proper name for a single individual: "the first man of all men have I called Adam, which is many," the Lord explains in Moses 1:34.

Although Joseph Smith's earlier writings largely accept the traditional language of the Fall, the doctrine of original sin was repudiated from the first. Without Adam's transgression and fall, there would have been no procreation and no opportunity for growth or joy (2 Ne. 2:22-25; Moses 5:10-11). Opposition is a metaphysical necessity for existence itself, and we could not progress without experiencing evil (2 Ne. 2:11-13).

Joseph Smith's two attempts to rework the Genesis creation story, found in the books of Moses and Abraham, provide a fascinating study of the evolution of his own doctrinal thinking. In his 1830 revision of the opening chapters of the Bible, later published as the book of Moses, Smith softened the overt mythology of a talking serpent by specifying that it was possessed, so to speak, by Satan. But he made little attempt to update the scientific details: the firmament still divides the waters above and below, and the events occur in the same skewed order as in Genesis 1. Doctrinal correction is evident, however. When God says "let us" in Moses 2:26, he is explicitly addressing his "Only Begotten." The discrepancies between chapters 1 and 2 of Genesis are resolved by making the first version a spiritual creation (Moses 3:5). It is this feature of Mormon scripture—the insistence that the description of creation in Genesis 1 is spiritual rather than physical—that belies the attempt to reconcile Genesis 1 with the scientific version of creation.

However, the succeeding description in the book of Moses, based on what we have attributed to J, is not clearly physical either. Of the garden the Lord planted and made to grow, he says, "it was spiritual in the day that I created it; for it remaineth in the sphere in which I, God, created it," implying that only with the Fall did the earth as we know it come into being (Moses 5:9). Such an interpretation, of course, would support a mythical view: it takes place in a realm where the rules of history are not yet operative.

Perhaps the most far-reaching difference in the creation account in Moses as compared to Genesis is the preexistence in Moses 4:1-4. This new motif was extensively developed in the account found in Abraham 3, which dates from 1842. Here the preexistent intelligences were organized and assigned to leadership roles and a plan to further their progression was explained. This plan had risks, since it involved the freedom to choose evil as well as good, the possibility of damnation as well as exaltation. The choice was not obvious at all, and many opted for Satan's safer alternative.

Linking this preexistence scenario with the Adam and Eve

story is important in terms of its mythical significance. The literary category of myth or prehistory in Genesis 2-3 corresponds to the doctrinal category of preexistence in the book of Abraham. The Garden of Eden story recapitulates the dilemma and choice we all faced in pre-earth life: whether to remain in static security or risk all and suffer pain, guilt, disappointment, and death in order to realize our full humanity and fulfill our potential to become as the gods. This constitutes the meaning of the Fall for Latter-day Saints and is the reason we reject the original sin dogma's pessimistic view of humanity. There is no other way to progress, to gain knowledge of good and bad, than to confront and experience evil directly and on our own, apart from God's presence. However, it is our choice; we cannot hold God responsible for the plan of salvation's negative aspects or our failings in the struggle.

The Book of Abraham version reflects a distinct attempt to make the creation story more rational and update its doctrinal points. The creator "gods" here do not get instantaneous results from a mere word: they "cause" things to be formed and watch to see that they are obeyed (4:4, 10, 18). Creation does not happen in just seven days but in eras or "times" (4:8, 13, 19, 23, 31; 5:2-3). When the lights are set in place during the fourth time, the gods again divide the day from the night, a specification that seems to recognize the problem of day and night preceding the creation of the sun.

The most striking aspect of the Mormon belief system concerning the creation myth is the temple endowment. This ritual presents the Genesis text in dramatic form reminiscent of ancient creation-new year ceremonies. It contains virtually all of the classic elements—purification, expiation of sin, dramatic reenactment of the creation and struggle between the forces of order and chaos, sanctification of marriage and the blessing of progeny, and even association with dead ancestors.[31] The endowment is clearly not intended to recite literal history. Except for replacing the serpent with Satan and the aside about the creation of Adam and Eve as figurative, little attempt is made to soften the mythological elements of Genesis 1-3. In contrast to the rest of biblical history, where communication with Deity is through visions or revelation, here everything takes place in direct confrontation between humans and God. The temple version has at various times gone well beyond even

Genesis, adding a variety of anachronisms to the Garden of Eden scenes, although recently some of these have been deleted. In true mythic fashion the endowment ceremony abolishes time as well as space: the temple is where heaven, earth, and hell meet, and all humankind—past, present, and future—convenes there. Only in this setting do we learn the true meaning of life.

What then shall we say about Missouri? After all Adam-ondi-Ahman is canonized in Doctrine and Covenants 116. There is even a song about it, number 49 in the new hymnal. However, despite my souvenirs procured from the very spot, I contend that the significance of this too belongs to the realm of mythical truths. Just as Brigham Young and the Mormon pioneers reenacted the Israelite trek through the wilderness, Joseph Smith's designation of the beginning, the original sacred space, the center (or navel) of the world, as being in America reinforces the idea of the New World as the promised land, the latter-day Zion. It is an elaboration of Book of Mormon doctrine: God established his covenant anew among the gentiles in a pristine land, a second Eden. As the tenth Article of Faith adds, this will be where the Lord returns at the last day to renew the earth to its paradisiacal glory. The end is to be a restoration and fulfillment of the beginning: creation redeemed.

Myth, properly understood, is a powerful means of religious expression and should not be dismissed as though it were the antithesis of truth. Myth is an important element of our religious heritage. To recognize the creation story in Genesis 1-3 as myth rather than history is not to denigrate its value, just as we do not reject the truth of Lehi's vision of the tree of life because it is only a dream or disregard the parables of Jesus because they are fictional. Rather these literary forms make the truths they teach all the more relevant to each of us.

Because myth and history deal with different levels of reality, it is still possible to consider Adam and Eve as actual historical figures while recognizing that the account of creation in Genesis is mythical in nature. In that sense the question of historicity is irrelevant. It is not necessary to believe in a literal Adam to keep the faith, and insistence to the contrary is shortsighted. Nor is a belief in creationism required of Latter-day Saints. Biblical faith and scientific evolution are not mutually exclusive but are two different approaches to truth. Science investigates the mechanisms of creation; Genesis discusses its purpose. We can learn from both if we do not confuse the two. Just as a literal reading of Genesis smacks of superstition, history completely demythologized is ultimately devoid of meaning.

NOTES

1. Lewis Carroll, *Alice's Adventures in Wonderland and Through the Looking Glass* (New York: Collier Books, 1962), 233.
2. Norman K. Gottwald, *The Hebrew Bible: A Socio-Literary Introduction* (Philadelphia: Fortress Press, 1985), 140, 170.
3. E. A. Speiser, *Genesis* (1967; rprt., New York: Doubleday, 1982), 14-15.
4. Or "she," if Harold Bloom's speculations on J are correct. See Bloom and David Rosenberg, *The Book of J* (New York: Grove Weidenfeld, 1990), 9-48.
5. Gottwald, *Hebrew Bible*, 137; Speiser, *Genesis*, xxvii.
6. Theodore H. Gaster, *Myth, Legend and Folklore in the Old Testament* (New York: Harper and Row, 1969), 3-50.
7. Bernhard W. Anderson, "Creation," in *The Interpreter's Dictionary of the Bible*, Vol. 1, ed. George Arthur Buttrick et al. (New York: Abingdon Press, 1962), 730.
8. Theodore H. Gaster, "Cosmogony," in *The Interpreter's Dictionary*, 702-709; Gottwald, *Hebrew Bible*, 474-76.
9. Gaster, *Myth, Legend and Folklore*, 36.
10. Bruce Vawter, *A Path through Genesis* (New York: Sheed and Ward, 1956), 64.
11. Claus Westermann, *Genesis 1-11*, trans. John J. Scullion (Minneapolis: Augsburg Publishing House, 1984), 152-54.
12. Vawter, *Path*, 54; Westermann, *Genesis*, 213.
13. James B. Pritchard, ed., *The Ancient Near East*, Vol. 1 (Princeton: Princeton University Press, 1958), 40-75.
14. Westermann, *Genesis*, 51-52; Bernhard W. Anderson, *Understanding the Old Testament*, 3rd ed. (Englewood Cliffs, NJ: Prentice Hall, 1975), 210.
15. Gerhard Von Rad, *Genesis*, rev. ed., trans. John H. Marks (Philadelphia: Westminster Press, 1972), 79-80; Gaster, *Myth, Legend and Folklore*, 27.
16. Anderson, "Creation," 726-27.
17. Roland M. Frye, ed., *Is God a Creationist? The Religious Case Against Creation Science* (New York: Charles Scribner's Sons, 1983), 92.

18. Gaster, *Myth, Legend and Folklore*, xxxiv.

19. Hermann Gunkel, *The Legends of Genesis: Biblical Saga and History*, trans. W. H. Carruth (Chicago: Open Court Publishing, 1901; New York: Schoken Books, 1964), 3.

20. Gaster, *Myth, Legend and Folklore*, xxxiv.

21. Northrop Frye, *The Great Code: The Bible and Literature* (New York: Harcourt, Brace, Jovanovich, 1982), 46.

22. Mircea Eliade, *The Myth of the Eternal Return, or, Cosmos and History*, trans. Willard R. Trask (New York: Bollingen Foundation Inc., 1954; Princeton, NJ: Princeton University Press, 1971); Hugh W. Nibley, *The Idea of the Temple in History* (Provo, UT: Brigham Young University Press, 1963).

23. Eliade, *Myth of Eternal Return*, 35, 52-74, 158.

24. Ibid., 59.

25. Gaster, "Cosmogony," 703.

26. Anderson, "Creation," 729.

27. Westermann, *Genesis*, 263.

28. II Enoch 30:8ff; Ecclesiasticus 49:16; Life of Adam 12ff; Apocalypse Baruch 17:3; II Esdras 3:4-21, 4:30, 7:11-12; Jubilees 3:28-29.

29. Keith E. Norman, "Toward a Mormon Christology," *Sunstone* 10 (Apr. 1985): 19-25.

30. G. W. H. Lampe, "Christian Theology in the Patristic Period," in *A History of Christian Doctrine*, ed. Cunliffe Jones (Philadelphia: Fortress Press, 1978), 162; Jaroslav Pelikan, *The Emergence of the Catholic Tradition (100-600)* (Chicago: University of Chicago Press, 1971), 300.

31. Eliade, *Myth of the Eternal Return*, 52; Nibley, *Idea of the Temple*.

13.
Astrophysics and Mormonism: Parallel Paths to Truth

R. Grant Athay

I BELONG TO A PROFESSION IN WHICH THERE IS SOME COMMON GROUND with religious teachings. In both subjects we deal with the origin and nature of the physical universe and with the origin and nature of life. I am qualified, as an astrophysicist, to speak only about the former of these—the origin and nature of the physical universe. Rather than launch into a discourse on astronomy, however, I prefer to talk about the areas of common ground where astronomy and religion each state their views.

In order to think about some of the complexity of the subject with which we are dealing, let me ask a series of questions. For the moment, think about the questions themselves, not about answers to them. How, for example, does one go about answering such questions:

1. What sorts of objects are stars? Are they vast and complicated like the sun, or much smaller, simpler objects?

2. Do stars vary in physical size?

3. Do stars other than our sun have planets that support life?

4. Have some stars ceased to exist and will new stars come into being?

5. What are the ages of stars?

6. Do stars rotate on an axis as the earth does?

These questions were common topics of discussion in Joseph

Smith's day, both among scientists and some segments of the general public. Speculation about the age of the universe ranged from a few thousand years to a few hundred thousand years. There was much debate about the nature, evolution, and sizes of stars and about the possibility of life elsewhere in the universe. Thus it should not be surprising to find that Joseph Smith himself was interested in these subjects.

It is not my intent to discuss at length the current scientific picture of the universe except in a general way. It is to me both remarkable and awe-inspiring to realize that the chemical elements of which we are made were manufactured billions of years ago inside a star, most likely several different stars. These stars lived out their life cycles, exhausted their nuclear fuel, and left as ashes the elements of which our sun, its planets, and we are made. In their death throes these dying stars sprayed much of their matter into outer space where æons later it coagulated to form our solar system and eventually to provide our present home.

This picture has been arrived at in science by a long, complicated path. It required that we find the means of answering most of the questions listed above, plus many other questions of equal or greater complexity. The scientific answer to these questions required sophisticated telescopes and ancillary equipment in addition to sophisticated theories, none of which were available to science in Joseph Smith's day. For many of the questions that needed to be answered, answers have come only in recent years. Prior to that, our knowledge and understanding of physics were not sufficiently good to answer the questions, even though much of the necessary data was at hand.

The merits of scientific information in the scriptures are best judged in terms of the level of science in the day in which the scriptures were produced. Let us then back up to the mid-1800s and ask what astronomers in that day knew and what tools they had to work with. Their telescopes were limited by today's standards. The largest lenses in use were about twelve inches in diameter. Knowledge of physics was still very limited. The structure of atoms and molecules was not known. Also the laws of thermodynamics, which are crucial in describing the state of matter in stars, were not known. Matter was believed to be both creatable and destructible. The velocity of light had been measured accurately, but the nature of light itself was not at all understood. Thus the messages carried in starlight were still unreadable to the scientist. As a result, nothing was known about the chemical composition or the physical nature of stars. Evolution of astronomical and physical objects was a common topic of discussion, but there was not sufficient physical foundation upon which a theory of stellar evolution could be based. Photography was just coming into use, and astronomers still relied mainly on their eyes to record whatever data they acquired.

By the mid-1800s the distance, size, and luminosity of the sun were reasonably well known. It was known also that the sun rotates on an axis. Scientists knew that the sun required a vast energy source, but the only sources of energy known were incapable of sustaining the sun more than a few hundred thousand years. This picture changed in 1853 when Helmholtz postulated that the sun was heated by its own contraction and found that such a mechanism could sustain the sun for approximately 18 million years. Even though this was still a crude and inaccurate picture, it represented a major step forward.

By the mid-1800s the distance to Alpha-Centauri, our nearest stellar neighbor, had been measured as being about four light years (23 million million miles), which is quite accurate. Herschel had shown from star counts in the Milky Way that the Milky Way was a vast star system exceeding 3,000 light years in width. Stars were known by this time to be sun-like objects at great distances and requiring, because of their distances, immense amounts of energy.

Rotation was believed to be a common property of all planets, but it could be studied for only three objects: the earth, moon, and sun. Orbital motions of planets and their moons and gravitational forces were known and reasonably well understood. By contrast, however, it was widely (but not universally) believed that stars were fixed, immovable objects.

In the early 1800s astronomers commonly (but erroneously) saw clouds and fortifications on the moon. Prior to about 1850 it was commonly believed that the interior of the sun was solid, cool, and habitable; only the outer atmosphere was thought to be hot and incandescent. Thus in the early 1800s the moon as well as the sun and all the planets were believed to be inhabited. By 1834, however,

Besel had shown that the moon had little or no atmosphere, and by 1850 the idea that the sun's surface was liquid (actually it is gaseous) rather than solid prevailed. At the time that Joseph Smith was working on the Book of Abraham (now contained in the Pearl of Great Price) the majority of scientists advocated a plurality of habitable worlds for humans, but this idea was opposed by many religious creeds.

The evolution of scientific thought concerning life in the universe has followed an interesting pattern. Pannekoek states that "In the mid-19th century the doctrine of a multitude of planetary systems, all inhabited by intelligent beings, formed part of the world concept often expressed in materialist and rationalist forms strongly antagonistic to the dominant religious creeds."[1] This concept of universal worlds changed dramatically over the next three-quarters of a century, and in 1927 Eddington stated his feeling that our planetary system is unique in the stellar universe and that hence the Earth, as an abode of living beings, is also unique as a world.[2] That view dominated scientific thought for several decades. Within the past thirty to forty years, our ideas have again given way to a widespread belief among scientists that habitable planets and life itself are relatively common features of the universe. The change in concept concerning life in the universe is not merely scientific whimsy. The questions involved are complex and cannot be answered with certainty without a deep understanding of the nature of the physical universe. Present evidence, however, indicates that Earthlike planets capable of sustaining life are far more common than Eddington had supposed.

The six questions we asked earlier in this essay were each the basis for lively discussions during Joseph Smith's lifetime. LDS scriptures produced by Joseph Smith contain information on these same questions. Let us then turn to the scriptures to see what information they give.

It would be a mistake, I believe, to attempt to interpret science literally as scripture or to interpret scripture as science. The two serve different purposes, and even though they describe the same events they need not describe them in the same way. With this note of caution, we glean the following "scientific information" from the books of Abraham and Moses in the Pearl of Great Price:

1. Stars are sun-like objects; some great and some small (Abr. 3:2).

2. Stars are numberless and extend endlessly into space (Moses 1:37, 38).

3. Stars occur in associations and some stars govern others (Abr. 3:3).

4. Stars rotate (Abr. 3:4).

5. Heavens (star systems) and populated worlds exist without number (Moses 1:37).

6. Stars are continuously being born, some have already died (Moses 1:38).

7. One star (Kolob) is the greatest of all. It rotates once each 1,000 years and is associated with many other great stars (Abr. 3:4, 16).

8. The sun borrows its light from Kolob (Abr. fasc. 2).

9. Kolob governs the annual revolutions of the moon, earth, sun, and fifteen other fixed planets or stars (ibid.).

An additional item of interest was printed in the *Times and Seasons* 5 (1844) on page 758. The following quote is from a letter from W. W. Phelps to William Smith, Joseph Smith's younger brother (Phelps was a scribe to Joseph Smith and worked with him on the Book of Abraham): "and that eternity, agreeable to the records found in the catacombs of Egypt, has been going on in this system (not the world) almost 2555 millions of years; and to know that deists, geologists and others are trying to prove that matter must have existed hundred of thousands of years:—it almost tempts the flesh to fly to God, or muster faith like Enoch to be translated and see and know as we are seen and known!" This is a remarkable statement, and we will return to it later.

The scientific information extracted from Abraham and Moses plus the information from the *Times and Seasons* answers each of the above six questions. Furthermore, they correspond with current concepts of astronomy. Only one question—the first one—was answered correctly by science in the early 1800s. In fairness, I should point out that this is why I chose to ask these particular questions—to show compatibility. I could have asked other questions the scriptures do not answer or answer incorrectly according to science. Also the scriptures give answers to questions I have not asked.

Of the nine statements listed above as scientific information, I understand what is meant by the first seven only. I have no idea what is meant by the statement that the sun "borrows" light from Kolob. As an astrophysicist I am perfectly content with the idea that the sun generates its own light from nuclear fusion in its deep interior and requires the help of no other star. Similarly, I have no idea what is meant by the statement that "governing power" from Kolob governs the moon, earth, and sun in their annual revolutions. For that matter, I do not even know what is meant by the "annual revolution" of the sun. The sun turns on its axis about once each month; it revolves with our Milky Way galaxy once each 200 million years or so, and it moves steadily about within our Milky Way. So far as astronomers know (and they have every reason to know how the sun moves through space) the sun has no "annual revolution," unless the word "annual" simply means period of time. The concept of a central governing star (Kolob) in our stellar system is not part of our current scientific picture. However, the central regions of our galaxy are heavily obscured by matter and are poorly understood.

It does not bother me particularly that I do not understand some of the statements in the Book of Abraham. That lack of understanding could reflect our own lack of knowledge of the universe. I personally doubt that this is the proper explanation, however. I see no reason to insist that all scriptural statements of a scientific nature be rigorous in today's concepts and couched in today's scientific jargon. Also I am content to allow Joseph Smith the freedom to miss one or two questions in the astronomy examination. That would not in any way diminish his greatness as a man or as a prophet.

Of far more importance to me than the things I do not understand in Abraham are the things I do understand. The problems considered are pertinent to topics of discussion in Joseph Smith's day. The questions asked were answered more correctly and completely by the books of Abraham and Moses than by mainstream science in the mid-1800s. In addition, the statement in the *Times and Seasons* that there have been goings-on in this system for almost 2555 million years predated science's reasonable estimate of the age of our local stellar system by almost a century.

The subject of astronomy is among the oldest of the sciences. It has taught us much about the nature and history of the universe.

In some ways, however, astronomy is still in its infancy. The universe is more complex than any of us are ready to admit. Even our sun, which is far better understood than any other star, is not at all well understood. As a specialist in solar physics, I readily admit my failure to understand much of what I, or others, observe to be happening on the sun. The sun is marvelously complex and provides us with one of our best laboratories for studying some of the less well-understood areas of physics.

Many stars seem more complicated than the sun and are even less well understood. Astronomy is a science in which we seem to have an increasing number of unsolved problems. In the course of finding the solution to one problem, we invariably uncover new problems to take its place. Thus as we create a collection of solved problems and piece them together to form a picture of the universe, we are seemingly faced with an ever-increasing number of new challenges.

Modern astronomy has been vastly increased in scope by the invention of radio telescopes and by our ventures into outer space where we now look at the universe with telescopes that are capable of seeing x-rays and extreme ultraviolet rays. These new devices provide new eyes through which we can study the universe. With these new eyes we are seeing new classes of objects with bizarre characteristics.

The newly-discovered objects in astronomy are beginning to play key roles in our understanding the universe and are upsetting our current picture. The foundation on which we have built the picture is beginning to shake a little. Some of the pieces that we thought were fitted snugly into place no longer seem to fit quite so well, and men and women of science are once again reexamining the most fundamental building blocks.

Our ventures into space have just begun, and radio astronomy is still relatively young. We have certainly not yet discovered all of the mysteries or even all the objects of our universe, and we have not yet answered the most important questions conclusively. Our children may learn a different brand of astronomy. They will undoubtedly look back on us as a group who made some progress but who were handicapped by limited experience and outmoded ideas. Their picture of the universe will differ from ours and will undoubtedly be more complete. It may well contain, as essential ingredients, objects and phenomena to which our scriptures do not even refer.

Until we developed radio and x-ray telescopes, we believed the universe to be completely dominated by objects that could be seen and studied with ordinary telescopes. This picture may still be partly true, but it seems also to be partly in error. How much the picture will evolve we cannot predict. Even if the picture were to change to the extent that stars, nebulæ, and galaxies no longer dominated, the understanding of Joseph Smith would not be diminished. He spoke and wrote of things scientific as they were known to him and his contemporaries. He had neither the need nor the proper framework for discussing objects unknown to the general populace even if he himself had known of them.

In the Book of Moses, when Moses sees the earth in all its detail and all its inhabitants, he is overcome with awe and wonder. After regaining his composure, he says, "Now, for this cause I know that man is nothing, which thing I never had supposed" (1:10). Moses was subsequently told of the complexity of the universe, of innumerable worlds some of which had already passed away and others which were yet to be born. He was carefully reassured by God that all things were created in wisdom and for a purpose and that they were numbered and known to God (vv. 31, 35). This, not science, is the message of the scriptures.

Science, on the other hand, reveals only the marvels and beauties of nature. It is the marvel and beauty of those creations and not God's hand in them that is the message of science. Let us not confuse the two and let us not find fault with either just because they seek different goals. Each is important by itself and in its own right. Together, however, they are both stronger and more beautiful to comprehend than either would be in the absence of the other.

NOTES

1. A. Pannekoek, *A History of Astronomy* (New York: Interscience), 402.

2. A. S. Eddington, *The Nature of the Physical World* (Cambridge, Eng.: Cambridge University Press, 1927), 178.

14.
Science: A Part of or Apart from Mormonism?

Richard Pearson Smith

Every art and science known and studied by the children of men is comprised within the Gospel.—Brigham Young (1868)

Beware of false science.—*Priests Study Course* (1973)

FOR MORE THAN THREE DECADES I HAVE MOURNED THE ABSENCE OF A benevolent spirit which helped me and my generation of Mormons find our way through life and our chosen professions in the scientific fields. I watch incessantly for its resurrection, only to see from time to time more nails driven into the coffin of isolationism.

When will I again see general authorities, church publications, teachers, and parents giving assurance to all that science blends beautifully with Mormonism? That's the way it was in the 1930s when I was a child in northern Utah, and on into the 1950s. That sort of support for science is unknown to today's young Mormons. Instead they hear that much of what the schools teach is wrong, and they had better not believe it. I am thankful that my faith was not subjected to that test and that I had help with my concerns about whether a scientist could be a Latter-day Saint. Are not today's students and scientists in greater jeopardy of failing to develop strong faith in the church?

I have watched and pondered science's banishment with

astonishment and frustration. It has seemed to run counter to basic Mormon teachings and to the church's general forward movement.

With pride I have watched my church come forth "out of obscurity and out of darkness." In my day it has changed from an obscure group in the western states, widely regarded as a cult, to a more-or-less respected international church. And it has moved from darkness into light in many ways, divesting itself of anachronisms and embracing new things found to be "of good report or praiseworthy."

Nowhere is progress more evident than in the use of technology, the fruit of science. Satellite television takes general conferences to a thousand stake centers. A million rolls of microfilm stored in Granite Mountain vaults preserve and centralize much of the world's genealogical information. Computers minimize work for membership and financial clerks while providing better reports for bishops. Prodigious genealogical databases under construction will some day be researchable from computer terminals everywhere. What other church creates and distributes sophisticated software for personal computers?

Then there is science. I have always loved science (by which I mean mostly the natural sciences). Perhaps that is because powerful (though not deliberate) forces at home were pushing me toward it from my earliest years. Perhaps those forces were strong partly because of the positive statements about science which some church authorities were making.

Many Mormons today ignore psychology and would say that I acquired my taste for science in the preexistence, but it seems to me it happened right in the Bear River Valley. Everyone liked science when I lived there. Long before then some church leaders had established a positive attitude toward science by preaching that it comes from God and that we should learn all we can about it.

We are told that the Protestant Reformation, the early global explorations, and the establishment of the United States helped prepare the way for the restoration of the latter-day gospel. Over the same period developments in science and technology came faster and faster until the pace was furious by 1830. President Young saw the church benefit from new technology, especially the steam locomotive and the telegraph. He sensed the hand of the Lord in that and made a number of comments to that effect in his sermons: "Where did the knowledge come from which has enabled man to accomplish such great achievements in science and mechanism within the last few years? We know that knowledge is from God."[1] He would love to have studied science in depth: "How gladly would we understand every principle pertaining to science and art, and become thoroughly acquainted with every intricate operation of nature, and with all the chemical changes that are constantly going on around us! How delightful this would be, and what a boundless field of truth and power is open for us to explore!"[2]

Praise for science and technology—and to the Lord for revealing them—continued. In their special centennial address on 6 April 1930 President Heber J. Grant and his counselors reviewed at length "the increase of scientific knowledge, invention, [and] industrial development" which had come about through "light, radiating from the presence of God, illuminating the minds of men, increasing intelligence and knowledge, which is the glory of God, and by the application of which the past one hundred years have been made the Miracle Century of the ages."[3]

At that time I was four years old. My mother had the finest flower garden around, and she told me the names of the many species and something about each one. She taught me about insects and birds and let me see the collections of pressed wild flowers and of minerals which she had made in school.

My father, Clarence E. Smith, was principal of Bear River High School. His education in psychology and history meant nothing to me in those childhood years. But his passion for technology, which he had acquired from his father, a blacksmith who had emigrated from Denmark, came across very well. He showed me the special tools in the wood and metal shops and how they were used, the amazing devices in the large physics equipment closets, and the chemistry laboratory with its many bottles of substances having interesting colors, textures, and odors. My interest in computers had its roots in watching him program the fascinating bell-controlling IBM clock by inserting metal tabs in slots in a revolving drum.

My involvement with science dates from one evening when I was seven and the family was returning home after an outing in Logan Canyon. An entire day of close association with both parents was uncommon. Not only did Father run a sizeable high school in a rather personal way but he presided over Bear River Stake with its fourteen rather far-flung wards. Looking up through the windshield, I noticed the stars for the first time in my life and asked what they were. Father explained the basic facts, which I thought the most interesting information I had ever learned. Right away I was given two nice astronomy books which were about on my level. I pored over them every day, the way we are supposed to study the scriptures. (Years later I heard Father expound on the importance of teaching a child about a matter at the very time he or she shows curiosity about it.)

It was not long before I had college astronomy books, a subscription to *Sky* magazine, a small telescope, and a notebook in which I recorded my observations. Concurrently my fascination with chemistry grew, and by the time I was ten or twelve I was doing experiments in the basement and at the high school. And Father introduced me to the high school biology teacher. Soon a friend and I were collecting insects. Father went to the wood shop and built a display case.

By the time I entered the University of Utah, high school classes in biology, chemistry, physics, and math had increased my love for those subjects to the point where I approached their study on a high level with awe and reverence, sensations akin to the strong spiritual feelings some people report having in the temple. The textbooks had far more information in them than I had seen before, all of it interesting, and I could find the names of some of the professors in books and see that they had made important discoveries. Work at the frontiers of knowledge was going on in the laboratories. It thrilled me through and through. I could not have even thought of majoring in a field outside the natural sciences. I chose chemistry.

I knew a fair amount about science and had an unassailable faith in its basic concepts and methods by the time I entered the university. Based on my observations of other students, I think that is usual for a science major. If anyone had urged me to test what I was learning against the scriptures or had told me that one should not seek to understand the origin of the universe or of life on the earth or had tried to convince me that no creature died on this planet until 6,000 years ago, I would have thought that a reason to question the scriptures, not science. Fortunately no one was saying such things.

Instead two apostles who were respected scientists were preaching the unity of science and true religion.

Four scientists have served as apostles: Orson Pratt, geologist James E. Talmage, chemist John A. Widtsoe, and physicist Joseph F. Merrill.[4] Pratt acquired a respectable education on his own; the other three earned doctoral degrees. The terms of the four in the Quorum of the Twelve covered practically the entire period from 1835 to 1952.

I knew of Elders Pratt and Talmage by reputation and by their writings (Talmage died when I was quite young). But Elders Widtsoe and Merrill were around until about the time I completed my formal education. Mother proudly spoke of how she had been taught geology and mineralogy by Talmage and physics by Merrill at the University of Utah in 1900 and 1901. It was impressive too that Elder Richard R. Lyman (after whom I had been named) was a Ph.D. engineer. As a child I was privileged to meet these brethren as they stayed overnight at our home and had Sunday meals with us when their turns came to visit our stake conferences. I wish I had been mature enough to discuss science and religion with them.

The very presence of well-educated and accomplished scientists among the apostles made it easier for me to take the church seriously. In addition their talks and writings helped with many of my specific concerns. Science students in the church do face problems as Widtsoe knew: "The struggle for reconciliation between the contending forces [science and religion] is not an easy one. It cuts deep into the soul and usually leaves scars that ache while life endures."[5]

As I see it the most serious difficulty for Mormon students is that a testimony of science is gained at an early age, as my personal story illustrates, while a testimony of religion comes later. A science student needs special help because the church requires belief in many things which a person with a scientific orientation is more likely to question.

For example, many people are able to take prayer for granted, but a student of science is almost sure to contemplate how it might work. If God is only as far away as the nearest star, timely response would seem to require communication at a speed greater than that of light. Orson Pratt thought that "if God foreknows all things, he must have foreknown all about our prayers millions of ages before we were born, and must also have foreknown the precise time when we would pray, and the kind of spirit or feeling, and the degree of faith that would accompany each prayer."[6] This idea presents its own difficulties. Does God have no real involvement with my affairs? Do I have genuine free agency? Did God precompute the times and places of accidents and their consequences? Other gospel concepts such as the reality of the spirit world and the possibility of moving mountains through faith present similar problems. The church teaches that a testimony of the reality of unseen things can be gained only by methods foreign to science.

Further questions arise in connection with the descriptions given in the scriptures of ancient events. Few science-oriented people are able to believe that the earth is very young, that evolution played no role in the creation of the species, that the earth stopped rotating for a while in Joshua's day, that Noah took two of every kind aboard the ark, or that the Flood covered the entire earth. Other Bible-believing churches have faced these problems and resolved them in various ways. But for Mormons there is the added complication that modern scriptures seem to reinforce some of the most troublesome biblical passages.

The modern scriptures also contain statements about the universe which are unique to Mormonism and which need to be pointed out to Mormon science students and discussed. Do they fit in with science, or do they present further problems? I am thinking especially of physics in the Doctrine and Covenants and astronomy in the Book of Abraham.

I became interested in the science-religion relationship while in my teens, a time of great increase in my awareness of the teachings of the church. I soon learned that Elder Widtsoe was active in seeking to help people feel comfortable in this area. He published numerous articles in the *Improvement Era* and elsewhere throughout the entire first half of this century, many of which dealt with science.

In his *Joseph Smith as Scientist*, based on early *Era* articles, Widtsoe explained that he saw opportunities not problems in the science in our scriptures, and he argued that the prophet had anticipated many of the findings of modern science. He said that "there is no real difference between science and religion. The great, fundamental laws of the Universe are foundation stones in religion as well as in science."[7] He accepted organic evolution within limits, not claiming any knowledge of just what those limits were, and he had no problem with a great age for the earth.

In his *Evidences and Reconciliations* books, Widtsoe explained that the earth did not necessarily pause in its rotation for Joshua; it would have been easier for the Lord to have created the illusion that the sun stopped. As for Noah's flood, he thought it "doubtful whether the water in the sky and all the oceans would suffice to cover the earth so completely." In keeping with the Mormon concept that the Flood was the earth's baptism, if there was a general downpour, "on sloping hill sides, it might have been only a fraction of an inch in depth,"[8] and that would have been sufficient.

In *Joseph Smith as Scientist*, Widtsoe argued that the concept of a space-filling ether is found in the Doctrine and Covenants, which he thought tended to confirm that Smith was a prophet, but by the time I came along science had abandoned the idea of ether. That did not bother me though. I knew that reinterpretation is a way of life for seekers of truth. Widtsoe's writings included provisional theories of his own, and one would expect some of them to turn out to be wrong. What was important to me was that Widtsoe, with his fine credentials both in science and in the church, believed science to be part of Mormonism and tried to help science students stay within the church by showing them how they could believe as he did.

Elder Merrill also was helpful but in a different way. In his 1945 radio talks he described in his uncommonly friendly style some of the wonders of the universe which had been discovered by physicists and astronomers, and then talked about how thrilled he was to see support for the existence of God in those wonders.[9] And he quoted famous scientists to show that they believed in God. As my studies broadened I learned that many scientists and philosophers could not see God in nature and that not all scientists believed in God. It was good to know that Merrill, intimately familiar with both Mormonism and science, did believe.

Perhaps illustrating my remark that a science student is likely to have extra difficulty gaining a testimony, Merrill stated in his final radio talk that beginning at age ten he had prayed daily for *nine years* for a testimony that God exists before receiving an answer. He wondered if unworthiness had stood in the way, but I suppose he was at least as worthy as most young people.

Further confirmation that Mormonism and science were compatible was provided by scientists who were not church leaders such as Frederick J. Pack, a University of Utah geology professor. Father owned Pack's book *Science and Belief in God* (1924), and when I was in my teens he suggested that I read it. It helped with some of the problems I have mentioned. For example, Pack reviewed the reasons for wondering if the Flood really covered the entire earth and concluded by doubting that it did. He showed to my satisfaction that Noah could not possibly have taken two animals of every kind aboard the ark. For one thing creatures are still being discovered by scientific expeditions—how could Noah have found them all in a short time? But Pack made it clear that his basic faith in the Bible was unshaken. I was happy to learn that I could be flexible in my understanding of some of the troublesome ancient stories and still be a good Latter-day Saint.

In addition to all the helpful books and articles by Widtsoe, Merrill, Pack, and others, there was a monthly column in the *Era*, "Exploring the Universe," by Franklin S. Harris, Jr., a University of Utah physics professor. It highlighted new developments in science and technology and therefore the church's interest in them.

While a soldier in Japan in 1946 I learned of Henry Eyring's move from Princeton to Utah, found a chapter by him in the library, and decided to do my graduate work with him. He was a theoretical chemist, and I considered theory to be the best part of science. A devout Mormon and a respected scientist, he helped me with my worries about science and religion from the time I entered graduate school until the end of his life. He gave many other people the benefit of his wisdom through his talks and articles in church magazines.[10]

Eyring did not try to get science and Mormonism to mesh in detail but pretty much kept them in separate compartments, believing that science is revealed through scientists not prophets. To Elder Richard L. Evans he wrote, "I never worry what the Brethren believe about my specialty today because it is part of the genius of the Lord's Church that both they and I will understand the entire situation better tomorrow."[11] At first I had difficulty accepting Eyring's philosophy because I shared Widtsoe's desire to merge science and Mormonism. Eventually I came to see much wisdom in it, as I learned (partly through the fate of Widtsoe's chapter on the ether) that one must not take too seriously any very specific ideas as to how Mormonism and science fit together.

Although Widtsoe, Eyring, and other church scientists differed in their styles, they preached the same basic message: science is a part of Mormonism. I began post-doctoral work at Harvard thoroughly imbued with that philosophy.

At Cambridge I found a remarkably talented group of Mormons. Branch president Melvin Herlin was a physics professor at M.I.T. The students, who represented many specialties, broadened my outlook. They taught me to see their disciplines too as dovetailing with Mormonism. A good number of them, building on that belief, went on to make distinguished careers for themselves while remaining true to the church.

One week Hugh Nibley visited our branch. I sat spellbound as he made me aware that the Book of Mormon is a gold mine, loaded with rich nuggets waiting to be picked up and analyzed and that every talent is needed. Perhaps I could make a contribution. Is there science in the Book of Mormon? The Nephite monetary system caught my eye. I found that it was based on the binary number system, and in the library I learned that the Egyptians had used that system in their mathematics. In basing their monetary system on this binary system, the Nephites had modified it, probably to minimize the number of coins needed for transactions, in exactly the way that the manufacturer of the sortable cards on which I kept my literature references had modified it to minimize the work of sorting out the cards in a given category. It was exhilarating to become actively involved with the science-Mormonism connection, adding a thread to it myself, and I gained a sense that a great many other points of contact await our discovery and investigation. I was more convinced than ever before that the marriage of science and Mormonism, which already was good, could only get better and better.

I was in for a big surprise. It came in 1954, just when I began teaching science and just when the publication of my little contribution had my optimism soaring at new heights.[12]

Elders Widtsoe and Merrill both died in 1952. Two years later President Joseph Fielding Smith of the Council of the Twelve published *Man: His Origin and Destiny*. I read the book with considerable discomfort. According to this book, much of science is quite apart from Mormonism.

President Smith felt that "Satan dominates the thinking of the world today." He saw that domination in several areas of science but most of all in biology. Satan, he said, authored the theory of evolution, which is "the most pernicious doctrine ever entering the mind of man" and "Satan's chief weapon in this dispensation in his attempt to destroy the divine mission of Jesus Christ."[13] I did not understand such sentiments. What did the truth or falsity of evolution have to do with whether the gospel was true? And I knew that many good people believed in evolution, including Eyring, whose thinking coincided with mine: "Organic evolution is the honest result of capable people trying to explain the evidence to the best of their ability. From my limited study of the subject, I would say that the physical evidence supporting the theory is considerable from a scientific viewpoint."[14]

It seemed to me as it had to Widtsoe that there must be evolution at least within some limits. I was willing to believe that the Lord guided it, but in my youth I learned as I collected butterflies that different species often are so much alike that they cry out to be seen as distant cousins. As a chemist I thought it unlikely that the fundamental reproductive processes could be perfectly protected from ever going astray a little bit. Mutations seemed inevitable. And I could not easily disbelieve all the evidences for evolution which I read about regularly in *Scientific American* and elsewhere, including direct laboratory observations.

Apparently President Smith objected to evolution mostly for reasons I still cannot quite grasp. He just knew that the Lord did not work that way. In addition he flatly repudiated evolution by asserting that the earth is only a few thousand years old and that there was no death for any creature prior to Adam's fall. President Smith ignored the existence of fossils over 6,000 years old, commenting only on skeletons such as the Piltdown hoax. Posing another problem for biologists, he asserted that prior to the Fall, Adam had no blood in his veins.[15]

He also denied a widely-held astronomical theory which Widtsoe accepted, insisting that stars never "become dead cold bodies" because the Lord "does not create anything to be destroyed."

He was sure that the earth really did pause in its rotation in Joshua's day. After all it will literally "reel to and fro as a drunkard" in the last days. He quoted and condemned Pack's ideas on the Flood.[16]

The names Talmage, Widtsoe, and Merrill were not in the index. The only entries under *scientists* were "claim Bible a myth," "faith in scriptures weakened by," "false concepts of God," "reject fall and atonement," "revelations attacked by," and "will formulate false theories as long as they ignore the Divine Creator."

Through long study and reflection and with the encouragement of apostles, I had come to see tentativeness as both permissible and necessary, especially regarding such prehistoric events as the Creation and the Flood. President Smith was denying that flexibility, and what he was saying would have required a drastic turnabout in my thinking which I felt I would be unable to make.

I was bothered not only by President Smith's rejection of science but by his implied rejection of teachings of past church leaders as well. President Young had not taken the writings of Moses so seriously: "How long it [the earth] has been organized is not for me to say, and I do not care anything about it. As for the Bible account of the creation we may say that the Lord gave it to Moses, or rather Moses obtained the history and traditions of the fathers, and from them picked out what he considered necessary, and that account has been handed down from age to age, and we have got it, no matter whether it is correct or not, and whether the Lord found the earth empty or void, whether he made it out of nothing or out of the rude elements; or whether he made it in six days or in as many millions of years, is and will remain a matter of speculation in the minds of men unless he give revelation on the subject."[17] I liked that statement. Couldn't I stick with it and with some things I had learned from Widtsoe which Smith evidently saw as false doctrine? But it bothered me to ignore precepts which the living president of the Quorum of the Twelve felt so strongly about. I asked Eyring how he handled that problem. As usual his reply was both witty and pithy: "Maybe it will turn out that everything Joseph Fielding Smith ever said was exactly right, and maybe when I go to be judged he'll be delegated to judge me. I'll just say, 'I'm sorry I was wrong. Now let's get this over with as quickly as possible!'"

In my innocence I finally concluded that despite Smith's high position, the publication of his book was an aberration which was not to be taken seriously. His views seemed to make little sense, and I figured that he must not have much support in them as no one had said such things before. While Eyring sprang into action defending science and scientists in talks and correspondence with Smith and other church leaders, I thought everything would soon be smoothed over and forgotten.[18]

I was wrong again.

Man: His Origin and Destiny has not often been quoted in church literature, perhaps owing to the protests made not only by Eyring but by many other scientists as well. Probably the majority of today's members have not read it, although many of them are familiar with its concepts through his son-in-law Elder Bruce R. McConkie's extensive quotations from it in *Mormon Doctrine* and elsewhere. Nevertheless as Duane Jeffery said in 1973, it "sparked a wave of religious fundamentalism that shows little sign of abatement." That wave continues unabated today.

President Smith said little more about science during his lifetime, but other church authorities proceeded to warn against evolution and to preach an earth history which most scientists find untenable. Their warnings and teachings have issued forth under increasingly impressive circumstances right down to the present time.

Even more disconcerting to me has been the lengthy and continuing silence which the remaining general authorities have maintained. Encompassing virtually all branches of science, this silence has worked in concert with the warnings to create the impression that all the Brethren are uncomfortable with science. And it is a rare day when a church publication has anything good to say about science or scientists, a notable exception being a 1984 *Ensign* article on James Fletcher.[19] It is usually in vain that I watch for some praise for science, for some attempts to show that science and Mormonism can be reconciled, and for some use of the wonders discovered by science to promote faith. No one is growing up in the Bear River Valley today with the advantages I had.

The change has surprised me partly because when I read *Man: His Origin and Destiny* I thought of it as an isolated bolt out of the blue, not knowing that evolution and related topics had long been vigorously debated by some of the church authorities. Enlightenment came years later when I was able to read interesting essays by Duane Jeffery, Richard Sherlock, and Jeffrey Keller, where I learned among other things that Smith had been pitted against Talmage and Roberts in arguments mediated by the First Presidency and the Quorum of the Twelve and that *Man* was based on an old manuscript which had long been held up, apparently due in part to opposition from Widtsoe and Merrill.[20]

I did know that at least a few authorities supported Smith. He noted in his preface that Elders Mark E. Petersen, Marion G. Romney, Milton R. Hunter, and Bruce R. McConkie had given him "encouragement and help." But still it surprised me when two of those four became ardent anti-science spokesmen. I guess I had just wanted to put that possibility out of my mind.

Elder Petersen, who wrote the foreword, sniped away at science from time to time through his *Church News* editorials for the remainder of his life. He particularly objected to efforts to understand the origins of the universe, of the earth, and of species: "No worm or similar lower form of life could, by accident or otherwise, evolve into such an intricate pattern as bird-life. No attempt at reason or research or hypothesis can provide the answer—only the divine creation." "We need no longer speculate as to the origin of life or the manner by which the earth and the heavens were created." Regarding the "big bang" theory: "Did explosions ever bring order out of chaos, or do they produce chaos?"[21] One wonders if he really supposed the astronomers had not thought of that.

Some of Peterson's editorials made me feel rather uncomfortable. He made scientists out to be foolish or at times evil. He was not in favor of some scientific activities which I and most scientists considered legitimate. And he seemed to be telling me that I should rid myself of some of my strong beliefs.

The views on evolution and related topics which Elder McConkie held are well known because of their prominence in *Mormon Doctrine*, an immensely popular book ever since its first publication. He completely dismissed all findings of science which seemed to conflict with what he saw in "the inspired word." In so doing he did not even comment on the obvious questions which are thereby raised. He was especially persistent in teaching that it is a "revealed truth that there was no death either for man or animals or plants or any form of life until some 6000 years ago when Adam fell."[22] That statement requires disbelief in thousands of findings of science. I doubt that very many Mormon science students were or will be persuaded to reject so much evidence. How about all the ancient fossils of myriads of species of living things? Isn't coal derived from ancient vegetation?

Mormon Doctrine is not church-published, and presumably the Church News editorials did not speak officially for the church. But in 1979 assertions with which most scientists would disagree appeared in more authoritative publications. Richard Sherlock has pointed out that denial of death prior to the Fall appears under "death" in the church's Bible Dictionary, which was bound with the 1979 and later editions of the Bible, and that anti-evolution quotations from Joseph Fielding Smith were published that year in a priesthood manual and in a Sunday school manual—and again in 1985.

In June 1982 McConkie's views on the Creation were published in the Ensign, giving them wide distribution and at least the appearance of still higher status.[23] He remarked that "an understanding of the doctrine of creation is essential to salvation" and that "we are duty bound to accept" the "revealed verities" he outlined. He explicitly dismissed evolution and taught that there was neither reproduction nor death for any species until after Adam's fall. (Did not baby dinosaurs grow into egg-laying adult dinosaurs?) Again we could presume a lack of official standing, but many Mormons assume that when McConkie spoke in the Ensign, he did so for the church.

Further escalation came at the October 1984 general conference through the words of two senior apostles—one apostle at each of the Sunday sessions.[24] The addresses reached an audience of unprecedented size thanks to satellite television. Using homey examples (chicks do not grow up to become horses or dogs), Elder Boyd K. Packer stressed that "the pattern for all life is the pattern of the parentage," a statement with which any biologist would agree. But Packer seemed to mean this statement in an absolute sense and to be using it as an argument against evolution following a pattern laid down by Smith and Petersen. He made clear his distaste for evolution by adding that "surely no one with reverence for God could believe that His children evolved from slime or from reptiles." He concluded with an enigmatic statement: "The theory of evolution, and it is a theory, will have an entirely different dimension when the workings of God in creation are fully revealed." I hope, as I imagine most religious biologists do, that he meant that the theory will survive and that it will be purified and expanded, allowing ever more clearly for the workings of God.

Elder McConkie's remarks were as usual unambiguous. In the course of outlining "some simple tests that all of us may take to determine if we are true to the faith," he said that "true believers know that this earth and man and all forms of life were created in an Edenic, or paradisiacal, state in which there was no mortality, no procreation, no death"—a state which ended only when Adam fell. By definition then anyone who believes that plants and animals were reproducing and dying millions of years ago is not a true believer.

Statements which are less than friendly to science have not been concerned solely with evolution and allied themes. A lesson for young men covered much more territory. It warned youths to test "the theories of men against the truths of the gospel, not the other way around," to "beware of false science," and that "to be learned is good only if we hearken to the council [sic] of God"—a bit of neo-Nephi which I do hope no one really believes.[25]

While some findings of science are condemned by some church authorities, other findings are widely ignored. Meanwhile, folk beliefs are endorsed. At a recent stake conference, I heard a local leader cite the personality differences among his children as proof of the preexistence. Another example: it was preached at a general conference and then repeated to the teachers quorums for several years that a smoker who does not quit will go to the spirit world plagued by a craving for tobacco, because it really is the *spirit* that is addicted.[26]

What will happen next, and what can we do? Since Mormonism and science are both basically true, they will converge eventually and then an even more benevolent attitude toward science than I knew in my youth will prevail in the church. At present though I feel great concern as I see movement in the wrong direction from time to time—and none in the right direction.

From 1954 until 1982 I dismissed, with some effort, the anti-science statements, assuming them to express only the personal opinions of a few leaders who were not following a 1931 First

Presidency directive to general authorities: "Leave Geology, Biology, Archaeology, and Anthropology, no one of which has to do with the salvation of the souls of mankind, to scientific research, while we magnify our calling in the realm of the Church."[27] What seriously concerned me then was the lack of a supportive climate for Mormons interested in science. That concern continues, but now there is a new worry—the teachings which I dismissed have appeared in the *Ensign* and have been preached in general conference. That raises the possibility that the authorities now unitedly approve them. It may be that the resurrection of the benevolent attitude toward science which I once knew will not occur soon.

How are today's Mormon science students getting by without science-religion reconciliations? Wouldn't it help them to be shown in a religious setting some of the wonders of the universe? Isn't it still a part of Mormon thought that "the heavens [and other natural wonders] declare the glory of God"? Shouldn't something be said in praise of science now and then as Presidents Young and Grant did? Wouldn't that help science students (and older scientists too) feel good about themselves and the church?

Instead a young person today learns in school of the thousands of researches proving that life, death, and reproduction have been going on for millions of years on this planet while learning that "the church" teaches otherwise. How that must strain the faith of many.

What can those of us do who are friendly to science? For one thing we can follow Eyring's example, explaining science and speaking and writing positively about it for Mormon audiences. *Reflections of a Scientist*, a masterful compilation of some of Henry Eyring's thought, will have much influence for good.

Discussions of Mormonism and science too often revolve about organic evolution and the age of the earth. Those topics are important, and scientists with expertise in the relevant areas should continue working for a more enlightened attitude. At the same time I would like to see more discussion of other areas of science which are uncontroversial. There are many areas where the risk of polarization is small and therefore the chance of doing good is great.

Modern technology could be discussed to good advantage. The church has always been comfortable with it, and we could show

how technology is based on science. The prophet Joseph Smith and his highest associates in the church traveled from Utica to Schenectady by rail on 29 July 1836 on one of America's first railroads, even before its inaugural run on 1 August 1836.[28] The transcontinental railroad and telegraph were both completed in Utah in time to be of great help to immigration—and so on with the automobile, air transportation, radio, television, the satellite, and the computer.

The Lord guided Luther, Columbus, and those who brought into being the United States government, according to Mormon teachings. Mormons believe a large part of the reason for doing so was to prepare the way for the church. Did God likewise guide the development of technology? Presidents Young and Grant thought so, and in 1975 President Spencer W. Kimball went further: "The telephone and telegraph and other such conveniences were permitted by the Lord to be developed for the express purpose of building the kingdom. Others may use them for business, professional or other purposes, but basically they are to build the kingdom."[29] There is much interesting material along these lines to speak and write about.

The divine guidance of pure science is another exciting concept which provides a natural framework within which to discuss science. For example, I think it thrilling to contemplate the enormous body of astronomical knowledge we have in connection with a statement the Lord made to Joseph Smith in 1839. At that time astronomers were just beginning to reach beyond the solar system and were discovering the very first facts about the stars—determining their distances from their relative apparent motions. To the prophet in Liberty jail, the Lord said, referring to the sun, moon, and stars: "All the times of their revolutions, all the appointed days, months, and years, and all the days of their days, months, and years, and all their glories, laws, and set times, shall be revealed in the days of the dispensation of the fullness of times" (D&C 121:31). Widtsoe pointed out that this revelation is remarkable in that it was given "many years before the fact that all celestial bodies are in motion was understood and accepted by the world of science."[30] Frank Salisbury further noted that "*now* is the dispensation of the fullness of times" and that "many of the things the Lord promised to reveal have already been discovered by modern astronomers."[31] It is overwhelming to read a modern overview of astronomy such as Isaac Asimov's *The Universe* and get a glimpse of the universe as scientists now know it.[32] Only scientists are able to ask the right questions and understand the answers. And God must have guided the astronomers and known what would happen.

I have given only two examples of the many marvelous resources unique to Mormonism which we can use to show the rising generation of students (our future leaders) that science mixes well with our religion. It is up to us to teach our convictions to as many people in the church as we can from young to old. Everyone needs to know that science really is part of Mormonism and that the Lord works through both prophets and scientists. All those good people in the Bear River Valley knew those facts when I was young. It saddens me that their grandchildren might not. We must do all we can to change that.

NOTES

1. *Journal of Discourses*, 26 vols. (Liverpool: LDS Book Depot, 1855-86), 12:257-58 (hereafter JD).

2. Ibid., 9:167.

3. B. H. Roberts, *A Comprehensive History of the Church of Jesus Christ of Latter-day Saints*, 6 vols. (Salt Lake City: Deseret News Press, 1930), 6:562-63.

4. See David J. Whittaker, "Orson Pratt: Prolific Pamphleteer," *Dialogue: A Journal of Mormon Thought* 15 (Autumn 1982): 27-41; Dennis Rowley, "Inner Dialogue: James Talmage's Choice of Science as a Career, 1876-1884," *Dialogue: A Journal of Mormon Thought* 17 (Summer 1984): 112-30;

5. John A. Widtsoe, *Joseph Smith as Scientist* (Salt Lake City: General Board of the YMMIA, 1908), preface.

6. Orson Pratt, *Absurdities of Immaterialism, or, A Reply to T. W. P. Taylder's Pamphlet, entitled, "The Materialism of the Mormons or Latter-day Saints, Examined and Exposed"* (Liverpool: R. James, 31 July 1849), 31.

7. Widtsoe, *Joseph Smith as Scientist*, preface.

8. John A. Widtsoe, *Evidences and Reconciliations: Aids to Faith in a Modern Day*, 3 vols. (Salt Lake City: Bookcraft, 1943-51), 1:109-11.

9. Joseph F. Merrill, *The Truth Seeker and Mormonism*, a series of radio talks delivered Sunday evenings, 1 July-30 Dec. 1945, KSL radio, Salt Lake City.

10. See Edward L. Kimball, "A Dialogue with Henry Eyring,"

Dialogue: A Journal of Mormon Thought (Autumn/Winter 1973): 99-108; "Harvey Fletcher and Henry Eyring: Men of Faith and Science," *Dialogue: A Journal of Mormon Thought* 15 (Autumn 1982): 74-86.

11. Henry Eyring to Richard L. Evans, 8 Apr. 1954, copy in my possession.

12. Richard Pearson Smith, "The Nephite Monetary System," *Improvement Era*, May 1954, 316-17.

13. Joseph Fielding Smith, *Man: His Origin and Destiny* (Salt Lake City: Deseret Book, 1954), 319, 133, 184.

14. Henry Eyring, *Reflections of a Scientist*, ed. Harden Romney Eyring (Salt Lake City: Deseret Book, 1983), 61.

15. Smith, *Origin and Destiny*, esp. chap. 24, 362.

16. Ibid., 272-73, 12, 414-15.

17. JD 14:115-17.

18. Steven H. Heath, "The Reconciliation of Faith and Science: Henry Eyring's Achievement," *Dialogue: A Journal of Mormon Thought* 15 (Autumn 1982): 87-99.

19. Dale Van Atta, "James C. Fletcher: Knowledge Lights the Way," *Ensign* 14 (Apr. 1984): 26-31.

20. Duane E. Jeffery, "Seers, Savants, and Evolution: The Uncomfortable Interface," *Dialogue: A Journal of Mormon Thought* 8 (Autumn/Winter 1973): 41-75; Richard Sherlock, "'We Can See No Advantage to a Continuation of the Discussion': The Roberts/Smith/Talmage Affair," *Dialogue: A Journal of Mormon Thought* 13 (Fall 1980): 63-78; Jeffrey E. Keller, "Discussion Continued: The Sequel to the Roberts/Smith/Talmage Affair," *Dialogue: A Journal of Mormon Thought* 15 (Spring 1982): 79-98.

21. *Church News*, 1 Sept. 1979, 20 Dec. 1980, 17 Oct. 1981.

22. Bruce R. McConkie, *Mormon Doctrine* (Salt Lake City: Bookcraft, 1958), 613-14.

23. Bruce R. McConkie, "Christ and the Creation," *Ensign* 12 (June 1982): 9-15.

24. Bruce R. McConkie, "The Caravan Moves On," *Ensign* 14 (Nov. 1984): 82-85; Boyd K. Packer, "The Pattern of Our Parentage," *Ensign* 14 (Nov. 1984): 66-69.

25. *Priests Study Course*, Series B (Salt Lake City: Church of Jesus Christ of Latter-day Saints, 1973).

26. *Teachers Study Course*, Series B (Salt Lake City: Church of Jesus Christ of Latter-day Saints, 1973). Hartman Rector, Jr., is quoted (44) from *Conference Report*, Oct. 1970, 73-74.

27. Jeffery, "Seers, Savants, and Evolution," 64.

28. Joseph Smith, Jr., *History of the Church of Jesus Christ of Latter-day Saints*, ed. B. H. Roberts, 2d ed. rev., 7 vols (Salt Lake City: Deseret Book, 1948), 2:463; Frank W. Stevens, *The Beginnings of the New York Central*

Railroad: A History (New York: G. P. Putnam's Sons, 1926), 125.

29. Spencer W. Kimball, address delivered at Regional Representatives Seminar, 3 Apr. 1975, 19, in *Teaching: No Greater Call* (Salt Lake City: Church of Jesus Christ of Latter-day Saints, 1978), 89.

30. Widtsoe, *Joseph Smith as Scientist*, 47-48.

31. Frank B. Salisbury, *The Creation* (Salt Lake City: Deseret Book, 1976).

32. Isaac Asimov, *The Universe*, 3d ed. rev. (New York: Walker and Company, 1980).

15.
Eternal Progression:
The Higher Destiny

L. Mikel Vause

Thus it is provided in the economy of God, that to progression there is no end. As a necessary consequence, man may advance by effort and by obedience to higher and yet higher laws as he may learn them through the eternities to come, until he attains the rank and status of Godship. "Mormonism" is so bold as to declare that such is the possible destiny of the human soul. And why not? Is this possibility unreasonable? Would not the contrary be opposed to what we recognize as natural law? Man is of the lineage of the Gods. He is the spirit-offspring of the Eternal One, and by the inviolable law that living beings perpetuate after their kind, the children of God may become like unto their Parents in kind if not in degree. The human soul is a God in embryo; even as the crawling caterpillar of the corpse-like chrysalis embodies the potential possibilities of the matured and glorified imago. We assert that there was more than figurative simile, and instead thereof the assured posssibility of actual attainment in the Master's words: "Be ye therefore perfect, even as your Father which is in heaven is perfect" (Matt. 5:48). —James E. Talmage[1]

MORMONISM HAS BEEN CALLED THE "AMERICAN RELIGION" BECAUSE of its unique theology. The beauty of early nineteenth-century America was the open intellectual atmosphere, particularly of New England with its Emersons, Thoreaus, Neals, Hawthornes, Fullers, and others. The loosening of Puritanism's strangle-hold allowed for more relaxed religions like Unitarianism and even more radical experiments connected to "transcendentalism" at Brook Farm and Fruitlands.

Much of Transcendentalism's "Romantic theory" centered around the infinite and divine qualities of the human mind. The failure of the Puritan experiment led to a re-examination of religious philosophies, particularly those limiting potential like innate depravity and pre-destination. Emerson and others, influenced by the English and German Romantics, sought a more hopeful—even "divine"—position for the human family.

Mormonism took this search further with the idea that humans are not only the literal offspring of God but in fact can become gods themselves. In 1835, some eight years before the teaching of eternal progression was fully introduced by Joseph Smith, Lorenzo Snow had the idea of the god-like potential of the human family. He recorded this realization in the form of an aphorism in couplet: "As man is now God once was; As God now is, man may become."[2] Emerson once called humans "Gods in ruin."[3]

The idea that humans can evolve, moving from, in Joseph Smith's words, "one small degree to another, and from a small capacity to a great one; from grace to grace and from exaltation to exaltation,"[4] is, for me, the greatest message of hope since the resurrection. The idea of an eternity of learning and progress seems the only logical end for a divinely directed creation.

In 1859, as Mormons were busy establishing Zion in the Rocky Mountains, the presses of John Murray of Albemarle Street, London, were producing the first edition of Charles Darwin's *On the Origin of Species*. After having spent five years as naturalist on the *H.M.S. Beagle,* Darwin took the next twenty-three years to compile his data. Only when forced by the work of Alfred Wallace did he publish his findings. The role of iconoclast was not one Darwin sought, nor did he seek to destroy the God of Christianity. Darwin endured attacks by not only religionists of his homeland but from around the world.

Andrew Dickson White, in his 1896 essay "The Final Effort of Theology," provides some examples of these attacks. Cardinal

Manning of the Anglican Church called the theory of evolution "a brutal philosophy—to wit, there is no God, and the ape is our Adam." The American branch of the Anglican Church called Darwin's views "infidelity," and claimed they turned the Bible into "unbearable fiction." Rev. Walter Mitchell of the Victoria Institute declared: "Darwinism endeavors to dethrone God." His attackers fired at him from France, Germany, Australia, and the United States. Even Pope Pius IX called Darwin's work "A system which is repugnant at once to history, to the tradition of all peoples, to exact science, to observed facts, and to Reason herself."[5]

Sir Charles Lyell, a respected geologist, ascribed to the creation theory presented in Genesis, and Darwin himself believed that the diversity in living things could be explained by the Bible. It was during his time on the *Beagle* and after his many careful observations that he found a problem with a literalist reading of the Bible, as finally did Lyell as well.

It is easy to see why evolution posed a problem for theologians of Darwin's day. With ideas like predestination, innate depravity, irresistible grace, and the several creeds that governed the Western religious world—evolution represented a major deviation. Evolution argued for a need for empirical evidence to explain earth's foundations. Fossil evidence pointed to pre-historic animal and plant life. Clerics argued for a literal acceptance of the biblical six-day creation and an earth age of 6,000 years.

On the Origin of Species has been called one of the most important books ever written and has influenced almost every field of scientific and philosophical study—biology, literature, law, psychology, sociology, theology. Noted for its readability, Darwin's work is the result of his five years aboard the *Beagle*, observing flora and fauna throughout the world and leading him to develop his idea that species are not immutable. In his introduction to the first edition Darwin noted: "I was much struck with certain facts in the distribution of the inhabitants of South America, and in the geological relations of the present to the past inhabitants of that continent. These facts seemed to throw some light on the origin of the species— that mystery of mysteries, as it has been called by one of our greatest philosophers."[6]

Like all scientists, Darwin built his theory upon those of his predecessors, and scientific opinion remains divided as to the precise contribution the *Origin* makes to the biological sciences, yet few books have had such far-reaching influence as Darwin's. In his introduction, he admits the possibility of mistakes and need for further investigation: "No doubt error will have crept in, though I hope I have always been cautious in trusting to good authorities alone. I can here give only the general conclusions at which I have arrived, with a few facts in illustration, but which, I hope, in most cases will suffice. No one can feel more sensible than I do of the necessity of hereafter publishing in detail all the facts, with references, on which any conclusions have been grounded; and I hope in a future work to do this."[7]

Throughout the work Darwin points out that the idea of evolution by natural selection is "one of long argument," that all the evidence has not been gathered. A quick sampling of chapter headings in *Origin* indicates the ambitious scope of the book: "Variation under Domestication," "Variation under Nature," "Struggle for Existence," "Divergence of Character," "Laws of Variation," "Organ of Extreme Perfection," "Geological Record," "Single Centers of Creation," "Embryology," and "Classification." In Darwin's later book, *The Descent of Man*, he wrote: "Authors of the highest eminence seem to be fully satisfied with the view that each species has been independently created. To my mind it accords better with what we know of the laws impressed on matter by the Creator, that the production and extinction of the past and present inhabitants of the world should have been due to secondary causes, like those determining the birth and death of an individual. When I view all beings not as special creations, but as lineal descendants of some few beings which have lived long before the first bed of the Silurian system was deposited, they seem to me to become ennobled."[8] The language and tone of *Origin* and *Descent* never suggest that God did not have a hand in creation, only that evolution by "Natural Selection" was the means by which life became what it is.

In *Descent* Darwin reinforces the idea that he is not attempting to destroy belief in God but is merely searching to understand the laws of creation. He hoped for the further growth and development of humanity:

"The main conclusion arrived at in this work, namely that

man is descended from some lowly-organized form, will, I regret to think, be highly distasteful to many persons. But there can hardly be a doubt that we are descended from barbarians. The astonishment which I felt on first seeing a party of Fuegians on a wild and broken shore will never be forgotten by me, for the reflection at once rushed into my mind—such were our ancestors. These men were absolutely naked and bedaubed with paint, their long hair was tangled, their mouths frothed with excitement, and their expression was wild, startled, and distrustful. They possessed hardly any arts, and like wild animals lived on what they could catch; they had no government, and were merciless to every one not of their own small tribe. He who has seen a savage in his native land will not feel much shame, if forced to acknowledge that the blood of some more humble creature flows in his veins. For my own part I would as soon be descended from that heroic little monkey, who braved his dreaded enemy in order to save the life of his keep; or from that old baboon, who, descending from the mountains, carried away in triumph his young comrade from a crowd of astonished dogs—as from a savage who delights to torture his enemies, offers up bloody sacrifices, practices infanticide without remorse, treats his wives like slaves, knows no decency, and is haunted by the grossest superstitions.

"Man may be excused for feeling some pride at having risen, though not through his own exertions, to the very summit of the organic scale; and the fact of his having thus risen, instead of having been aboriginally placed there, may give him hopes for a still higher destiny in the distant future. But we are not here concerned with hopes or fears, only with the truth as far as our reason allows us to discover it. I have given the evidence to the best of my ability; and we must acknowledge, as it seems to me, that man with all of his noble qualities, with sympathy which feels for the most debased, with benevolence which extends not only to other men but to the humblest living creature, with his god-like intellect which has penetrated into the movements and constitution of the solar system—with all these exalted powers—Man still bears in his bodily frame the indelible stamp of his lowly origin."[9]

Darwin, having been the target of criticism for more than twenty years, in these concluding lines of *Descent* recognizes and praises the progress of humanity and postulates "hopes for a still higher destiny in the distant future."

Joseph Smith, upon revealing the doctrine of "eternal progression," explained that the human "higher destiny" is Godhood. The fact that God was once a man and that he progressed through life experiences to the station of God by gaining a knowledge of the truth is illustrated in the life of Jesus. The example set by the birth and life of the Savior, his being born in a natural fashion, his progression through life, learning by experience (Heb. 5:8), and his return to the Godhead established a model for humanity to follow. Such a model also provides the ultimate sense of hope and wellbeing for the human family when faced with struggles and trials, knowing that Christ "has descended below them all" (D&C 122:8).

Darwin's tone of eternal hope for further development of humankind is not incompatible with Joseph Smith's vision of human potential. Mormons, least of all among Christians, should be the last to oppose the postulates of Darwin and his intellectual descendants. Seen in the light of the doctrine of eternal progression, the theology of Mormonism and the theory of evolution are not mutually exclusive but could well blend together to form a harmony of faith and reason.

NOTES

1. James E. Talmage, *The Philosophical Basis of Mormonism* (Salt Lake City: 1915), 18-19.

2. Joseph Smith, *The King Follett Discourse* (Salt Lake City: Magazine Printing Co., 1963).

3. Ralph Waldo Emerson, "Prospects," in *Selections from Ralph Waldo Emerson*, Stephen E. Wheeler, ed. (Boston: Houghton Mifflin Co., 1960), 63.

4. Joseph, Smith, *The Teachings of the Prophet Joseph Smith*, Joseph Fielding Smith, ed. (Salt Lake City: Deseret Book, 1971), 346-47.

5. Andrew Dickson White, "The Final Effort of Theology," in *Darwin*, Philip Appleman, ed. (New York: W. W. Norton, 1979), 362-67.

6. Charles Darwin, *On the Origin of Species* (Cambridge: Harvard University Press, 1981), 1.

7. Ibid., 2.

8. Ibid., 488.

9. Charles Darwin, *The Descent of Man and Selection in Relation to Sex*, Vol. 2 (London: John Murray, Albemarle Street, 1871), 404-405.

16.
Science and Mormonism:
A Review Essay

Craig J. Oberg and *Gene A. Sessions*

THE VOLUME OF WRITINGS IN MORMON LITERATURE ON THE SUBJECT OF science and religion seems prodigious. If nothing else, it illuminates the depth and breadth of concern about the issue. While by no means exhaustive, the following review includes some of the more noticeable works that have appeared on the subject, particularly in recent times.

A vast portion of LDS literature on science has sought to debunk notions of organic evolution and the geologic timetable. Akin to the "creation science" prevalent among fundamentalist Christian groups, many Mormon writers have attempted to present their own "scientific" evidence against current biological and geological paradigms in order to reinvigorate literalist ideas about the Creation. A leader of this group is Melvin A. Cook, longtime professor of metallurgy at the University of Utah. In a series of three works (the last co-authored with M. Garfield Cook), Cook proposes a much younger earth by putting forth a number of new scientific models against standard ideas of evolution and earth age, particularly in his *Prehistory and Earth Models* (London, 1966). Cook's thirty-six-page pamphlet *Creation and Eternalism* (Salt Lake City, 1970) argues that the Mormon books of Abraham and Moses are antagonistic to the Lyell-Darwin-Wallace-Huxley doctrine. In *Science and Mormonism* (Salt Lake City, 1973) the Cooks use a comprehensive literalist approach to analyze correlations, conflicts, and conciliations between science and Mormonism, again demonstrating "proof" for a much younger earth than contemporary science suggests.

An earlier work that followed the same tack is Gilbert Green's *Science Uprooted* (Salt Lake City, 1938). While not as sophisticated in its creation science, it argues that modern science is off-track and that there was no life on earth 50,000 years ago. Similar to Green's approach is Dean R. Zimmerman, *Evolution: A Golden Calf* (Salt Lake City, 1976), which examines scientific arguments for evolution and dating of the earth then uses standard anti-science rhetoric to show that the theories are false. In the guise of attempting reconciliation, R. Clayton Brough and Rodney D. Griffin, *Scientific Support for Scriptural Stories* (Bountiful, UT, 1992), present rather standard creation-science arguments reminiscent of similar efforts among fundamentalist Christian organizations. More overtly anti-science is Clark A. Peterson, *Using the Book of Mormon to Combat Falsehoods in Organic Evolution* (Salt Lake City, 1992), who classifies the theory of evolution as one of the "works of darkness" against which the Book of Mormon warns.

More typical of anti-science works among Mormon authors are those based on the incompatibility argument, such as Reid E. Bankhead, *The Fall of Adam, the Atonement of Christ, and Organic Evolution* (Levan, UT, 1978), in which the basic doctrine of the Fall and the Atonement comes forth to deny the possibility of the evolution of humankind. Similarly crafted, Ernst Eberhard Jr.'s *The Origin: A Mormon's View on Evolution* (Salt Lake City, 1981) compares divine creation and organic evolution and concludes that the latter is a doctrine of the devil that denies the fatherhood of God and the need for a savior. Hyrum L. Andrus, BYU religion professor, follows much the same tack in a chapter on the Creation in *God, Man, and Universe* (Salt Lake City, 1968).

Most examples of recent LDS literature that might be classed as antagonistic to science take their lead from Joseph Fielding Smith's *Man: His Origin and Destiny* (Salt Lake City, 1954) which affirms the most literal interpretation of the scriptures relative to creation and states unequivocally that evolution is a trick of the devil. Smith's son-in-law Bruce R. McConkie reinforced this view in *Mormon Doctrine* (Salt Lake City, 1975) and "The Seven Deadly Heresies," *BYU Speeches of the Year* (Provo, UT, 1980), which assert that any attempt to reconcile organic evolution with gospel truth is heretical and impossible. Using basically the same frame of reference, Boyd K. Packer's October 1984 conference address, "A Pattern of Our Parentage," and his address at BYU in October 1988 detailed his own notions of a special creation for humankind while allowing science to propose tentative answers for the rest of nature.

Other church authorities have cast doubts on contemporary science without the direct anti-science tilt. For example, Alvin R. Dyer's *The Meaning of Truth* (Salt Lake City, 1973) includes a chapter entitled "Scientific Concepts: A Part of the Gospel in All Ages," suggesting that evolution is not adequate to explain the origins of humankind. For another, David O. McKay, *Gospel Ideals* (Salt Lake City, 1953), 49-52, outlines the limitations of science and challenges Darwin's concept of humans as mortal animals. Ezra Taft Benson's April 1958 conference address similarly calls into doubt science's answers to questions best posed to God and the scriptures.

Not all recent mainstream church leaders have been so anxious to debunk science. Spencer W. Kimball, *Modern Scientific Findings Harmonize with Revelation through the Ages* (Salt Lake City, 1962), recalls an earlier epoch when church doctrine was shown to coincide with scientific discovery, although Kimball's focus is away from biology and geology and toward astronomy, electronics, and the like. The unpublished work of B. H. Roberts on the immutability of scientific discovery is chronicled in Richard Sherlock, "'We Can See No Advantage in a Continuation of the Discussion:' The Roberts-Smith-Talmage Affair," *Dialogue: A Journal of Mormon Thought* 13 (Fall 1980): 63-78, and Jeffrey E. Keller, "Discussion Continued: The Sequel to the Roberts-Smith-Talmage Affair," *Dialogue: A Journal of Mormon Thought* 15 (Spring 1982): 79-98. Earlier, Roberts had tackled the seeming inconsistencies between scripture and science in *The Gospel and Man's Relationship to Deity* (Liverpool, 1888) by constructing a pro-science yet anti-evolutional set of ideas surrounding the Creation. Roberts suggests that the earth was made from fragments of an earlier world. Later editions include a series of articles Roberts wrote for *The Contributor* on "Man's Relationship to Deity" that further extrapolate his theories for an alternative scientific explanation of the Creation.

Anxious to defend both faith and science were a trio of twentieth-century apostles who were also professional scientists.

Joseph F. Merrill, *The Truth-Seeker and Mormonism* (Salt Lake City, 1945), consists of a series of radio addresses which dealt with science and religion. Perhaps the most prolific was John A. Widtsoe. Volume 1 of his *Evidences and Reconciliations: Aids to Faith in a Modern Day* (3 vols., Salt Lake City, 1943-51) contains a chapter devoted to science, including a charitable view of the church's attitude toward science, discussions of the age of the earth, of the origin of life, and of evolution, which reveals Widtsoe to be an evolutionary creationist. His *In Search of Truth* (Salt Lake City, 1963) gives insight into his views on science and his faith in its methods while stressing how hypotheses change over time. *In a Sunlit Land: The Autobiography of John A. Widtsoe* (Salt Lake City, 1953) illuminates clearly his feelings about the importance of science, as does his *Joseph Smith as Scientist* (Salt Lake City, 1909) and "Science and Religion," in *Man and the Dragon, and Other Essays* (Salt Lake City, 1945). While not as publicly outspoken on the subject, James E. Talmage expressed similar devotion to science, as revealed in John R. Talmage, *The Talmage Story: Life of James E. Talmage, Educator, Scientist, Apostle* (Salt Lake City, 1972), and Dennis Rowley, "Inner Dialogue: James Talmage's Choice of Science as a Career," *Dialogue: A Journal of Mormon Thought* 17 (Summer 1984): 112-30.

A collection of writings and talks of prominent Mormon scientists who defend their adherence to both faith and reason is Paul R. Green, *Science and Your Faith in God* (Salt Lake City, 1958). Among such scholarly-inclined Latter-day Saints are several who published their own reconciliations, including Eldon J. Gardner, *Organic Evolution and the Bible* (Logan, UT, 1960); William E. Harris, *From Man to God: An LDS Scientist Views Creation, Progression and Exaltation* (Bountiful, UT, 1989); Henry Eyring, *Reflections of a Scientist* (Salt Lake City, 1983), and *The Faith of a Scientist* (Salt Lake City, 1967); Nels Nelson, *Scientific Aspects of Mormonism* (New York, 1904), and *What Truth Is* (Salt Lake City, 1947); Frederick J. Pack, *Science and Belief in God* (Salt Lake City, 1924); Frank B. Salisbury, *The Creation* (Salt Lake City, 1976); Richard P. Smith, "Science: A Part of or Apart from Mormonism?" *Dialogue: A Journal of Mormon Thought* 19 (Spring 1986): 106-22. All of these scientists affirm the compatibility of scientific and religious knowledge and typically come down on the side of "evolutionary creationism."

Writings about specific Mormon intellectuals and their reconciliations include Ralph V. Chamberlin, *The Life and Philosophy of
W. H. Chamberlin* (Salt Lake City, 1925); Steven H. Heath, "The
Reconciliation of Faith and Science: Henry Eyring's Achievement,"
Dialogue: A Journal of Mormon Thought 15 (Autumn 1982): 87-99;
Edward L. Kimball, "Harvey Fletcher and Henry Eyring: Men of Faith
and Science," *Dialogue: A Journal of Mormon Thought* 15 (Autumn
1982): 74-86, and "A Dialogue with Henry Eyring," *Dialogue: A Journal
of Mormon Thought* 8 (Autumn/Winter 1973): 99-108; Erich Robert
Paul, "Early Mormon Intellectuals: Parley P. and Orson Pratt, a
Response," *Dialogue: A Journal of Mormon Thought* 15 (Autumn 1982):
42-48; Clyde Parker and Brent Miller, "Dialogues on Science and
Religion," *Dialogue: A Journal of Mormon Thought* 8 (Autumn/Winter
1973): 109-33.

Hugh Nibley occupies a unique position along the spectrum
with his many works on the subject, including "Before Adam," *Old
Testament and Related Studies* (Salt Lake City, 1986), and "Treasures
in Heaven: Some Early Christian Insights into the Organizing of
Worlds," *Dialogue: A Journal of Mormon Thought* 8 (Autumn/Winter
1973): 76-98.

A later generation has written in defense of the scientific
method in the face of growing antagonism. Perhaps most prolific
among these has been William Lee Stokes, a University of Utah
geology professor, whose works include *The Creation Scriptures: A
Witness for God in the Scientific Age* (Salt Lake City, 1979); "An Official
Position," *Dialogue: A Journal of Mormon Thought* 12 (Winter 1979):
90-92; *The Genesis Answer: A Scientist's Testament for Divine Creation*
(Englewood Cliffs, NJ, 1981); *Evolution? The Scriptures Say Yes!* (New
York, 1988); *So God Created Man: Latter-day Alternatives* (Salt Lake City,
1988); *Joseph Smith and the Creation* (Salt Lake City, 1991). In league
with Stokes's ardent defense of science and its harmony with true
religion are J. L. Farmer, W. S. Bradshaw, and F. B. Johnson, "The
New Biology and Mormon Theology," *Dialogue: A Journal of Mormon
Thought* 12 (Winter 1979): 71-75. Keith E. Norman, "Adam's Navel,"
Dialogue: A Journal of Mormon Thought 21 (Summer 1988): 81-97,
suggests that a simple understanding of myth unlocks the mystery.
More tentative in their defense of science but just as anxious for
harmony are Rodney Turner, *The Footstool of God* (Orem, UT, 1983);

and R. Kenneth Walter, *Science, Saints, and Sense* (Salt Lake City, 1973).

In addition to several articles mentioned elsewhere in this essay, a special issue of *Dialogue: A Journal of Mormon Thought* (Autumn/Winter 1973) contained introductory essays by Robert Rees, "Science, Religion and Man," James L. Farmer, "Science and Religion: Introduction," and Richard F. Haglund, Jr., "Religion and Science: A Symbiosis." It also included three brief notes on science/religion subjects by William E. Dibble, "The Book of Abraham and Pythagorean Astronomy," William Lee Stokes, "Geological Specimen Rejuvenates an Old Controversy," and Benjamin Urrutia, "The Structure of Genesis, Chapter 1."

In 1979 a two-volume collection of pro-science essays came forth entitled *Science and Religion: Toward a More Useful Dialogue* (Geneva, IL). The first volume, edited by Wilford M. Hess and Raymond T. Matheny, *Background for Man: Preparation of the Earth*, contains a series of articles written primarily by BYU professors hoping to show how science and religion interface, earth chronology (methods of geological and fossil dating), evidences for evolution throughout the earth record, and astronomy. Volume 2, edited by Hess, Matheny, and Donlu D. Thayer, *The Appearance of Man: Replenishment of the Earth*, is a continuation of the first volume in three parts. Part 1 contains five essays searching for reconciliations between science and evolutionary findings, while Part 2 involves a closer examination of the evolution of life on earth. The last portion consists of four essays about human evolution. Similarly valuable to students hoping to find a path to harmony are Erich Robert Paul, *Science, Religion, and Mormon Cosmology* (Urbana, IL, 1992), a comprehensive analysis of the "intimate connections between the development of modern science and the shaping of Mormon theology"; and David H. Bailey, "Scientific Foundations of Mormon Theology," *Dialogue: A Journal of Mormon Thought* 21 (Summer 1988): 61-80.

While the writers in the Hess-Matheny collection seem to find no difficulty harmonizing Mormonism and science, other authors chronicle the challenges. The teaching of evolution at BYU, for example, created an early nineteenth-century crisis, discussed in Gary James Bergera and Ronald Priddis, *Brigham Young University: A House of Faith* (Salt Lake City, 1985). In connection with that episode, see also R. V. Chamberlin, *The Meaning of Organic Evolution* (Provo, UT, 1911), and "The Present Attack on the Doctrine of Evolution," *Bulletin of the W. H. Chamberlin Philosophical Association* 1 (1922): 1-46.

Although Ann Weaver Hart, "Religion and Education: The Scopes Controversy in Utah," *Utah Historical Quarterly* 51 (Spring 1983): 183-98, demonstrates that a strong fundamentalist reaction to evolution did not occur in Utah, others have chronicled the considerable angst generated among Mormons. Among these are Cedric I. Davern, "Evolution and Creation: Two World Views," *Dialogue: A Journal of Mormon Thought* 17 (Spring 1984): 44-50; Duane E. Jeffery, "Seers, Savants and Evolution: The Uncomfortable Interface," *Dialogue: A Journal of Mormon Thought* 8 (Autumn/Winter 1973): 41-75; Keith E. Norman, "Mormon Cosmology: Can It Survive the Big Bang?" *Sunstone* 10 (Oct. 1985): 18-23; Richard Sherlock, "A Turbulent Spectrum: Mormon Reactions to the Darwinist Legacy," *Journal of Mormon History* 5 (1978): 33-59; Erich Robert Paul, "Science: Forever Tentative?" *Dialogue: A Journal of Mormon Thought* 24 (Summer 1991): 119-23. A good example of contemporary concern over the challenge evolution presented to late nineteenth-century Mormonism is Joseph Stanford, "Evolution and Creation," *The Contributor* 12 (Sept., Oct. 1891): 409-15, 451-56.

Interestingly enough, official church magazines have occasionally joined in the search for harmony between science and Mormonism. See, for example, Jay M. Todd, ed., "In the Beginning," *The Improvement Era* 73 (Jan. 1970): 33-48; George R. Hill III, "Solutions from the Scriptures," *Ensign* 18 (May 1988): 72-73; Morris S. Petersen, "I Have a Question," *Ensign* 17 (Sept. 1987): 28-29. According to Petersen, conflict between Mormonism and science "arises only when we assume that God has revealed all he is going to reveal on the subject or forget that scientific theories change as new discoveries are made."

Epilogue:
An Official Position

William Lee Stokes

NOTHING HAS SO BAFFLED AND FRUSTRATED PEOPLE AS THE QUESTION of origin. It is doubly troublesome because both science and theology feel impelled to solve it by offering two totally opposed solutions. Believers in Judaeo-Christian scriptures find an answer in the first two chapters of Genesis which they interpret as a story of divine origin for the human family. Science has discovered another possibility in the form of the theory of organic evolution. Ordinary citizens, caught between two certified sources of truth, have trouble deciding what they can safely believe.

Latter-day Saints are caught in the evolution/anti-evolution conflict in much the same way as other Bible-based religions but to an intensified degree. The LDS doctrine of eternal progression is peculiarly body oriented. Before birth the spirit is said to be unembodied. It is embodied at birth, disembodied at death, and reembodied in resurrection. That every worthy spirit should receive a proper human body is such an important, fundamental necessity that the possibility of its coming by chance or by accident, without divine provision, is unthinkable.

In the minds of most Mormons, organic evolution leaves God out of the picture and reduces the human body to the level of a lower animal. And yet the arguments for evolution are so persuasive and voluminous that many waver in their opposition. In the face of conflicting evidence and in a state of painful indecision, many if not most members would welcome a decision from a credible authority wiser or better informed than they. Many therefore believe that such a decision actually exists and that it is set down in the statements of general church authorities. The impression is widespread that organic evolution has been officially condemned by the church and that evolutionists are holding their views in opposition to duly constituted authority. But is this so?

In 1957 as head of the Department of Geology at the University of Utah, I became aware of the need to know the position of the church. This feeling was intensified by publication in 1954 of the book *Man, His Origin and Destiny*, by Joseph Fielding Smith, then president of the Quorum of the Twelve and later president of the church. I decided to inquire of President David O. McKay, not only for my own personal satisfaction but on behalf of thousands of college students who are entitled to correct information. I asked President McKay if the church had taken a position and if Elder Smith's book had the weight of an official pronouncement. He answered with the following letter:

THE CHURCH OF JESUS CHRIST OF LATTER-DAY SAINTS
47 EAST SOUTH TEMPLE STREET
SALT LAKE CITY, UTAH

DAVID O. McKAY, PRESIDENT
February 15, 1957

Professor William Lee Stokes
2970 South 15th East
Salt Lake City, Utah

Dear Brother Stokes:
    Your letter of February 11, 1957, has been received.
    On the subject of organic evolution the Church has officially taken no position. The book "Man, His Origin and Destiny" was not published by the Church, and is not approved by the Church.
    The book contains expressions of the author's views for which he alone is responsible.

Sincerely your brother,
[Signed, "David O. McKay"]
(President)

I believe President McKay answered with the intention that his statements would be used by me in connection with my official duties as a teacher in a public institution, but he did not specifically grant me permission to publish his response. Rightly or wrongly I forwarded copies of his letter to those interested enough to ask for them and the letter thus gained fairly wide distribution. At no time did I personally broadcast the letter or give it publicity even though I think I would have been justified in doing so.

Anti-evolution sentiment continued to grow in the 1950s and was strengthened by further publications by church authorities such as *Doctrines of Salvation*, a compilation of Elder Smith's writings by his son-in-law, Elder Bruce R. McConkie, and by McConkie's own book, *Mormon Doctrine*. In *Mormon Doctrine* (1958) after quoting from President John Taylor (*Mediation and Atonement*, 160-61), McConkie stated: "This aptly expressed and plainly worded statement from President John Taylor summarizes the official doctrine of the Church as to the falsity of the theory of organic evolution."[1]

In the face of what appeared to me as a contradiction of authorities or at least a serious difference of opinion, I continued to feel a need to publish the McKay letter but was restrained by the idea that I had no clear permission to do so. On 13 October 1968 I again wrote to President McKay and asked for permission to publish the essential statements from his 1957 letter. At this time he was so ill (he would die on 18 January 1970) that I scarcely expected a reply. However, on 18 October I received a letter over the signature of Joseph Anderson, secretary to the First Presidency, stating that he had been directed to tell me that there was no objection to my use of the quotation—"on the subject of organic evolution the Church has officially taken no position"—in a book I was then writing.

I have since been accused of taking unfair advantage of President McKay. Let readers judge. I am personally grateful that the church has not taken a stand that might prove to be wrong. This has already happened to fundamentalist churches among whose ranks I am happy not to be included. It is also faith promoting to me to know that God expects men and women to sift and study many subjects for truth and that he does not solve all our problems by official pronouncements.

NOTE

1. Bruce R. McConkie, *Mormon Doctrine* (Salt Lake City: Bookcraft, 1958), 230; the second edition of *Mormon Doctrine* (1966), 248, dropped the term "official" but conveyed virtually the same message: "This aptly expressed and plainly worded statement from President John Taylor expresses the same views and perspective found in the writings and sermons of Joseph Smith, Brigham Young, Orson Pratt, Parley P. Pratt, Charles W. Penrose, and many of our early day inspired writers."

CONTRIBUTORS

R. GRANT ATHAY, retired, was employed by the High Altitude Observatory, National Center for Atmospheric Research. He served as president of the Commission on the Structure of the Solar Atmosphere, International Astronomical Union, and chaired the Solar Physics Division, American Astronomical Society. "Astrophysics and Mormonism: Parallel Paths to Truth" is adapted from *Astrophysics and Mormonism: Parallel Paths to Truth, Commissioner's Lecture Series* (Salt Lake City: Church Educational System, 1973).

DAVID H. BAILEY is a computer scientist at NASA Ames Research Center in Mountain View, California. "Scientific Foundations of Mormon Theology" first appeared in *Dialogue: A Journal of Mormon Thought* 21 (Summer 1988): 61-80.

GARY JAMES BERGERA is director of publishing at Signature Books, Inc., Salt Lake City. "The 1911 Evolution Controversy at Brigham Young University" is adapted from Gary James Bergera and Ronald L. Priddis, *Brigham Young University: A House of Faith* (Salt Lake City: Signature Books, 1985), pages 134-48.

WILLIAM S. BRADSHAW is professor of zoology at Brigham Young University, Provo, Utah. "The New Biology and Mormon Theology" was first published in *Dialogue: A Journal of Mormon Thought* 12 (Winter 1979): 71-75.

JAMES L. FARMER is professor of zoology at Brigham Young University, Provo, Utah. "The New Biology and Mormon Theology" first appeared in *Dialogue: A Journal of Mormon Thought* 12 (Winter 1979): 71-75.

ELDON J. GARDNER was professor of zoology at Utah State University in Logan. "Organic Evolution and the Bible" is adapted from Eldon J. Gardner, *Organic Evolution and the Bible* (Logan, UT: Utah State University Press, 1960).

STEVEN H. HEATH is associate professor of mathematics at Southern Utah University in Cedar City. "Agreeing to Disagree: Henry Eyring and Joseph Fielding Smith" was first published as "The Reconciliation of Faith and Science: Henry Eyring's Achievement" in *Dialogue: A Journal of Mormon Thought* 15 (Autumn 1982): 87-99.

DUANE E. JEFFERY is professor of zoology at Brigham Young University, Provo, Utah. "Seers, Savants, and Evolution: The Uncomfortable Interface" first appeared in *Dialogue: A Journal of Mormon Thought* 8 (Autumn/Winter 1973): 41-75.

F. BRENT JOHNSON is professor of microbiology at Brigham Young University, Provo, Utah. "The New Biology and Mormon Theology" was first published in *Dialogue: A Journal of Mormon Thought* 12 (Winter 1979): 71-75.

JEFFREY E. KELLER, M.D., specializes in emergency medicine in Idaho Falls, Idaho. "The B. H. Roberts/Joseph Fielding Smith/James E. Talmage Affair" is adapted in part from his "Discussion Continued: The Sequel to the Roberts/Smith/Talmage Affair," *Dialogue: A Journal of Mormon Thought* 15 (Spring 1982): 79-98.

EDWARD L. KIMBALL is professor of law at Brigham Young University, Provo, Utah. "Harvey Fletcher and Henry Eyring: Men of Faith and Science" first appeared in *Dialogue: A Journal of Mormon Thought* 15 (Autumn 1982): 74-86.

KEITH E. NORMAN holds a Ph.D. in early Christian studies from

Duke University. "Adam's Navel" was first published in *Dialogue: A Journal of Mormon Thought* 21 (Summer 1988): 81-97.

MORRIS S. PETERSEN is professor of geology at Brigham Young University, Provo, Utah. "Fossils and the Scriptures" first appeared in the *Ensign* 17 (Sept. 1987): 28-29.

DENNIS ROWLEY is a writer and an archivist who lives in Provo, Utah. "Inner Dialogue: Jame's Talmage's Choice of Science as a Career, 1876-84" was first published in *Dialogue: A Journal of Mormon Thought* 17 (Summer 1984):112-30.

RICHARD SHERLOCK is professor of philosophy at Utah State University, Logan. "The B. H. Roberts/Joseph Fielding Smith/James E. Talmage Affair" is adapted in part from his "'We Can See No Advantage to a Continuation of the Discussion': The Roberts/Smith/Talmage Affair," *Dialogue: A Journal of Mormon Thought* 13 (Fall 1980): 63-78. "A Turbulent Spectrum: Mormon Reactions to the Darwinist Legacy" first appeared in *Journal of Mormon History* 5 (1978): 33-59.

RICHARD PEARSON SMITH, retired, was a physical chemist with the University of Utah and later Exxon Research and Engineering in Linden, New Jersey. "Science: A Part or Apart from Mormonism?" was first published in *Dialogue: A Journal of Mormon Thought* 19 (Spring 1986): 106-22.

WILLIAM LEE STOKES, retired, was professor of geology at the University of Utah. "An Official Position" first appeared in *Dialogue: A Journal of Mormon Thought* 12 (Winter 1979): 90-92.

L. MIKEL VAUSE is associate professor of English at Weber State University in Ogden, Utah. "Eternal Progress: The Higher Destiny" has not been published previously.